PURITY IN RABBINIC JUDAISM

SOUTH FLORIDA STUDIES IN THE HISTORY OF JUDAISM

Edited by
Jacob Neusner
William Scott Green, James Strange
Darrell J. Fasching, Sara Mandell

Number 95

Purity in Rabbinic Judaism

by

Jacob Neusner

PURITY IN RABBINIC JUDAISM

A Systematic Account

The Sources, Media, Effects, and
Removal of Uncleanness

by

Jacob Neusner

Scholars Press
Atlanta, Georgia

PURITY IN RABBINIC JUDAISM

A Systemic Account

The Sources, Media, Effects, and Removal of Uncleanness

Publication of this book was made possible by a grant from the Tisch Family Foundation, New York City. The University of South Florida acknowledges with thanks this important support for its scholarly projects.

Library of Congress Cataloging in Publication Data

Neusner, Jacob, 1932-
    Purity in rabbinic Judaism : a systematic account : the sources, media, effects, and removal of uncleanness / by Jacob Neusner.
        p. cm. — (South Florida studies in the history of Judaism ; no. 95)
    Includes index.
    ISBN 1-55540-929-6
    1. Purity, Ritual—Judaism. 2. Rabbinical literature—History and criticism. I. Title. II. Series.
BM702.N446   1993
296.7'4—dc20   93-40720
                                     CIP

Printed in the United States of America
on acid-free paper

Table of Contents

Preface

This is the first in a planned two-part description, formed in exactly the same way and using identical categories, of purity in Judaism and Zoroastrianism, works themselves intended to provide the basis for a collaborative essay in comparison of religions at a point at which they intersect. Here I systematically describe the purity laws of Rabbinic Judaism, following a scheme that will govern the counterpart description of the purity laws of Zoroastrianism by Dr. A.V. Williams, University of Manchester. When the two matching descriptions are complete, Dr. Williams and I will undertake to make observations, each on the results of the other, which then will form the foundation for a study of comparisons and contrasts. But the basic descriptions prepared to facilitate comparison at the same time will stand on their own, and in this book I present mine of Judaism.

Both Zoroastrianism and Judaism accord to the theme of purity a central place, and that theme bears a formidable burden of what each religion wishes to say. Not only so, but at numerous points, each religious system concurs with the other in detail, and the structure of purity for both follows a single pattern, attending in both religions to the organizing questions. Judaism and Zoroastrianism set forth complete statements of these constitutive principles of purity: [1] sources of uncleanness, [2] affects and effects of uncleanness (what is subject to uncleanness and the consequences of uncleanness for what contracts it), and [3] modes of the resolution of uncleanness and the restoration of cleanness. Those three categorical questions define the main lines of thought – legal and theological alike – characteristic of each religious system's treatment of the common theme. Accordingly, we describe, analyze, and compare one of the fundamental and constitutive components equally characteristic of two religious systems. Judaism finds representation in its classical statement, the Pentateuchal books of Leviticus and Numbers, for the written part of the Torah, and the Mishnah and Tosefta, for the oral part of the Torah. Zoroastrianism in its fullness speaks through counterpart documents, to be read in the way I read those of Judaism. This comparison aims at gaining perspective on two subjects, Judaism and Zoroastrianism, in particular, and purity in religion, in general.

For the purposes of comparison, we compose not side-by-side histories of the formation of purity law in the two great religions that focus on that protean matter, but comparison of how in fully exposed systemic statements the two treat a common theme. We undertake in this volume and its planned counterpart for Zoroastrianism the comparison and contrast of those two systems because we seek perspective on the two systems that treat purity as a critical consideration and that resort to the same category formation as well. My purpose is to investigate what we learn about the differences between entire religious systems from an important native category that is defined in the same way by each. Since the three-part category formation just now set forth serves equally well to organize both system's data on a single topic defined in much the same terms, the comparison is both appropriate and illuminating.

The plan of the book is simple. I begin, in the Introduction, with a careful statement of the premises and method of our planned description and comparison of the Zoroastrian and Judaic systems. I explain comparison, define religious systems, and justify the comparison of Judaism and Zoroastrianism in particular. Finally, I explain my purpose in asking one set of questions, not some other, and I want readers to know precisely what I claim to accomplish, therefore to understand the reason I do this work in one way, rather than in some other. The terms having been defined, we proceed in Parts One, Two, and Three to set forth concise accounts of the causes, affects and effects, and resolution of uncleanness in the law of Rabbinic Judaism. A single pattern governs, and the same will dictate the program of Dr. Williams's account of Zoroastrianism and purity.

I wish at the very outset briefly to make clear what I do not do, a point spelled out in the Introduction. I do not address questions of parallels, intersections, origins, influences or borrowings, for example, how Zoroastrianism influenced Leviticus in Achaemenid times, or the framers of the law of the Mishnah in Parthian and earliest Sasanian times; how Judaism borrowed the idea of light and darkness as generative symbols from Zoroastrianism; how Zoroastrianism influenced Mithraism or Gnosticism or Manichaeism or any of the other -isms and -ities of antiquity. It may have been the fact that the authors of materials now collected in Leviticus and Numbers, or in the Mishnah Division of Purities, got ideas from Magi; but we cannot show it, so we do not know it. And what we do not know as fact, we cannot undertake then to interpret either. Nor do I propose to infer theories of origin on the strength of (alleged) parallels. These paths have long been explored, and they have yielded whatever solid results they are likely to set forth. If I thought that comparative work to date has rested on sound conceptual foundations in method, I should have followed the available models. For reasons I spell out, I find deep flaws in the conceptions of comparison and contrast that have guided prior work (such as it is) on Zoroastrian and Judaic comparison and on the comparison of religions in general, a field awaiting rediscovery and reexploration.

A second negative qualification is in order. I speak not of "Judaism" in general, surveying everything that pertains to our subject in all the writings of those two large, massive, and protean traditions. What I describe here and Dr. Williams will describe in his companion volume are ideal types, specifically, the systemic statements of the two traditions as these emerge in specific, canonical writings representative of the whole. We construct these ideal types out of the specified documents and compare the two ideal types. As an initial project in the comparative study of kindred religions through a collaboration of specialists in each, this book promises a clear picture of the main points of the two systems. We do not at this point offer a fully articulated, detailed survey of everything on the common theme that is found in the respective writings of each. We plan to undertake a responsible description of the system of purity in Judaism and in Zoroastrianism as these may be compared; that means categories that are common to the two will define what can be described in a productive way.

Categories of data that are particular to the one or the other tradition cannot be treated in this context, even though, in an overall systemic comparison, they will figure. But, in all, our aim is simple. We do not compare everything with everything, but systems with one another, in their fundamental documentary articulation. As always, the best is the enemy of the good. Here the work begins; it does not end.

Our ultimate purpose, realized here and in the companion work on Zoroastrianism only in a preliminary way, is threefold: to gain perspective, first, on the two religions that are compared, second, on purity as a category of (some) religious systems, and, third, on religion. Our interest in the study of religion through comparison of religions should be explicit. Our goal is to find out what religions that utilize the purity theme in important systemic ways have in common, and how they may (in theory at least) be supposed to differ from religions that ignore that theme. The Judaism of the Dual Torah, Zoroastrianism, Islam, and Hinduism then will have to be compared by reason of their shared interest in the theme; but so far as purity is other than sexual, Christianity's disinterest in the matter (indeed, its Founder's explicit disdain for the category, purity, when it comes to the very matters important to the priestly code, for example, menstrual uncleanness, cleanness of foods and utensils) classifies that family of religions in another category, and what we learn from that fact (if it is a fact) remains to be considered.

Obviously, I do not for one minute argue that the comparison of purity systems should encompass only the two religions treated here, only that the comparison is apt and appropriate for, among other religions, the ones at hand. It goes without saying that speciating religions by the stated criterion – presence or absence of attention to the clean and the unclean as defined inductively by the data of two or more religious systems – invites yet another comparison: religions that pay ample attention to that category compared to those that do not; but that work must wait for another occasion. Here I do the first part of an attempt to join the forces of specialists in two kindred religions to deal with a category important to both. Our results when they become available with Dr. Williams's completion of his part of the work and then with our shared comparison as well may prove fruitful for further comparative research of this kind.

I acknowledge with thanks the ongoing support for this research that is provided by the University of South Florida. That is by the University's providing ideal conditions – including a generous research expense fund – in which to pursue research. I further expresses thanks to colleagues in the Department of Religious Studies and in other departments of the University of South Florida for their ongoing friendship and stimulating conversation.

JACOB NEUSNER

Distinguished Research Professor of Religious Studies
UNIVERSITY OF SOUTH FLORIDA
Tampa, FL 33620-5550 USA

Introduction

In Preparation for the Systemic Comparison of Kindred Religions

This book takes the first step in the planned comparison of two religions' treatment of a single important topic. The two religions are Zoroastrianism and Judaism, and the comparison deals with purity in each of these kindred religions, both of which assign an important place to the matter of cultic and personal purity. The comparison that is planned is systemic and phenomenological, not historical. These two methodological points – the positive matched by the negative – require careful definition, since the plan of this book is devoted to making possible the comparison that is coming. And that comparison means that the subject must be treated in the correct manner. Since in these pages I devote myself to spelling out the subject in one way, rather than in some other, I have at the outset to explain the program of comparison that is undertaken here and in the planned, companion work.

A systemic comparison juxtaposes complete systems, rendered not as they may have existed at some one point in its history but as ideal types. What are compared are systems as they are set forth out of their internal evidence, through their own category formation of their own phenomena, not defined by external categories, circumstances or contexts. "Systemic description" takes up as a whole and complete working statement the details of the principal components of purity as these coalesce along lines of logically necessary categories; systemic comparison then compares two or more such systems: How does each treat a single important category in fact native to both. A systemic comparison furthermore inquires into the place of purity in the larger systemic statements of the two religions as a whole. How does each utilize the purity theme to say what it wishes to say about all themes?

A systemic comparison, therefore, identifies how an entire statement on purity is put together, using a simple, functional logic to specify its main categories or constitutive elements. Such a comparison asks each of the two religions to fill in its answer to a common set of questions. Viewed as a simple structure, any system of uncleanness – so naked logic suggests – will have to answer three questions to cover the ground of its topic: [1] What are the sources of uncleanness? [2] How is uncleanness transmitted, to what objects or persons, and with what consequences? and [3] How is uncleanness removed or resolved? A system may, and ordinarily does, raise a variety of other questions, but these seem to us, if not sufficient, then at least necessary: cause, effect, remission. That claim concerning how any system in theory must divide up the subject of purity and formulate its details lies beyond demonstration and forms a premise of my work. I cannot prove that claim in the manner of nominalism, by showing that every known system of uncleanness answers these particular questions. I offer that claim as a matter of logic, in philosophy: this is how all such systems ought to be. But for the work at hand, I need not pursue the issue to the end. It suffices that I maintain only a simple proposition. It is that how Zoroastrianism and Judaism treat purity is adequately set forth within the stated category formation. I further show through the shank of this book that that category formation is not only necessary to my data, but sufficient for most of them: hence a philosophical category formation that corresponds to the native categories that intelligibly organize the facts of the two systems.

That formulation of the method of describing purity – within a structure that equally well fits both systems – produces answers of only a descriptive, analytical, and interpretative nature. I promise to describe the facts of uncleanness that fit into the system just now set forth; to analyze through comparison and contrast how each system expresses its larger conceptions through the details covered by the systemic description; and to interpret the points of likeness and difference by proposing broader theses on the comparison of the two religions. This yields, at the very end, some tentative suggestions on the taxonomic study of religion to which all comparison of specific religions ought to contribute.

Five matters require attention at the outset: [1] the definition of religion or (as I prefer) "religious system"; [2] an initial, and primitive, inductive definition of purity and impurity in general; [3] the basis and purpose of comparison of religions in general; [4] the justification for comparing Judaism and Zoroastrianism in particular; and [5] the purpose of comparing the two religions in particular: what I propose to do and not to do in this joint effort of ours.

I. Defining a Religion or Religious System

In general, people define religions by saying what people believe: Zoroastrianism believes in the reality of good and evil, Judaism posits monotheism, for instance. But belief is too abstract and general, but also too small a conception of what a religion is and accomplishes. First, religion is public, social, shared, an objective fact of the social order, while what people believe tells us only about what individuals think. Religion governs what people do, telling them who they are and how they should live, while what people believe tells us only about attitudes. Religion is always specific and particular, making its statement through the details of the everyday and the here and now. Religion therefore encompasses not only beliefs or attitudes – matters of mind and intellect – but also actions and conduct. Religion combines belief or attitude, worldview, which I may call "ethos," and also behavior or way of life or right action, which I may call in a broad and loose sense, "ethics," and it always serves to formulate in an integrating account the theory of the social entity that lives in accord with the ethics and views the world in the light of the ethos.

I call this third component of a religious system, referring to the social entity that realizes the religious system, by the word "ethnos." It is the starting point of any description, analysis, and interpretation of a religious system. For, because religion – ethos, ethics, ethnos —forms the basis of life of not individuals or families in the abstract but people otherwise unrelated to one another, it must be seen as an account of a social entity or a social group, for instance, a church or a holy people or a nation. Religion imputes relationships that are other than those that come about through physical proximity (territorial, for example), or through natural, familial processes (genealogy). Religion to the contrary invokes other than this-worldly relationships or validates in different terms the this-worldly ones.

What integrates the ethics, ethos, and ethnos, forming a single cogent statement of the social order, is two things: an urgent question, addressed implicitly at every point, and a self-evidently valid answer, delivered in each and every detail. Self-evidence pertains to the truths that (as represented in the evidence that attests a system) demand no articulation, no defense, no argument but form premises for all discourse. What is self-evident forms the system and defines its generative exegetical principles. And if I want to know what people find self-evident, I also have to uncover the questions they confront and cannot evade. These questions will dictate the program of inquiry, the answers to which then follow after the fact. The system holds together at the union of urgent question and self-evidently valid answer. So, if I know

what issues of social existence predominate, I can also uncover the point
– the circumstance – of origin of a religious system. To be sure, no one
claims to know the source of urgent questions: whether political, whether
cultural, whether formed within the received condition of the faith,
whether framed by forces outside. Debates on such issues of beginnings
rarely yield consensus. The reason is simple. In the end no one is
present at the beginning, so I have no information to settle any important
questions. I work my way back from the known to the unknown. But all
I wish to know is whether what I trace is old and continuous, as its
apologists invariably claim, or essentially new and creative, a testimony
to human will and human power and human intellect, as I maintain it is:
a new religious system, for a new circumstance.

So to summarize the special language that governs here: a religious
system comprises a worldview, explaining who people are, where they
come from, what they must do, a way of life, expressing in concrete
deeds that worldview and linking the life of the individual to the polity,
and a particular social group. A Judaic system, or simply, a Judaism,
therefore comprises a worldview, a way of life, and a group of Jews who
hold the one and live by the other. When I speak of a Judaism, therefore,
I point to not the time and circumstance but the systemic statement in
which a given worldview, way of life, and social group coalesce in a
definitive way to answer in a self-evidently valid way an urgent and
inescapable question: How do I discern that coalescence? I look for the
resort to a striking and also distinctive symbol, something that expresses
the whole all together and all at once. For the symbol – whether visual or
verbal, whether in gesture or in song or in dance or in the definition of
the role of woman – will capture the whole and proclaim its special
message: its way of life, its worldview, its definition of who is Israel.

To give a concrete example of how in a very small detail a system
makes its statement, so that a religion transforms, and socializes,
otherwise commonplace relationships, I address ways in which one
relates to a person in accord with special rules, formed out of mythic and
not everyday reality. In the following cases, the relationship of the father
to the son is treated as the generative metaphor for the relationship of the
teacher to the student, which is transformed into the language, the
master (teaching revelation) and the disciple (hearing God's word from
the master). The comparison of the relationship of father to son and
master to disciple comes to expression, in the Rivayat that accompanies
the Datastan-i Denig,[1] in the revelation by Ohrmazd to Zoroaster on the

---

[1] All translations are by A.V. Williams, *The Pahlavi Rivayat Accompanying the
Dadestan i Denig* (Copenhagen, 1990: The Royal Danish Academy of Sciences and

rule – parallel in the two relationships – governing lawsuits between persons of said classifications. The tradition tells the judge how to adjudicate a case in which each party presents evidence of the same weight as that of the other. In that case, the judge is to favor the master or the father, who has nurtured him. Indeed, the father, and, by extension, the master, owns the earnings of the son or disciple and the merit of his good deeds, as though the father or the master had done those deeds himself:

Chapter Twenty-Nine
The Privileges of Seniority

> This also (is) revealed, Ohrmazd said to Zoroaster: "If a father is engaged in a lawsuit with his son, or a herbad with his pupil, or a father-in-law with his son-in-law, and if the father (has) one witness on his side, and the son one witness on his, make the decision in favour of the father, and entrust the property (at stake) to the father, for this reason that the good that the father does for his son, the son can never repay that goodness. He has nurtured him from childhood and immaturity until that (time) when he becomes an adult. Indeed according to this saying: 'Until a son is 15 years old his nurture (comes) from his father,' then also so long as he [i.e., the father] (is) alive the (son's) earnings belong to the father, and all the good deeds which the son does will thus belong to the father as if he had done them with his own hands."

What attracts our attention is two facts, first, the reason – the father has nurtured the son, and the master is in the status of the father and so is deemed to have nurtured him, too – and second, the consequence, the father or master owns the son's earnings and merits. I find the same issue worked out along intersecting lines in the following:

Mishnah-tractate Baba Mesia 2:11

A. [If one has to choose between seeking] what he has lost and what his father has lost,
B. his own takes precedence.
C. [If he has to choose between seeking] what he has lost and what his master has lost,
D. his own takes precedence.
E. [If he has to choose between seeking] what his father has lost and what his master has lost,
F. that of his master takes precedence.
G. For his father brought him into this world.
H. But his master, who has taught him wisdom, will bring him into the life of the world to come.
I. But if his father is a sage, that of his father takes precedence.

Letters through Munksgaard) I. *Transliteration, Transcription, and Glossary*; II. *Translation, Commentary, and Pahlavi Text.*

J.   [If] his father and his master were carrying heavy burdens, he removes that of his master, and afterward removes that of his father.

K.   [If] his father and his master were taken captive,

L.   he ransoms his master, and afterward he ransoms his father.

M.   But if his father is a sage, he ransoms his father, and afterward he ransoms his master.

The issue is framed in different terms, of course, since it is the son who has the decision to make, not the judge. At issue is when the son (not the judge) has to choose between his father and his master. The Mishnah rule carries forward the same principle as the Zoroastrian one: the master enters into the status of the father. Here is a good example of how religion intervenes to transform public and social relationships. In that sense, as this case indicates, religion explains the social world made up by people who believe certain things in common and act in certain aspects of their lives in common

Religion therefore accounts for the social entity, which I may call, for the sake of symmetry, ethnos. These three things together – ethos, ethics, and ethnos – define the religious system that forms the foundation of the life of social entities in humanity. A religious system – way of life, worldview, theory of the social entity that lives by the one and believes in the other – identifies an urgent and ongoing question facing a given social group, and provides an answer that for the faithful is self-evidently valid. To study any vital religion is to address a striking example of how people explain to themselves, by appeal to God's will or word or works, who they are as a social entity. Religion as a powerful force in human society and culture is realized in society, not only or mainly in theology; religion works through the social entity that embodies that religion. Religions form social entities – "churches" or "peoples" or "holy nations" or monasteries or communities – that, in the concrete, constitute the "us," as against "the nations" or merely "them." Within communities, religions also transform relationships to conform to mythic patterns, for example, the natural relationship of one who acquires information and one who provides it is recast into the supernatural relationship, intervening in ordinary patterns of obligation and action, of disciple to master, disciple in the faith and master of the teaching of the faith (in context). And religions carefully explain, in deeds and in words, who that "us" is – and they do it every day. To see religion in this way is to take religion seriously as a way of realizing, in classic documents, a large conception of the world.

Now to the matter of "a religious system": religion may represent itself as a tradition, meaning, the increment of the ages. That represents an apologia, in the claim that religion has come forth whole and complete, and has been preserved from its pure beginnings in truth to the present day: linear, harmonious, incremental. A religious system also may come forth as a cogent statement, a well-crafted set of compelling answers to urgent questions. A religious tradition covers whatever the received sedimentary process has handed on. A religious system addresses in an orderly way a worldview, a way of life, and a defined social entity. And both processes of thought, the traditional or the systematic, obey, each its own rules. The life of intellect may commence morning by morning. Or it may flow from an ongoing process of thought, in which one day begins where yesterday left off, and one generation takes up the task left to it by its predecessors.

A system of thought by definition starts fresh, defines first principles, augments and elaborates them in balance, proportion, above all, logical order. In a traditional process, by contrast, we never start fresh but only add, to an ongoing increment of knowledge, doctrine, and mode of making judgment, our own deposit as well. And, in the nature of such an ongoing process, I never start fresh, but always pick and choose, in a received program, the spot we choose to augment. The former process, the systematic one, begins from the beginning and works in an orderly, measured and proportioned way to produce a cogent and neatly composed statement, a philosophy for instance. Tradition by its nature is supposed to describe not a system, whole and complete, but a process of elaboration of a given, received truth: exegesis, not fresh composition. And, in the nature of thought, what begins in the middle is unlikely to yield order and system and structure laid forth *ab initio*. In general terms, systematic thought is philosophical in its mode of analysis and explanation, and traditional thought is historical in its manner of drawing conclusions and providing explanations.

So far as "tradition" refers to the matter of process, it invokes, specifically, an incremental and linear process that step by step transmits out of the past statements and wordings that bear authority and are subject to study, refinement, preservation, and transmission. In such a traditional process, by definition, no one starts afresh to think things through. Each participant in the social life of intellect makes an episodic and ad hoc contribution to an agglutinative process, yielding, over time, (to continue the geological metaphor) a sedimentary deposit. The opposite process I may call systematic, in that, starting as if from the very beginning and working out the fundamental principles of things, the intellect, unbound by received perspectives and propositions, constructs a free-standing and well-proportioned system. In terms of architect the difference is between a city that just grows and one that is planned; a scrapbook and a fresh composition; a composite commentary and a work of philosophical exposition.

The one thing a traditional thinker in religion, as against a system builder in religion, knows is that he or she stands in a long process of thought, with the sole task of refining and defending received truth. And the systematic thinker affirms the task of starting fresh, seeing things all together, all at once, in the right order and proportion, a composition, not merely a composite, held together by an encompassing logic. A tradition requires exegesis, a system, exposition. A tradition demands the labor of harmonization and elaboration of the given. A system begins with its harmonies in order and requires not elaboration but merely a repetition, in one detail after another, of its main systemic message. A tradition does not repeat but only renews received truth; a system always repeats because it is by definition encompassing, everywhere saying one thing, which, by definition, is always new. A system in its own terms has no history; a tradition defines itself through the authenticity of its history. In this book, I read some of the classic documents of Judaism as systemic, meaning, documents that form part of a religious system and cohere within that system; in the anticipated work, the same will be done for Zoroastrian writings.

II. Toward an Inductive Definition of Purity: First Steps

From one abstraction, the matter of religion and religious system, I proceed to another. But this time, instead of a theoretical definition loosely set upon facts, I work from data to their definition, in an inductive manner. To begin with, let me propose a definition based on the working of words in the languages before us – languages of religion; I deal with abstractions, involving changes of status. The best way to proceed is to take up passages in the two religious languages in which cleanness figures and work from the case to the rule. The Rivayat accompanying Datestan i Denig presents the following law concerning the transmission of uncleanness through being affected by the motion of, without direct contact with, the source of uncleanness:

> If they are carrying a dead (body) over a bridge of wood or of stone, if it trembles, if everyone who is standing on the bridge (is standing) still (they are) not polluted, but if anyone keeps going he will indeed be polluted.

The principle here is that the corpse uncleanness is conveyed through motion, but not at rest; the criterion (who has to be moving) is, the person who is a candidate for contamination. If a corpse is carried across the bridge, and if others are moving on it, too, if the bridge trembles under the weight of the corpse, then all other persons on the bridge are made unclean, the movement of the bridge transmitting the corpse uncleanness to third parties if they, too, are moving. But if they are not moving, then the uncleanness is null. It then follows that [1] if the bridge is firm and does not shift, [2] and if occupants of the bridge also do not move, then others standing on the bridge are unaffected. The upshot is simple. Corpse uncleanness is transmitted through the motion of an object that bears its weight. Now if on the basis of this case, I had to define our unknown, which is "uncleanness," I should say, "X" derives from a corpse, is transmitted invisibly to objects or persons, and is conveyed through unseen, but clearly physical waves or emanations. I do not know the consequence of being affected by this "X."

A comparable source in the Mishnah provides the same information. That is, in the following the same principle of the physics of the transmission of uncleanness pertains, though it works itself out somewhat differently. The datum is the category of uncleanness described at Lev. 15, called in Hebrew the Zab, a person afflicted with flux uncleanness. Such a person transmits uncleanness to objects that bear his weight, even though not touching those objects – just as the corpse does in the Zoroastrian case – if the other party also is in motion by reason of the same cause, the movement of the ship or the raft or the beast.

Mishnah-tractate Zabim 3:1

A. The Zab and the clean person who sat in a ship or on a raft,
B. or who rode [together] on a beast,
C. even though their clothes do not touch –
D. lo, these are unclean with midras uncleanness.
E. [If] they sat on a plank, or on a bench, or on a bed frame, and on the beam,
F. when they are infirm –
G. [if] they climbed up on a tree which was shaky,
H. on a branch which was shaky on a firm tree –
I. [if they climbed up] on an Egyptian ladder when it is not fastened with a nail,
J. on the bridge,
K. and on the beam,
L. and on the door,
M. when they are not fastened with clay –
N. they are unclean.
O. R. Judah declares clean.

At Eff. I come to precisely the case before us: the Zab and the clean person are on the same plank, bench, bed frame or beam or tree or ladder or bridge: if these are shaky, then the clean person is made unclean. Why? Because the uncleanness of the Zab is transmitted to the clean person through the motion of the infirm bridge or other object. And that is the exact counterpart to the Zoroastrian detail, if the persons on the bridge are moving, too. The point of difference proves equally obvious:

for the Mishnaic law, it is the bridge that is moving, for the Zoroastrian, the afflicted parties. For the one, the uncleanness is transmitted by the movement of the weight bearing component of the tableau, for the other, the movement of the candidate for uncleanness. In the following, I find the same principle:

M. Negaim 13:7

A. The unclean [person] stands under the tree, and the clean person passes –
B. he is unclean.
C. The clean person stands under the tree, and the unclean passes –
D. he is clean.
E. If he stood, he is unclean.
F. And so with the stone which is afflicted with plague – he is clean.
G. And if he put it down, lo, this one is unclean.

Now if the unclean person is at rest (put the corpse down on the bridge) and the clean person walks by (add: and overshadows it, in line with Num. 19), then the clean person contracts uncleanness. The opposite is also the rule: if the uncleanness is in motion and the clean person or object at rest, then the clean person or object remains clean. Here again, this condition, "X," derives from a person in an unspecified condition; but it is transmissible to others through certain contextual conditions, for example, transferred through motion or other media of emanation.

A considerable inductive labor would be required to accomplish a proper definition, but it suffices even now to point out that, in both religious systems, there is an invisible, intangible, yet real emanation, deriving from persons (in our case) that have been transformed into sources of that emanation, and affecting persons that have not earlier been affected by that same emanation. If now I were to ignore the conventions of translation and drop the language of pure and impure or clean and unclean (clearly not hygienic in any sense at all), I could as well borrow the language of atomic physics and cast these emanations into the language of radiation. All that changes is the metaphor. The facts remain the same. An emanation from a source of (radioactive) contamination affects persons and things, in consequence of which the status (health, use) of persons and things is changed (for the worse!). Whatever metaphor I use, the language, "purity" and "impurity," or "cleanness" and "uncleanness," refers to status affected by what is impalpable but very real, and with consequences that are material and substantial: if one is "pure" or "clean," he or she may do certain things that, if impure or unclean, may not be done.

On an inductive basis, we may at this point say only that we deal with an invisible, intangible emanation, with everyday consequences, affecting persons and things. That emanation originates in what is physical or tangible (for example, a corpse) but is transmitted, as in radio waves, in intangible form. And, we may further surmise, persons or things affected by that emanation suffer restrictions that do not apply to those unaffected: a matter of status effected by what is invisible and intangible but exceeding real. Even though that definition is partial, it serves to tell me what data, in the writings we examine, belong, and what do not: what concerns an invisible, intangible emanation that affects one's status with concrete results will come under study. That definition excludes what is tangible, on the one side, and what is inert and ineffective, on the other.

III. The Basis and Purpose of Comparing Religions

The fact that the distinction as to status imputed by reason of an intangible, invisible emanation recurs in documents of two distinct religions and makes the same difference, (but, for the Judaic system, in reverse) justifies the enterprise of comparing the opinions on that same phenomenon in the two sets of writings. And, as a matter of fact, as the pages of this book will show in rich detail, I can readily identify, even in the most remote and hermetic chapters of the law of uncleanness of Iran and Israel, more than a few points of intersection, where the same principles and the same cases generate decisions that are either the same or the opposite: a fine problem for comparison and contrast indeed. Obviously, until I have formed a theory of the whole, each system compared in its entirety to the other, these details remain inert facts, generating nothing beyond themselves. That is why, for the present purpose, a clear view of what I wish to find out has always to remain in plain sight. It is to compare the two traditions when they go over the same theme and reach comparable conclusions, a comparison that, once more, shows us how the documents differ where they are alike. By showing the two religious systems to be alike, I validate comparing them; by showing that they are, where they are alike, also unlike, I validate the process of comparison by yielding contrast bearing meaning.

Let me broaden this observation and speak in more general terms. When we compare one thing to another, it is to gain a measure of perspective on each; we seek an account of likeness and difference, and then we want to explain the difference. What we compare are never things that are identical, but things that are different in interesting ways. When we propose to compare and differentiate, it is because we postulate a fundamental commonality. When we compare, we do so because we perceive basic points of difference that bear significance; comparison in a methodical way then is methodical manipulation of difference. A sound definition of the labor of comparison and differentiation requires a clear notion of what we do when we compare. Subject to the comparison and contrast are diverse systems (in the sense just now defined). Because these systems are alike, they can be shown to differ; because there will be points of difference, we can point also to traits of sameness. What the one thing shows me can be applied to two things only when both things show the same one thing.

There are three dimensions of comparison, diachronic, synchronic, and systemic. We ignore the first two and concentrate only on the third. A diachronic comparison will deal with two systems as they unfold, comparing how, through time, each solves the same problem or produces the same phenomenon. It is then a historical comparison, that is, a comparison of separate histories. A synchronic comparison will address how two systems appear at the same time, for example, in the same historical period. It, too, is a comparison, but not of separate histories, but of different things within the same moment of history. A systemic comparison turns away from historical context and describes systems as ideal types, comparing them not as they have unfolded through time (diachronically) or as they existed at one moment in time (synchronically), but as they appear in the fullness of their development: in theory.

I select systemic comparison partly because synchronic or diachronic comparison is not feasible.[2] As to feasibility: to accomplish diachronic comparison, I should require a common and well-documented context definitive for both religious systems. That is, they should share a single or closely comparable historical and geographic, cultural, political, economic, and social setting. I should then legitimately compare what existed at a particular place and time of proximate uniformity; then the exercise of differentiation becomes possible: then, but only then, I may apply what the one thing shows me to the case of two things. But for our cases, that is not possible, because the literary evidence upon which we must rely for the formation of our comparable ideal types comes from widely separated times, the Mishnah being a second century C.E. document, the comparable Zoroastrian writings having been produced in the ninth century C.E., for example.[3] The two systems flourished in

---

[2]We also find ourselves unpersuaded by the meaning of the results of synchronic or diachronic comparison, as we shall explain in Part Five of this chapter.

[3]True, the documents under study contain "traditions" that "go way back," but allegations to that effect rarely are accompanied by clear instructions on how we know which laws represent such ancient traditions and quite how far back they go. So the entire matter of "tradition" is indeterminate and provides no guidance on how things really were at some determinate time and place, that is, a single moment at which both religious systems were saying enough of the same things, in a sufficiently comprehensive systemic statement, to validate comparison and

different places, under different political circumstances, in worlds remote in their cultural characteristics. True, one might wish to compare Zoroastrian purity laws of the time of the Achaemenids and the corresponding laws of Leviticus, since these come from more or less the same period. But then we should be comparing not Zoroastrianism's fully exposed system, nor that of Judaism, but only one phase of the one and one phase of the other. And I propose a complete, systematic comparison of a systemic character, not a partial one, and the systems I have chosen are not the Priestly Code of the Book of Leviticus against the Avesta, also deriving from Achaemenid times, but Judaism as fully formulated in the Dual Torah and Zoroastrianism as wholly set forth in the counterpart writings.

All comparison begins in establishing likeness – as my cases already have done – which then legitimates finding what is unlike in the like. Finding what is like in the unlike, by contrast, is not legitimate. A simple observation explains why. In the former case the datum – the fact from which I commence all work – is similarity; that is not imposed, imputed or invented. It is obvious and superficial. In the latter case the datum on which I build my structure of comparison is difference. But this point of unlikeness may be random and episodic; it may be imposed, imputed, and invented; it is subjective and deep. If I wish to compare, my mental experiment requires me to differentiate among available similarities, things that trigger my interest by obvious likeness (intersecting theories of the transfer of invisible, viscous waves that emanate from a corpse and change the status of those affected by said waves). We cannot condemn ourselves to wander aimless in search of connections among things that are fundamentally unlike one another. The infinity of possibilities – cars and cantaloupes, manholes and mangos, for instance – makes the work merely silly; the metaphors are all there is. Contrasting things that have not to begin with been compared and found comparable seems too much a labor of imagination to serve well in the work of analysis.

What are common grounds that make possible the mapping of diverse contours? If, as in this study of religious ideas about intangible but real forces,[4] I compare artifacts of intellect, then in common should be, if not a common language and mode of discourse, then at least common attitudes, established to begin with. In the case at hand, we

---

therefore also contrast. So the allegation as to a linear, incremental, unitary tradition represented by the documents of a much later period, while plausible, is not very helpful and bears no important consequences for the descriptive work that makes contrast plausible.

[4]Readers will have recognized how many metaphors we have had to use to speak of our subject-matter; the task of Chapter Eight will be to move beyond metaphor and toward language dictated by inductive analysis of our data.

shall see some evidence of common attitudes, but much evidence of systemic commonality: both religious systems set forth purity systems, and the two systems are in fact identical in their basic organization, structure, and systemic components. Any comparison, moreover, requires that we have sufficient data, and data of a comparable order. There has to be a rough proportionality to secure plausible comparison. I cannot compare a system that is rich in data of one kind to one that is rich in data of some other kind, for example, a purity system that tells us much about rites of purification but little about sources of uncleanness against one that is informative about the transfer of uncleanness but offers little differentiation in rites of purification. My case, as this book shows, allows us to compare truly comparable systems.

I therefore accept as a challenge to this enterprise in particular the general question phrased by Jonathan Z. Smith:

> We know better how to evaluate comparisons, but we have gained little over our predecessors in either the method for making comparisons or the reasons for its practice. There is nothing easier than the making of patterns...but the "how" and the "why" and above all the "so what" remain most refractory.... It is a problem to be solved by theories and reasons, of which we have had to little.[5]

The why here is: these are two religious systems that concern themselves with the same things in the same ways. The how is, a phenomenological comparison of systems represented as ideal types. But what about the "so what"?

To phrase matters in my own way: Having defined an arena for comparative study, why is it urgent to do this work of comparison? That is to say, what do we think we learn, which we did not know before, when we juxtapose two congruent facts of systemic analysis? What questions can we answer that we could not answer before the act of juxtaposition, yielding comparison and contrast, such as we offer here? Or more accurately: What else do we know, what more do we know than we knew before we tried to apply what the one thing shows me to the case of two things? To state the question simply: What else do I know, what more do I know than I knew before, when I find out that one thing, for example, the fact that corpses contaminate, is the case of two things (Judaism, Zoroastrianism)? That is the issue of this book.[6]

Judgments based on comparison are required if we are to understand any single religious system; in the study of religion, everybody concurs, one who knows only one religion understands no religion. But these

---

[5]Jonathan Z. Smith, *Imagining Religion* (Chicago, 1986: University of Chicago Press), p. 35.
[6]Worked out in Chapter Eight.

judgments may prove somewhat impressionistic and offhand, even the result of an apologetic bias. To give one important example, the simple fact that the eschatological doctrines of Zoroaster occur in four great religions, Judaism, Christianity, Islam, and Zoroastrianism, is addressed by the great scholar of Zoroastrianism, Mary Boyce, in these words:

> Zoroaster's eschatological teachings...became profoundly familiar through borrowings to Jews, Christians, and Muslims, and have exerted enormous influence on the lives and thoughts of men in many lands. Yet it was in the framework of his own faith that they attained their fullest logical coherence.[7]

Now the allegation, "...in the framework of his own faith that they attained their fullest logical coherence" is a judgment of comparison (or a mere encomium!) and therefore requires evidence, and the evidence must come from the kind of comparative work I do here. First, we have to describe the four systems; then we have to identify the place of the eschatology of Zoroaster in each system; third we have to know the systemic logic that holds that myth in place in each of the religious systems, respectively; we further have to assess, as best we can, the coherence, within each system, of the myth of eschatology; and then, but only then, we shall have reason to maintain that it is in this system, rather than that, that the eschatology attains its "fullest logical coherence." Merely saying so does not prove it, though expressing the judgment does stimulate inquiry of a fresh and interesting order: comparison.

What is at stake? First, of course, only through comparative inquiry of an inductive character into the use and consequence of language can we know that, in two systems, the same words may appropriately be used, for example, unclean and clean (or any words that are so used as to signify the same things, for instance, describing the same effects in concrete terms). So comparative work on two or more systems is what makes possible the formation of a single language to cover a number of religions. Without a work of comparison, we may actually impose upon several religions the category formation, inclusive of the language that contains said formation, of a single religion.

Second, only through comparative study can we fully understand what we are seeing in a given religious system. For in comparison we see roads taken and not taken. When we take account of the things people might have done, we may make sense of the things they actually did do. Confronting the range of choices, we make sense of the chosen. Since a given group does some one thing, constructing the requisite

---

[7]Mary Boyce, *A History of Zoroastrianism* [= *Handbuch der Orientalistik*. Erste Abteilung. VIII.1. Lieferung 2, Heft 2A] (Leiden, 1975: E. J. Brill) 1:246.

group of choices is rarely possible within the range of artifacts of a single group. Perhaps in theory all the things all social entities or religious systems might choose would constitute the true range of alternatives, a social and religious counterpart to the unlimited range of sounds that at birth we are able to replicate. But in practice, a broader context, established through commonalities and contrasts, defines the proximate range of alternatives – equal equivalent to the sounds we actually hear, which deprive us of our innate power to make all sounds ever heard. I apply what the one thing shows me to the case of two things by demonstrating that, faced with both things, one group chose one thing, one group the other. In the comparison and contrast of groups standing within a single, clearly defined continuum, I am able to make sense of one group by playing it off against the other.

Let me state the case very simply: the useful end of the game of comparison is to discover, through the might-have-beens of culture, the meaning of what was.

IV. The Justification for Comparing Judaism and Zoroastrianism in Particular

Two religions that exhibit numerous, important affinities, Zoroastrianism and Judaism, concur that certain sources of uncleanness produce concrete effects in everyday life. They agree that corpse matter and menstrual fluids convey uncleanness; uncleanness affects food and drink, persons and objects, so changing their status, for example, their utility; and they concur that, under certain circumstances and in specified ways, uncleanness can be removed. Those points of agreement in detail invite comparison of the larger structures of which the details form a part.

For heavily laden with what we roughly call "ritual," both Judaism and Zoroastrianism concur on such propositions as the correspondence between the ethical and moral and the concrete and practical aspects of everyday life, regarding ritual as consequential, also insisting that ritual convey what is right and true. Joining (in terms of the Hebrew Scriptures) the priestly concern for cult, law, and justice, with the prophetic insistence on the priority of right over rite, both religions hold together and in balance the material and the moral aspects of religion. Not only so, but at important points, they concur that rite affects everyday life; consequential theology is lived theology; actions express truth in the workaday world; rules draw into harmony what God wants and what people do – or call attention to their divergence.

Before proceeding, let me give a single, very concrete example to show the profound congruence of attitudes that links the two religions:

the self-evidence of the correlation between rite and right. That correlation is expressed in cases particular to the respective traditions, which make precisely the same point. It is the specificity of the parallel that makes the comparison consequential. In the present case, an act of rite that God desires is rejected if it is based on a wrongful action. First comes the Zoroastrian, then the Judaic, formulation of the same point:

Offering Stolen Firewood unto the Fire

Question: If one offers unto the fire libation and fuel that are stolen and robbed and obtained through deceit and wickedness, then does any meritorious deed accrue therefrom or not?

Answer: No, surely it is a sin. The fire of Ohrmazd scorches him just as when he holds heat. And he who would offer me the libations procured through theft, robbery, ravishing, raid, and brought from a liar. He who offers libation unto my fire originating from theft, robbery, ravishing, deceiving, depriving men [they deprive mankind in price] and carrying through fraudulence, burns me thus with so much burning, just as thereby...and defilement of the Evil Spirit comes upon men. My fire scorches that man with so much scorching, just as mankind whom the Destructive Spirit defiles.[8]

And, along these same lines the law of Judaism rejects the use for purposes of piety of what is unlawfully acquired:

M. Sukkah 3:3A-B

A.   A stolen or dried up willow branch is invalid [for use in the celebration of the festival of Tabernacles].
B.   And one deriving from an asherah or an apostate town is invalid.

Now the sentiment is the same: one cannot serve God through things gained unlawfully. That commonplace need not capture our attention; what makes it interesting is that the same idea is expressed through the same medium: a case that, changing the details, proves interchangeable from writing to writing. The setting is of course particular, each to its own system. The Zoroastrian formulation has God instruct Zoroaster, the Judaic one just states a rule in a laconic, factual way – a mighty difference indeed. It follows that, at particular points – a great many, as a matter of fact, as we shall see even in the severely curtailed survey given here – Judaism and Zoroastrianism intersect and commonly concur on the same principle, each making the same point through its own idiom.

---

[8]Kaikhusroo M. Jamaspa and Helmut Humbach, *Pursishniha. A Zoroastrian Catechism* (Wiesbaden, 1971: Otto Harrassowitz), Part I. *Text, Translation, Notes*, pp. 36-37.

The specific subject of comparison is purity and impurity, or cleanness and uncleanness in an other-than-material or hygienic, but cultic or ritual sense. It suffices here to say only that the comparison can be, and is, uniform, because the same category formation serves each religious system. That is why we compare both whole systems and also the matching parts of which they are comprised. This sustained and systematic systemic comparison is possible also for reasons of proportion: both religions in their classical statements make much of purity; through that subject, both communicate important elements of their larger systems and messages. Comparing how each treats a topic addressed by the other affords perspective on both religions and also enriches our understanding of the uses of the category, purity, in religion.

To summarize: the comparative study of religion begins by comparing religions that sustain interesting comparison. That is to say, religions that are alike also differ in consequential ways; those that exhibit no basis for comparison, being utterly unlike in fundamental ways, also cannot stand contrast. To give a concrete example, a religion that regards food and sex as matters of indifference to its god will not afford interesting points of comparison and contrast with one that regards food and sex as principal points of concern for its god. All we know when we undertake the comparative study of those two religions is that the one legislates, the other does not, on matters of nourishment and procreation. If, by contrast, two religions formulate their systemic statements through detailed and close attention to those subjects, then the comparison will yield differentiated, therefore interesting points of systemic likeness and difference. And, in the light of that differentiated comparison, the systemic character of each religion will be seen in shades and nuances that the flat light of the level plane does not reveal.

The particular affinities between Zoroastrianism and Judaism that in my view validate comparison and thus contrast concern the matter of purity, meaning, the absence of impurity: its sources, effects, and resolution. Purity and impurity bear a variety of meanings in diverse contexts, since these words may refer to matters both public and private, material and immaterial, physical and spiritual; in diverse contexts they cut across a variety of other categories, for example, the physically pure or impure, the morally pure or impure, the pure or impure act of sex, eating, the bodily secretions that are pure or impure, and on and on. The indeterminate uses or meanings of the words pure and impure find simplest illustration in the following perfectly intelligible phrases: pure gold, pure soul, pure land, pure genealogy, pure faith, pure food, pure water, and pure intention. Categories conveyed by the adjectives pure and impure, therefore, prove so diverse and incoherent that the adjectives themselves lose all indicative sense and precise meaning.

It follows that the statement, Zoroastrianism and Judaism in common invoke the categories, pure and impure, or use in common language that we translate by those words (or clean/unclean) in no way validates the comparison between the two religious systems, so far as such comparison rests on shared traits. The adventitious character of words deriving from several different systems and their languages that, coming into our own language are translated by the same words in English bears no consequence whatsoever.

V. The Purpose of Comparing Judaism and Zoroastrianism: Diachronic, Synchronic, Systemic

It remains to spell out what I do not promise to provide in my comparison and contrast, so that readers will not expect what is not here. In the case of both religions, therefore, I set forth not the history of how a given detail of the law may have developed, but a phenomenological account of the structure and form of the system as set forth in its systemic statement recast as an ideal type. The comparison I undertake does not concern historical unfolding; I do not ask about points of contact at given moments in time, let alone issues of influence or borrowing. Accordingly, what I propose to accomplish – the comparison of systems and structures – requires that I also explain what I do not undertake. Since I identify a fixed statement of Judaism's structures of purity and their systems (how they are comprised, how they function), I set aside three important considerations, together with the questions that they answer. Describing matters at a determinate moment eliminates the need to specify how things reached this formation rather than some other. Doing so further sets aside questions of influence and borrowing. Finally, it dismisses as heuristically null the claim to explain how something is by reference to how it was or whence it derived or how it developed – its past – on the one side, or the contributory sources of its components, on the other.

Clearly, a single agendum, defined by a simple logic of what (in theory at least) *any* treatment of a given subject must address, governs. I maintain that (in the abstract) any structure of cleanness and uncleanness in an other-than-hygienic framework (for example, a framework that is cultic or ritualistic and not one-dimensionally palpable or material or physical) will have to answer my three questions of cause, effect, and remission: sources of uncleanness and how uncleanness contaminates; what difference uncleanness makes; and how uncleanness is removed. Admittedly, that allegation that my theoretical structure (in terms of logic) should serve universally borders on the disingenuous, since the specified categories serve very well for both religions subject to study here and encompass nearly all of the data set forth by each; I have already alleged that the comparison is possible because of that very fact. So the logic of the phenomenon in general may in fact be particular to the shared cases of Judaism and Zoroastrianism. Of that I cannot be sure before examining other systems besides those under study here. My premise forms a starting point that is legitimated by my data; but my definition of what is at stake requires that my premise become a matter of hypothesis to be investigated in its own terms; once more, the best is the enemy of the good. And that is why, in the actual doing of the descriptive work, this simple analytical structure comes prior to the approach to any set of data and applies equally to each set of facts. I accordingly form my data into a cogent picture, deriving from the two systems, so showing how the two religions take up a single program. In theory, I should gladly invite into the comparative enterprise at hand specialists in other religious systems that devote substantial attention to the clean and the unclean.

The phenomenological organization of the data that I have defined of course represents only one way of comparison and contrast. It is neither synchronic nor diachronic, since one system, the Judaism of the Dual Torah, Scripture and the Mishnah, that is, written and oral, reached its nearly complete statement in books that came to closure by the late second century C.E. [= A.D.], while the other, Zoroastrianism, is here represented by writings that took shape over a long period of time and reached fullness only in the ninth century C.E. So the comparison by definition is not synchronic. And for the same reason, it is not diachronic, since I do not maintain that I and my co-worker in time to come are comparing systems that unfolded over a long period of time along parallel lines, a development in the thinking of the one, for example, on sources of contamination, forming a counterpart to a development in the thinking of the other.

Diachronic (and also synchronic) comparison might be possible if I knew for sure the point at which, in each system, the conclusion was reached that (by way of example) menstruation or corpse matter was a principal source of uncleanness. If I determined that in a given system that conclusion was reached at a given time, and in a juxtaposed system, known to have been in the same time and place, the same conclusion was reached at that same time, diachronic comparison would prove feasible. Then it might be claimed as a matter of fact that a major book of the Judaism of the Dual Torah set forth the uncleanness of those sources at the same time that a major book of Zoroastrianism reached the same conclusion. And, if I knew that as fact, I might also wonder how come the two religions came to the same point at the same time and so commence speculation on issues of influence, intersection, and parallelism. Such questions, once legitimated by facts, take on a logic of their own. But what we cannot show, we do not know, and I prefer to concentrate on the hard facts in hand: the documents in their fullness, at their point of closure – therefore phenomenological comparison. Admittedly, the more familiar mode of comparison is historical and contextual: synchronic and diachronic. If such comparison were possible in the case it hand, it might win attention; but it is not, and for that reason I have preferred the phenomenological to the historical mode of description, analysis, and interpretation.

But feasibility is not the only argument that favors phenomenological comparison and prevents the historical – diachronic or synchronic. In my view, the upshot of comparison is perspective on the things compared, on the one side, and on the contrast between the things legitimately compared (by reason of having sides in common) and things not compared at all (not having aspects that legitimate comparison). Perspective is not afforded by mere detail, for example, at a given and determinate time, this system gained this detail, and that system gained that; systemic description is required to accommodate the comparison of details, or all I know is the fact at hand – likeness or unlikeness – but not what is at stake in that fact, its meaning or consequence. Historical explanation aims at showing borrowings or influences, confluence and diffusion. But that explanation ignores the system altogether, fixing, rather, upon a different question from the one of systemic description, analysis, and interpretation. I ask why this, not that? So what? Historical explanation wants to tell us where something has come from, how one thing may be explained by appeal to the character of some other and its influence.

But when I know that fact X has come to system B from system A, I still know nothing about either system other than the simple allegation at hand: system B has "borrowed from" or "been influenced by" system A. How I understand system B better than I did before, or whether I understand it at all by reason of this new fact, is surely to be explained, not merely gainsaid. This kind of historical explanation looks suspiciously akin to the reduction of system B to the question, where did it get (some of) its materials? But I want to know, what is this system and how is it to be described, analyzed, and interpreted? And the answers to that question derive from the system that is subject to study, not from other systems that may have contributed data to the formation of said system. The heuristic value remains to be shown: If I know something, then what else do I know? In my case, a clear answer is to be given, and it is not a reductionist one.

Specifically, what I seek from the facts adduced by comparison and contrast is perspective upon the religions that have yielded those facts, each in its system and context – a greater depth than a one dimensional angle of vision affords. And, as is clear, I hope also to contribute to the comparative study of religion by comparing comparable religions and pointing to contrasts with incomparable ones. That explains why for this part of the comparative study I have formed a general theory of what any purity system ought to cover – admittedly, framed out of the facts I had in advance about what the Zoroastrian and Judaic systems do address – and explored that theory.

Accordingly, I dismiss as irrelevant to my work two important and commonplace principles of description and explanation. These are history, on the one side, development, and influence, on the other. Once I identify that determinate moment at which the two systems will be compared and contrasted and specify the documentary evidence that expresses the system, I treat as a settled, stable fact whatever those documents tell us. I acknowledge all of the facts emerge from a long history of development; but that history does not help us describe how things are, only how they came to be. But origins explain nothing; only systemic position and structure do. If historical origins are set aside as irrelevant, then of course questions of development and change, prior to the fixed point at which the description is undertaken, do not have to be asked.

And, it goes without saying, I claim to know nothing of points at which a given system may have intersected with some other (either one with the other, or both with a third system). Since parallel lines do not meet, where I find parallels I have to explain them: A borrowed from B, B from A, or both from C. When I know that, what more do I know? Assuming system B has borrowed a fact from system A, I do not know why that has taken place, or, more important, what system B has done with the fact shared with system A that testifies to the distinctive character of system B. The system is itself; its systemic statement is always in its native language, even though words in that language have come from some other, indeed many other languages. A language is prior to its vocabulary, and a system is prior to its components. That explains why I do not understand how knowing what is borrowed and what is "original" contributes to the description, analysis, and interpretation of what is: that is, of the system as it makes its appearance, whole and complete, cogent and harmonious, in its selected and determinate moment of full expression: in the selected documents.

It is important to make these observations, since imperial claims have extended the boundaries of Zoroastrian hegemony hither and yon, over more territory than Cyrus conquered, over a far longer period of time than the Achaemenids ruled. Matters have reached such an extreme that, wherever light contrasts with darkness, whenever a dualism characterizes theology, for example, we are asked to recognize "Zoroastrian influence." But once we have done so (even only for the sake of argument), then we must wonder how we understand that which supposedly has been so influenced in some other, better way than we did before we knew that fact. The heuristic consequence of borrowings, influences, intersections, parallels, and the like has been broadly assumed but has not been fully explained. If it is taxonomic – religions affected by Zoroastrianism distinguished from those not – and depends upon my concurring on the dubious taxic premise that the contrast of light and dark signals Zoroaster's presence, then we have made a taxic distinction that yields no heuristic difference. A classification that holds nearly everything speciates nothing.

A wraith, a chimera, an evanescent shadow, Zoroaster then is supposed to be present everywhere. But, if he is, then he is allowed to make a consequential, differentiating impact nowhere. Portrayed in such cosmic and abstract terms, Zoroastrianism stands for too much beyond its own specificities to help me understand either the religions supposedly shaped in response to Zoroastrianism, on the one hand, or Zoroastrianism itself, on the other. The claims of vast influence turn out to trivialize and homogenize what is a differentiated and very specific religious system (at least, at the point at which, in these pages, that system is represented). Let me close with a single concrete example of how issues of history, development, borrowing, and influence yield a reading I find inconsequential, because too abstract and schematic to matter. If we are told that the creation narrative of Genesis, which distinguishes light from darkness and maintains one God created both, responds to, and forms a judgment upon, the theology that explains the distinction between light and darkness in a different way – the one stands for one God, the other, for a competing God – then what do we know that helps us better to understand either the Genesis narrative or the Zoroastrian dualism (for that matter)? The information is trivial, inert, banal, and commonplace; all we learn is that the religions differ, and the one religion takes up a different position from the other. If it is alleged that the emphasis of the Genesis story responds to the Zoroastrian view, the "therefore" we are supposed then to propose, the consequence for describing, analyzing, and interpreting the Genesis story, hardly leaps upward to articulate definition.

That kind of comparison – diachronic, synchronic – I therefore do not undertake; the comparison that is meant to meant to yield evidence of borrowing, influence, contact or intersection, I do not promise. If, therefore, readers want to find out how, for example, Zoroastrianism influenced Judaism, or if they wish to follow debates on how Judaism reshaped into a statement of its own what it borrowed from Zoroastrianism, they will be best advised to read some other book than this one. My purpose must be clear: it is comparative and interpretative, not historical, not even contextual. So I do not deal with the formation of either system at diverse points in time, but only in what I conceive to be its final and full statement. My co-worker and I are not writing parallel histories of the two systems, for example, what came first, what was later on added, to the final system of purity put forth by Judaism in Scripture and the Mishnah. We do not pretend to know those parallel histories, and for our purpose, we find them monumentally irrelevant.

Nor, in consequence, do we compare out of systemic context one detail of the one religion's purity rules with a counterpart of the other's (even though, in the foregoing remarks, I have done just that three times over). I do not propose to explain how systems grew and changed through the passage of time ("history"), or what each did with components both may have borrowed from some third party or one from the other ("parallels"). That is not only for methodological reasons already spelled out – our preference for phenomenological over historical description. It is also for a much simpler consideration, also adumbrated just now: I simply doubt the facticity of much that is alleged about matters of origins and influences and borrowings. Indeed, it is so easy to demolish theories of origins, influences, parallels, borrowings, and the like that I regard such work as facile and sterile. I prefer to set forth theories for others to utilize and criticize and improve.

I cannot overstate the grounds for abandoning all interest in the study of mere parallels and speculation on unanswerable questions of origins, points supposedly in common, alleged divergences from a common path, and the like. Allegations of facts of these kinds – parallels, borrowing, origins, and the like – prove facile. They hardly pass the simplest tests of verification, for example, is borrowing or influence the only explanation or indeed the best explanation for what appear to be parallels? Are the parallels contextually parallel at all? How should I know whether an allegation as to influence or borrowing might be falsified? The answers to these questions – borrowing or influence are not the only or best possible explanations; parallels upon closer examination prove divergent; possibilities for falsification are nil – hardly win my confidence. Parallel lines do not meet; diverse explanations present themselves as candidates for understanding a given confluence of facts; and things that look alike often deceive. And, it follows the results must be sterile, since, once we know (or think we have proven) that X has borrowed from Y, what more we know about either X or Y is unclear. That is why I call into question the heuristic interest of proposed answers to such questions as, who borrowed from or influenced whom, and where did this idea or rule originate? I have in mind, therefore, offering an example of a different way of comparing religions than is presently commonplace. Accordingly, I have chosen a different route in this comparative study, the systemic comparison I have now defined. Now to deal with Judaism in particular.

1

An Overview of Judaism: Definitions, Sources, and Purity Systems

I. Defining Judaism

Defining Judaism requires us to survey thousands of years of continuous human existence. Over the span of thirty-five hundred years of an ongoing life of a group, much changes, and little, if anything, remains the same. When we speak of "Judaism," therefore, we must ask ourselves what we mean. We wonder how we may define the whole despite the diversity of the parts. One solution to this problem is not to pretend that many things are really one, but to find a way of describing, analyzing, and interpreting diversity within a realm of commonality. That is to say, there never has been a single encompassing Judaism, present beneath the accidents of difference. There have been only diverse Judaisms. But these Judaisms do form a whole, in that, seen all together over time and all at once in comparison to other religion cultures, they do bear traits that distinguish all of them from all others and permit us to identify them as a cogent set of systems. That requires us to define not Judaism but a Judaism, that is to say, a single religious system, composed of three elements: a worldview, a way of life, and a social group that, in the here and now, embodies the whole. The worldview explains the life of the group, ordinarily referring to God's creation, the revelation of the Torah, the goal and end of the group's life in the end of time. The way of life defines what is special about the life of the group. The social group, in a single place and time, then forms the living witness and testimony to the system as a whole and finds in the system ample explanation for its very being. That is a Judaism.

How shall we know when we have a Judaism? The answer to that question draws us to the data – the facts – we must locate and describe, analyze, and interpret. The first requirement is to find a group of Jews who see themselves as "Israel," that is, the Jewish People who form the family and children of Abraham, Isaac, Jacob, Sarah, Rebecca, Leah, and Rachel, the founding fathers and mothers. That same group must tell us that it uniquely constitutes "Israel," not an Israel, putting forth "Judaism," not a Judaism. The second requirement is to identify the forms through which that distinct group expresses its worldview. Ordinarily, we find that expression in writing, so we turn to the authoritative holy books that the group studies and deems God-given, that is, the group's Torah or statement of God's revelation to Israel. Since we use the word Torah to mean biblical books, starting with the Five Books of Moses (Genesis, Exodus, Leviticus, Numbers, and Deuteronomy), we must remind ourselves that the contents of the Torah have varied from one Judaism to the next. Some groups regard as holy what other groups reject or ignore. But all Judaisms appeal to the Pentateuch in particular, whatever other scriptures they call "the Torah." Let me specify the periods of the history of Judaism relevant to this study.

586 B.C.E. The destruction of the first Temple in Jerusalem by the Babylonians.

The ancient Israelites, living in what they called the Land of Israel, produced Scriptures that reached their present form in the aftermath of the destruction of their capital city and Temple. Whatever happened before that time was reworked in the light of that event and the meaning imputed to it by authors who lived afterward. All Judaisms, from 586 B.C.E. forward, appeal to the writings produced in the aftermath of the destruction of the first Temple. Therefore we must regard the destruction of that Temple as the date that marks the beginning of the formation of Judaism(s).

70 C.E. The destruction of the second Temple in Jerusalem by the Romans.

The Jews' leaders – the political classes and priesthood – after 586 B.C.E. were taken to Babylonia, the homeland of their conquerors, where they settled down. A generation later, Babylonia fell under the rule of the Persians, who permitted Jews to return to their ancient homeland. A small number did so, where they rebuilt the Temple and produced the Hebrew Scriptures. The second Temple of Jerusalem lasted from about 500 B.C.E. to 70 C.E., when the Romans – by that time ruling the entire Middle East, including the Land of Israel, mainly through their own friends and allies – put down a Jewish rebellion and, in the war, destroyed Jerusalem again. The second destruction proved final and marked the beginning of the Jews' history as a political entity defined in social and religious terms, but not in territorial ones. That is, the Jews formed a distinct religious social group, but all of them did not live in any one place, and some of them lived nearly everywhere in the West, within the lands of Christendom and Islam alike.

THE FIRST AGE OF DIVERSITY begins with the writing down, in more or less their present form, of the Scriptures of ancient Israel, beginning with the Five Books of Moses. Drawing upon writings and oral traditions of the period before the destruction of the first Temple of Jerusalem, in 586 B.C.E., the authorship of the surviving leadership of that Temple and court, the priests, produced most of the books we now know as the Hebrew Bible ("Old Testament," or "Tanakh"), specifically, the Pentateuch or Five Books of Moses, the prophetic writings from Joshua and Judges through Samuel and Kings and Isaiah, Jeremiah, Ezekiel, and the twelve smaller books of prophetic writings; and some of the other Scriptures as well. During this same period a number of diverse groups of Jews, living in the Land of Israel as well as in Babylonia, to the east, and in Alexandria, in Egypt, to the west, took over these writings and interpreted them in diverse ways. Hence during the period from the formation of the Torah book to the destruction of the second Temple, there were many Judaisms.

THE AGE OF DEFINITION, beginning with the destruction of the second Temple in 70, saw the diverse Judaisms of the preceding period give way, over a long period of time, to a single Judaism. That was the system worked out by the sages who, after 70, developed a system of Judaism, linked to Scripture but enriched by an autonomous corpus of holy writings in addition. This Judaism is marked by its doctrine of the dual media by which the Torah was formulated and transmitted, in writing on the one side, in formulation and transmission by memory, hence, orally, on the other. The doctrine of the Dual Torah, written and oral, then defined the canon of Judaism. The Written Torah encompassed pretty much the same books that the world at large knows as the Old Testament. The Oral Torah added the writings of the sages, beginning with the Mishnah, a philosophical law code produced at ca. 200 C.E., two massive commentaries on the Mishnah, the two Talmuds, one produced in the Land of Israel and called the Yerushalmi, or Jerusalem Talmud, ca. 400 C.E., the other in Babylonian and called the Bavli, or Talmud of Babylonia, ca. 600 C.E. In that same age, alongside Mishnah commentary, systematic work on Scripture yielded works organized around particular books of the Written Torah, parallel to works organized around particular tractates of the Mishnah. These encompassed Sifra, to the book of Leviticus, Sifré, to Numbers, another Sifré, to Deuteronomy, works containing statements attributed to the same authorities who stand behind the Mishnah, to be dated sometime between 200 and 400, as well as Genesis Rabbah and Leviticus Rabbah, discursive works on themes in Genesis and Leviticus, edited between 400 and 450, Pesiqta deRav Kahana, a profoundly eschatological treatment of topics in Pentateuchal writings, of about 450, and similar works. These writings all together, organized around, first, the Mishnah, and, then, Scripture, comprised the first works of the Oral Torah. That is to say, the teachings of the sages, originally formulated and transmitted in memory, were the written down contents of the Oral Torah that God had revealed – so the system maintained – to Moses at Sinai. During the age of definition, that Judaism of the Dual Torah reached its literary statement and authoritative expression.

The Jewish people form a very small group, spread over many countries. One fact of Jews' natural environment is that they form a distinct group in diverse societies. A second is that they constitute solely a community of fate and, for many, of faith, but that alone, in that they have few shared social or cultural traits. A third is that they do not form a single political entity. A fourth is that they look back upon a very long and in some way exceptionally painful history. A worldview suited to the Jews' social ecology must make sense of their unimportance and explain their importance. It must explain the continuing life of the group, which in important ways marks the group as different from others, and persuade people that their forming a distinct and distinctive community is important and worth carrying on. The interplay between the political, social, and historical life of the Jews and their conceptions of themselves in this world and the next – that is, their worldview, contained in their canon, their way of life, explained by the teleology of the system, and the symbolic structure that encompasses the two and stands for the whole all at once and all together – these define the focus for the inquiry into the ecology of the religion at hand, that is, the ecology of a Judaism.

One idea predominates in nearly all Judaic religious systems, the conception that the Jews are in exile but have the hope of coming home to their own land, which is the Land of Israel (a.k.a. Palestine). The original reading of the Jews' existence as exile and return derives from the Pentateuch, the Five Books of Moses, which were composed as we now have them (out of earlier materials, to be sure) in the aftermath of the destruction of the Temple in 586 B.C.E. and in response to the exile to Babylonia, the experience selected and addressed by the authorship of the document is that of exile and restoration. But that framing of events into the pattern at hand represents an act of powerful imagination and interpretation. That experience taught lessons people claimed to learn out of the events they had chosen and, in the Pentateuch, which took shape in 450 B.C.E. when some Jews returned from Babylonia to Jerusalem, for their history: the life of the group is uncertain, subject to conditions and stipulations. Nothing is set and given, all things a gift: land and life itself. But what actually did happen in that uncertain world – exile but then restoration – marked the group as special, different, select.

That experience of the uncertainty of the life of the group in the century or so from the destruction of the First Temple of Jerusalem by the Babylonians in 586 to the building of the Second Temple of Jerusalem by the Jews, with Persian permission and sponsorship returned from exile, formed the paradigm. With the promulgation of the "Torah of Moses" under the sponsorship of Ezra, the Persians' viceroy, at ca. 450 B.C.E., all future Israels would then refer to that formative experience as it had been set down and preserved as the norm for Israel in the mythic terms of that "original" Israel, the Israel not of Genesis and Sinai and the end at the moment of entry into the promised land, but the "Israel" of the families that recorded as the rule and the norm the story of both the exile and the return. In that minority genealogy, that story of exile and return, alienation and remission, imposed on the received stories of pre-exilic Israel and adumbrated time and again in the Five Books of Moses and addressed by the framers of that document in their work over all, we find that paradigmatic statement in which every Judaism, from then to now, found its structure and deep syntax of social existence, the grammar of its intelligible message.

No Judaism recapitulates any other, and none stands in a linear and incremental relationship with any prior one. But all Judaisms recapitulate that single paradigmatic experience of the Torah of "Moses," the authorship that reflected on the meaning of the events of 586-450 selected for the composition of history and therefore interpretation. That experience (in theological terms) rehearsed the conditional moral existence of sin and punishment, suffering and atonement and reconciliation, and (in social terms) the uncertain and always conditional national destiny of disintegration and renewal of the group. That moment captured within the Five Books of Moses, that is to say, the judgment of the generation of the return to Zion, led by Ezra, about its extraordinary experience of exile and return would inform the attitude and viewpoint of all the Israels beyond. Looking back on Scripture and its message, Jews have ordinarily treated as special, subject to conditions and therefore uncertain what (in their view) other groups enjoyed as unconditional and simply given. Why the paradigm renewed itself is clear: this particular view of matters generated expectations that could not be met, hence created resentment – and then provided comfort and hope that made possible coping with that resentment. To state the thesis with appropriate emphasis: *Promising what could not be delivered, then providing solace for the consequent disappointment, the system at hand precipitated in age succeeding age the very conditions necessary for its own replication.*

There have been many Judaisms, each with its indicative symbol and generative paradigm, each pronouncing its worldview and prescribing its way of life and identifying the particular Israel that, in its view, is Israel, bearer of the original promise of God. But each Judaism retells in its own way and with its distinctive emphases the tale of the Five Books of Moses, the story of a no-people that becomes a people, that has what it gets only on condition, and that can lose it all by virtue of its own sin. That is imposes acute self-consciousness, chronic insecurity, upon what should be the level plane and firm foundation of society. That is to say, the collection of diverse materials joined into a single tale on the occasion of the original exile and restoration because of the repetition in age succeeding age also precipitates the recapitulation of the interior experience of exile and restoration – always because of sin and atonement. So it is the Pentateuch that shaped the imagination of Jews wherever they lived, and it is their social condition as a small and scattered group that made the question of raised by the Pentateuchal narrative urgent, and the power of the Pentateuch both to ask but also to answer the question that made the answer compelling whenever and wherever Jews (that is to say, "Israel") lived.

II. The Sources of Judaism on Purity [1]:
The Pentateuchal Priestly Code (Leviticus and Numbers)
[Ca. 450 B.C.E.]

The way of life of the Judaism that set the norm for the Second Temple period was that holy way of life depicted in the Five Books of Moses, the Pentateuch. The Pentateuch encompasses four sources, originally distinct, three, J, E, and D, or the Yahwist, the Elohist, and the Deuteronomist, deriving from the period before 586, one, the priestly, from the period afterward. But from our perspective, the Judaic system represented by the Pentateuch came into being when the several sources became one, that is, the Five Books of Moses as we now know them. That work was accomplished by priests in the time of Ezra, around 450 B.C.E. The worldview derived from the account of heaven and earth and definition of Israel presented in the Pentateuch. The Israel of that Judaism found its definition in the same Scripture: Israel encompassed the family of an original father, Abraham. Israel now consisted of the genealogical descendants of that original family. Thus the Scripture of the first Judaism was the Five Books of Moses, the setting encompassed Israel after the exile and return to Zion, and the system centered on the explanation of those rules that would keep Israel holy, that is separate for God alone. Central to that life of holiness was the "tabernacle," conceived as the model for the post-exilic temple.

While making ample use of ancient tales, the priests, who were the final framers of the Pentateuch as we now know it, conceived as their systemic teleology the return to Zion and the rebuilding of the temple – hence the centrality in the wilderness narratives of the tabernacle and its cult. So the setting of the Judaism of the priests imparts to the scripture of that first setting its ultimate meaning: response to historical disaster followed by (to the Jews' mind) unprecedented triumph. Their vision is characterized as follows:

> In the priests' narrative the chosen people are last seen as pilgrims moving through alien land toward a goal to be fulfilled in another time and place, and this is the vision, drawn from the ancient story of their past, that the priests now hold out to the scattered sons and daughters of old Israel. They, too, are exiles encamped for a time in an alien land, and they, too, must focus their hopes on the promise ahead. Like the Israelites in the Sinai wilderness, they must avoid setting roots in the land through which they pass, for diaspora is not to become their permanent condition, and regulations must be adopted to facilitate this. They must resist assimilation into the world into which they are now dispersed, because hope and heart and fundamental identity lay in the future. Thus, the priestly document not only affirms Yahweh's continuing authority and action in the lives of his people but offers them a pattern for life that will ensure them a distinct identity.[1]

The net effect of the Pentateuchal vision of Israel, that is, its worldview seen in the aggregate, lays stress on the separateness and the holiness of Israel, all the while pointing to dangers of pollution by the other, the outsider. The way of life, with its stress on distinguishing traits of an Israel distinct from, and threatened by, the outsider corresponds. The fate of the nation, moreover, depends upon the loyalty of the people, in their everyday life, to the requirements of the covenant with God, so history forms the barometer of the health of the nation. In these ways the several segments of the earlier traditions of Israel were so drawn together as to make the point peculiarly pertinent to Israel in exile. It follows that the original Judaic system, the one set forth by the Pentateuch, answered the urgent issue of exile with the self-evident response of return. The question was not to be avoided, the answer not to be doubted. The

---

[1]W. Lee Humphreys, *Crisis and Story. Introduction to the Old Testament* (Palo Alto, 1979: Mayfield Publishing Co), p. 217.

center of the system, then, lay in the covenant, the contract that told Israel the rules that would govern: keep these rules and you will not again suffer as you have suffered. Violate them and you will. At the heart of the covenant was the call for Israel to form a kingdom of priests and a holy people. That conception assigned to purity systemic priority.

If we read the priestly viewpoint as it is contained in the books of Leviticus and Numbers, as well as in priestly passages of Genesis and Exodus, this is the picture we derive. The altar was the center of life, the conduit of life from heaven to earth and from earth to heaven. All things are to be arrayed in relationship to the altar. The movement of the heavens demarcated and celebrated at the cult marked out the divisions of time in relationship to the altar. The spatial dimension of the Land was likewise demarcated and celebrated in relationship to the altar. The natural life of Israel's fields and corrals, the social life of its hierarchical caste system, the political life (this was not only in theory by any means) centered on the Temple as the locus of ongoing government – all things in order and in place expressed the single message. The natural order of the world corresponded to, reinforced, and was reinforced by, the social order of Israel. Both were fully realized in the cult, the nexus between those opposite and corresponding forces, the heavens and the earth.

The lines of structure emanated from the altar. And it was these lines of structure which constituted high and impenetrable frontiers to separate Israel from the gentiles Israel, which was holy, ate holy food, reproduced itself in accord with the laws of holiness, and conducted all of its affairs, both affairs of state and the business of the table and the bed, in accord with the demands of holiness. So the cult defined holiness. Holiness meant separateness. Separateness meant life. Why? Because outside the Land, the realm of the holy, lay the domain of death. The lands are unclean. The Land is holy. For the Scriptural vocabulary, one antonym for holy is unclean, and one opposite of unclean is holy. The synonym of holy is life. The principal force and symbol of uncleanness and its highest expression are death. So the Torah stood for life, the covenant with the Lord would guarantee life, and the way of life required sanctification in the here and now of the natural world. It was in that setting that the purity system functioned.

III. The Sources of Judaism on Purity [2]:
The Mishnah [Ca. 200 C.E.]

The Mishnah is a six-part code of descriptive rules formed towards the end of the second century C.E. by a small number of Jewish sages and put forth as the constitution of Judaism under the sponsorship of Judah the Patriarch, the head of the Jewish community of the Land of Israel at the end of that century. The reason the document is important is that the Mishnah forms the foundation for the Babylonian and Palestinian Talmuds. It therefore stands alongside the Hebrew Bible as the holy book upon which the Judaism of the past nineteen hundred years is constructed. The six divisions are: (1) agricultural rules; (2) laws governing appointed seasons, for example, Sabbaths and festivals; (3) laws on the transfer of women and property along with women from one man (father) to another (husband); (4) the system of civil and criminal law (corresponding to what we today should regard as "the legal system"); (5) laws for the conduct of the cult and the Temple; and (6) laws on the preservation of cultic purity both in the Temple and under certain domestic circumstances, with special reference to the table and bed.

The Mishnah is made up of sayings bearing the names of authorities who lived, as I just said, in the later first and second centuries. (The book contains very little in the names of people who lived before the destruction of the Temple of Jerusalem in C.E. 70.) These authorities generally fall into two groups, namely, two distinct sets of names, each set of names randomly appearing together, but rarely, if ever, with names of the other set. The former set of names is generally supposed to represent authorities who lived between the destruction of the Temple in 70 and the advent of the second war against Rome, led by Simeon Bar Kokhba, in 132. The latter set of names belongs to authorities who flourished between the end of that war, ca. 135, and the end of the second century. The Mishnah itself is generally supposed to have come to closure at the end of the second century, and its date, for conventional purposes only, is ca. C.E. 200. Now, of these two groups of sages from 70-130, and from 135-200, the latter is represented far more abundantly than the former. Approximately two thirds of the named sayings belong to mid-second century authorities. This is not surprising, since these are the named authorities whose (mainly unnamed) students collected, organized, and laid out the document as we now have it. So, in all, the Mishnah represents the thinking of Jewish sages who flourished in the middle of the second century. It is that group which took over whatever they had in hand from the preceding century and from the whole legacy of Israelite literature even before that time and revised and reshaped the whole into the Mishnah.

The topical program of the document is easily summarized. The critical issue in the economic life, which means, in farming, is in two parts, revealed in the first division. First, Israel, as tenant on God's holy Land, maintains the property in the ways God requires, keeping the rules which mark the Land and its crops as holy. Next, the hour at which the sanctification of the Land comes to form a critical mass, namely, in the ripened crops, is the moment ponderous with danger and heightened holiness. Israel's will so affects the crops as to mark a part of them as holy, the rest of them as available for common use. The human will is determinative in the process of sanctification.

Second, in the second division, what happens in the Land at certain times, at Appointed Times, marks off spaces of the Land as holy in yet another way. The center of the Land and the focus of its sanctification is the Temple. There the produce of the Land is received and given back to God, the one who created and sanctified the Land. At these unusual moments of sanctification, the inhabitants of the Land in their social being in villages enter a state of spatial sanctification. That is to say, the village boundaries mark off holy space, within which one must remain during the holy time. This is expressed in two ways. First, the Temple itself observes and expresses the special, recurring holy time. Second, the villages of the Land are brought into alignment with the Temple, forming a complement and completion to the Temple's sacred being. The advent of the appointed times precipitates a spatial reordering of the Land, so that the boundaries of the sacred are matched and mirrored in village and in Temple. At the heightened holiness marked by these moments of Appointed Times, therefore, the occasion for an affective sanctification is worked out. Like the harvest, the advent of an appointed time, a pilgrim festival, also a sacred season, is made to express that regular, orderly, and predictable sort of sanctification for Israel which the system as a whole seeks.

If for a moment we now leap over the next two divisions, the third and fourth, we come to the counterpart of the divisions of Agriculture and Appointed Times. These are the fifth and sixth divisions, namely Holy Things and Purities, those which deal with the everyday and the ordinary, as against the special moments of harvest, on the one side, and special time or season, on the other. The fifth division is about the Temple on ordinary days. The Temple, the locus of sanctification, is conducted in a wholly routine and trustworthy, punctilious manner. The one thing which may unsettle matters is the intention and will of the human actor. This is subjected to carefully prescribed limitations and remedies. The division of Holy Things generates its companion, the Sixth division, the one on cultic cleanness, Purities. The relationship between the two is like that between Agriculture and Appointed Times, the former locative, the latter utopian, the former dealing with the fields, the latter with the interplay between fields and altar.

Here too, in the sixth division, once we speak of the one place of the Temple, we address, too, the cleanness which pertains to every place. A system of cleanness, taking into account what imparts uncleanness and how this is done, what is subject to uncleanness, and how that state is overcome that system is fully expressed, once more, in response to the participation of the human will. Without the wish and act of a human being, the system does not function. It is inert. Sources of uncleanness, which come naturally and not by volition, and modes of purification, which work naturally, and not by human intervention, remain inert until human will has imparted susceptibility to uncleanness, that is, introduced into the system, that food and drink, bed, pot, chair, and pan, which to begin with form the focus of the system. The movement from sanctification to uncleanness takes place when human will and work precipitate it.

This now brings us back to the middle divisions, the third and fourth, on Women and Damages. They take their place in the structure of the whole by showing the congruence, within the larger framework of regularity and order, of human concerns of family and farm, politics and workaday transactions among ordinary people. For without attending to these matters, the Mishnah's system does not encompass what, at its foundations, it is meant to comprehend and order. So what is at issue is fully cogent with the rest. In the case of Women, the third division, attention focuses upon the point of disorder marked by the transfer of that disordering anomaly, woman, from the regular status provided by one man, to the equally trustworthy status provided by another. That is the point at which the Mishnah's interests are aroused: once more, predictably, the moment of disorder. In the case of Damages, the fourth division, there are two important concerns. First, there is the paramount interest in preventing, so far as possible, the disorderly rise of one person and fall of another, and in sustaining the status quo of the economy, the house and household, of Israel, the holy society in eternal stasis. Second, there is the necessary concomitant in the provision of a system of political institutions to carry out the laws which preserve the balance and steady state of persons.

The two divisions which take up topics of concrete and material concern, the formation and dissolution of families and the transfer of property in that connection, the transactions, both through torts and through commerce, which lead to exchanges of property and the potential dislocation of the state of families in society, are both locative and utopian. They deal with the concrete locations in which people make their lives, household and street and field, the sexual and commercial exchanges of a given village. But they pertain to the life of all Israel, both in the Land and otherwise. These two divisions, together with the household ones of Appointed Times, constitute the sole opening outward toward the life of utopian Israel, that diaspora in the far reaches of the ancient world, in the endless span of time. This community from the Mishnah's perspective is not only in exile but unaccounted for, outside the system, for the Mishnah declines to recognize and take it into account. Israelites who dwell in the land of (unclean) death instead of in the Holy Land simply fall outside of the range of (holy) life. Priests, who must remain cultically clean, may not leave the Land and neither may most of the Mishnah.

When we listen to the silences of the system of the Mishnah, as much as to its points of stress, we hear a single message. It is a message of a system that answered a single encompassing question, and the question formed a stunning counterpart to that of the sixth century B.C.E. In both cases the urgent question pertains to the sanctification of Israel: land, people, way of life. This brings us to the meeting point of the Written Torah and the Mishnah, the first document of the Oral Torah. Both writings were brought into being in response to enormous catastrophes in ancient Israel's life. The Five Books of Moses were brought together as the Torah after the destruction of the Temple (586 B.C.E.) by Ezra, the scribe, in Jerusalem, at about 450 B.C.E. So the Written Torah began as a statement in the face of calamity, explaining what the event meant. The Mishnah, too, came into being in the aftermath of a catastrophe (70 C.E.), at about 200 C.E. So the Pentateuchal system addressed one reading of the events of the sixth century, highlighted by the destruction of the Jerusalem temple in 586 B.C.E.

At stake for both components of the Torah was how Israel as defined by that system related to its land, represented by its temple, and the message may be simply stated: what appears to be the given is in fact a gift, subject to stipulations. The precipitating event for the Mishnaic system was the destruction of the Jerusalem temple in C.E. 70, but at stake now was a quite fresh issue. It was, specifically, this: What, in the aftermath of the destruction of the holy place and holy cult, remained of the sanctity of the holy caste, the priesthood, the holy land, and, above all, the holy people and its holy way of life? The answer was that sanctity persists, indelibly, in Israel, the people, in its way of life, in its land, in its priesthood, in its food, in its mode of sustaining life, in its manner of procreating and so sustaining the nation.

The Mishnah's system therefore focused upon the holiness of the life of Israel, the people, a holiness that had formerly centered on the Temple. The logically consequent question was, what is the meaning of sanctity, and how shall Israel attain, or give evidence of, sanctification. The answer to the question derived from the original creation, the end of the temple directing attention to the beginning of the natural world that the temple had (and would again) embodied. For the meaning of sanctity the framers therefore turned to that first act of sanctification, the one in creation. It came about when, all things in array, in place, each with its proper name, God blessed and sanctified the seventh day on the eve of the first Sabbath. Creation was made ready for the blessing and the sanctification when all things were very good, that is to say, in their rightful order, called by their rightful name. An orderly nature was a sanctified and blessed nature, so dictated Scripture in the name of the Supernatural. So to receive the blessing and to be made holy, all things in nature and society were to be set in right array. Given the condition of Israel, the people, in its land, in the aftermath of the catastrophic war against Rome led by Bar Kokhba in 132-135, putting things in order was no easy task. But that is why, after all, the question pressed, the answer proving inexorable and obvious. The condition of society corresponded to the critical question that obsessed the system builders.

IV. The Judaic System of Purity: An Overview of the Parts

Viewed in gross and general terms, the Scriptural and Mishnaic systems correspond in important ways. First, both make provision for and supply definitions of sources and loci of uncleanness and modes of purification. The principal constituent elements in the two systems are the same. Second, the sources of uncleanness of the former with no variation are replicated in the latter. Third, the loci in general are the same, since the Mishnaic materials self-evidently presuppose that cleanness is to be kept in the cult, and the Scriptural ones are clear that cleanness is to be kept outside of the cult. But the emphases are strikingly different. The importance of cleanness in the cult is central in the Priestly Code, and cleanness outside the cult depends upon that inside it. The former is explained as necessitated by the latter. The Mishnah has a different focus altogether. Its interest is in the table, in that its primary discussions of what becomes unclean pertain to cooking utensils, on the one side, and food and drink, on the other. Sexual acts which produce uncleanness scarcely appear in that Order, and the language of clean and unclean is not a primary expressive formulary in that on Women.

While the systems of the Pentateuch and the Mishnah are structurally identical, it is only with sources of uncleanness that the Mishnah's and Scripture's systems coincide in detail. The emphasis in the matter of loci of uncleanness is strikingly at variance, and the Mishnah's modes of purification are quite distinct from those of Scripture. The Mishnah's system therefore rests upon, but is not identical to, Scripture's. It is at the points at which we discern variant emphases and wholly fresh conceptions that Mishnah wishes to say something new and to state a worldview different from that in Scripture. And, it follows, it is in the locus of cleanness, and, only secondarily, in the modes of purification, which depended upon and are generated by that locus, that the important new conceptions will emerge. From what we have said, it already is obvious that what is fresh in the Mishnah is interest in cultic cleanness at the table. Issues of dietary cleanness, inclusive of both domestic utensils and food and drink, predominate, not to the exclusion, of course, of sexual uncleanness. The shift is one of focus and emphasis. What is given is given: Scripture is the foundation. But the structure built thereon rises along lines hardly determined by that foundation.

Let us now survey the tractates of the Mishnah's Division of Purities. That is where we find the purity system of three principal parts: sources of uncleanness, objects and substances susceptible to uncleanness, and modes of purification from uncleanness. So it tells the story of what makes what unclean and what makes it clean. The tractates on these several topics are as follows: (1) sources of uncleanness – Ohalot, Negaim, Niddah, Makhshirin, Zabim, Tebul Yom; (2) objects and substances susceptible to uncleanness – Kelim, Tohorot, Uqsin; and (3) modes of purification – Parah, Miqvaot, Yadayim.

SOURCES OF UNCLEANNESS

OHALOT is to be dealt with in two parts, its treatment of sources of uncleanness and modes of their transfer, and its interest in the theory of the tent (Numbers 19). The former segment develops the notion that things which are like a principal source of uncleanness impart uncleanness as does that to which they are likened. A tent is defined as something so small as a handbreadth squared; by contrast, we confront the generative problematic of this tractate. The matter begins in the notion that corpse uncleanness flows through such a small space, or may be prevented from passing through such a small space. Conceived as a kind of fluid, corpse uncleanness then will be stopped up in such a way as to be forced to flow perpendicularly – that is, under pressure – or it will be so contained that it affects all the sides of its container – that is, not under pressure.

NEGAIM, NIDDAH, MAKHSHIRIN, ZABIM AND TEBUL YOM: Mishnah-tractates Negaim (the uncleanness described at Leviticus 13-14), Niddah on the menstruating woman, as Leviticus 15, and Zabim, devoted to the uncleanness of the Zab (person afflicted with the flux described at Lev. 15) and how that uncleanness is transferred, like the beginning and end of Ohalot, do not work out a problematic in connection with their respective themes, the uncleanness of the person with *nega*, the menstruating woman, and the Zab. There is nothing people want to know about these sources of uncleanness other than rules for their definition and application. An important notion is (M. Neg. 13) the issue of whether that which affords protection from uncleanness also is more susceptible to uncleanness than that which does not afford protection from uncleanness or than that which is not susceptible to uncleanness to begin with. We deal in Negaim with the following subjects: rules applying to all plagues, with special attention to the role of the priest, the process of inspection, the susceptibility of gentiles, the matter of doubts: the issues of colors and their definition and interrelationship; the character of bright spots and the signification that they are unclean; the boil and the burning; bald spots; clothing; houses; and, last, purification rites. Rulings are founded on the laws of Lev. 13 and 14.

NIDDAH constitutes an extended commentary, not in exegetical form, to be sure, upon the basic law of Scriptures, in particular Lev. 12 and 15. I see no important idea which does not derive directly or derivatively from Scripture. At no point does the tractate raise questions not provoked by Scripture or the extension, by analogy or contrast of Scripture's definitions and conceptions. Niddah presents a discourse on unclean body fluids and on doubts in reference to unclean body fluids.

ZABIM. Zabim is to be considered in two parts, first, its definitions of how a man becomes unclean as a Zab and modes of transfer of his uncleanness in general, and, second, how a Zab imparts uncleanness through pressure in particular. The former part, like Niddah and Negaim, presents a series of refinements and amplifications of Scripture's basic definition of the Zab. The latter part in chapters 3 and 4 deals with the nature of pressure. The matter of pressure begins with the view that pressure need not be formal, in the sense that the Zab exerts physical pressure upon a bed. If the Zab's weight is indirectly transferred to something which might be used for lying or sitting, even though that object is not utilized at present for that purpose then the uncleanness has been transferred. After the definition of the problem of pressure in general, we find a full working out of the logical possibilities. Either (1) we hold that any pressure, even of both a Zab and a clean person on one side of an object, involves the transfer of uncleanness. Or (2) only if the Zab presses against a clean person or object is there such a transfer. That is to say, only if the clean person certainly has borne the weight of the unclean one are the person and his clothing unclean.

MAKHSHIRIN: The theme of Makhshirin is liquids which impart to dry produce susceptibility to uncleanness. The problematic is the role of human intention in the application of said liquids so that they function to render produce susceptible, and, secondarily, the role of human intention in the definition of effective liquids. The working out of the problematic is in terms of the interplay between what a person wants to do and what he actually does. One possible position is that we interpret the effects of what is done in terms of what is intended. A second and opposite position is that we define what is intended in terms of the ultimate result. These are the possible positions yielded by the logical requirements of the problematic. There are no others. The determinative problematic, whether or not liquids must be applied intentionally, thus is itself redefined in terms of a still more profound and fundamental question. The process begins in the position that we take account only of water which has actually conformed to a person's original intent, ignoring the presence of water which is peripheral to the accomplishment of one's purpose. The process then is completed by the inquiry into this position, specifically the meaning of intent; the limitations upon the capacity of water to impart susceptibility imposed by one's original intent in drawing the water. There are three possibilities. First, one's action can produce a different effect from one's original intention. Or, second what happens is retrospectively deemed to define what one wanted to happen. Or, third, what one wanted to happen affects the assessment of what actually has happened. There are no other logical possibilities contained within the original problematic.

TEBUL YOM: The theme of Tebul Yom is the person or object which has immersed in an immersion pool on that selfsame day and must await sunset for the completion of the process of purification, hence, one who has immersed on that selfsame day. Its first element is whether the tebul yom is essentially clean or essentially unclean. If he is essentially unclean, then the matter is concluded. He functions to impart uncleanness as does any other source. But if he is essentially clean, then the next stage unfolds. We distinguish between what is primary and what is secondary in a mixture. If what is primary is affected, then what is secondary likewise is unclean. But if what is secondary is affected, what is primary remains clean. Now this distinction is distinctively related to the tebul yom, who, because of his own ambiguous status, is able to illuminate the ambiguities presented by the stated distinction as to connection. If the tebul yom touches what is secondary in a mixture, what is primary is unaffected and vice versa.

WHAT IS SUBJECT TO UNCLEANNESS: FOOD, DRINK, UTENSILS

KELIM: What Kelim (utensils) wants to know about utensils in general is when they become unclean, the status of their parts in relationship to the uncleanness of the whole utensil, when they cease to be unclean, and the status of their sherds and remnants in relationship to the uncleanness of the whole. The uncleanness of a utensil depends upon two criteria: the form of the utensil and the materials of which the utensil is composed. A utensil which forms, or has, a receptacle can contain uncleanness. A utensil which is fully processed and available for normal use is susceptible to uncleanness. Full processing must impose on the utensil a distinctive function. The criterion is the human conception of function. An object which is fully manufactured, routinely used, for a fixed purpose, by man, is susceptible. Diverse materials, to be sure, exhibit different traits, but only within these criteria. The refinement of this view will deal with gray areas, for example, imperfect receptacles, the status of parts of a utensil or of subsidiary functions, the distinction between the time at which a utensil serves man and the time at which it does not, and the revision of the distinctive purpose, for example, by a change in the form of an object. The assessment of the status of parts of a utensil or of things affixed to a utensil represents a further refinement. A part must be firmly affixed. Parts which are going to be removed, because they interfere with the functioning of a utensil, are not taken into account as susceptible to uncleanness. A part which is essential to the use of utensil is deemed integral to it. Having completed the consideration of when a utensil is susceptible to uncleanness, we turn to the point at which it ceases to be susceptible. We simply state systematically the negative of the foregoing propositions. A utensil which is useless is insusceptible. One which is broken is useless. One which no longer serves its original function is no longer susceptible as it was before. When we assess uselessness, we focus upon human intention in working with said utensil. Sherds and remnants are subject to the same criteria of uselessness. We determine whether or not the utensil's sherd continues to be useful on its own.

TOHOROT: The three paramount themes of Tohorot, on the uncleanness of food, are to be treated separately. The first, the issue of removes of uncleanness and levels of sanctification, is fully worked out in the interplay between the one and the other. Once the levels of sanctification are defined, the structure demands completion through the specification of corresponding, and opposite, removes of uncleanness. It further will want to know how the two interrelate. At that point the system is complete. The secondary question of whether that which is unconsecrated may be raised, through appropriate deliberation and protection, to the level of sanctification not only of heave-offering but of holy things, is further worked out. The second theme, the relationship between the nonobservant Israelite and the observant one, begins in two conflicting principles. The former, the *am ha'ares*, in general will act in such a way as to respect the cleanness of the property of the latter, the *haber*. Or the former is indifferent to the matter of cleanness. The problematic is to be stated in exactly those simple terms. It can be worked out in a myriad of cases, but no significant conceptual advance is possible or undertaken. The third theme, the resolution of doubts, is open ended. Once we postulate that matters of doubt are to be worked out through the application of diverse principles, then the number of potential principles is scarcely limited.

UQSIN: this tractate is coherent and exhibits traits of sophisticated formulary and redactional work. It treats, first, the status of inedible parts of food, whether they are susceptible because they are connected to edible parts or insusceptible because they are inedible. The second aspect is joined to the first: How do we treat these inedible parts when we estimate the bulk or the volume of food? Accordingly, the issue is the status of what is joined to food but is not to be eaten. The logical possibilities, that these inedible parts are deemed (1) wholly part of the produce to which they are connected; (2) wholly separate from said produce; or (3) under some circumstances part, and under some circumstances not part, of the edible part of the food, are fully worked out.

MODES OF PURIFICATION

PARAH treats the conduct of a sacrifice outside of the Temple in a place of uncleanness, its requirements and limitations. The deep structure of the tractate is readily discerned, for at each point, the issue is how the requirements of a rite of sacrifice done in the Temple determine the necessities of burning the cow and mixing its ashes with suitable water, that is, a rite of sacrifice done outside of the Temple. Do we do outside the Temple exactly what we do inside? Do we do the opposite? Do the Temple's requirements of cleanness define those of the burning of the red cow? Do they stand lower or higher in the progression of strictness? The tractate also contains rules required by the theme, but not by the problematic, of the red cow, such as defining the water, spelling out how the purification water is used, and other prescriptions that hardly relate in detail to the overriding question. The principal foci of the tractate, the principle that labor extraneous to the rite spoils the rite of the burning of the cow and spoils the drawn water, and the conception that cleanness rules of unimagined strictness are to be observed, relate to that crucial point of interest, which is the analogy to the Temple.

The tractate centers upon the conception that human intervention in the process of preparing the purification water is absolutely essential. The utensil used for collecting the water and mixing the ashes must be a human construction. The act of drawing the water, by contrast to the act of forming an immersion pool, must be with full human deliberation. If at any point the human participant fails to devote his entire and complete attention to the work and so steps outside of the process, the whole process is spoiled. Once man is intruded, moreover, his attention is riveted to what he is doing by the omnipresent danger of contamination. If he touches any sort of object whatsoever – which is to say, if at any point he does anything at all which is not connected to the requirements of the rite – he automatically is made unclean. This is the rule for objects used for lying and sitting. The participant cannot cease from his labors in connection with the rite, for he cannot sit down on a chair. He cannot lie down on a bed. He must at all times be active, standing and alert, moving from the well from which he has drawn the water to the place at which he will mix it with the ash. It may also be the case that if he touches any sort of object which can become unclean, not only a bed or a chair, he is eo ipse unclean. Even though this is subject to dispute, the issue is secondary to the one on which all parties agree. Moreover, the assumption is that he will have burned the cow, and only then have gone off to collect the necessary water. So the process is continuous, from selecting the cow and burning it – which the tractate places first in its sequence of themes – to the gathering of the water and the mixing of the water with the ash.

MIQVAOT: What Miqvaot wants to know about the immersion pool is the sort of water which is to be used. This issue carries in its wake the question of the role of man in the process of purification. By contrast to the foregoing tractate, here man is rigidly excluded from the process of making the pool. Water drawn by man is not to be used in the pool. It will follow that we must answer these questions: What sort of water is to be used? How much of such water is needed? What is the rule if acceptable water is mixed with unacceptable water? Can the former purify the latter? If so, in what volume? Does the latter render the former irreparably unfit, or is there a way to take an unfit pool and make it fit? This range of issues explores the deeper question of the role of suitable water in effecting purification. Once we say that a certain kind of water – specifically, that which man has not affected – is to be used, then we ask a range of questions dependent upon the workings of the suitable water, its relationship to unsuitable water, and its power to restore the suitability of unfit water. In asking these questions, moreover, we enter the inquiry into the actual workings of the immersion pool, for we want to know exactly what power the pool has even over its own constituent element, water, and, all the more so, over things which are different from its constituent element. The route to the analysis of the working of the pool, therefore, is the inquiry into the character of the water which is used in the pool and its power over all other things which enter therein.

YADAYIM: The theme of Yadayim, the uncleanness of hands, is spelled out in the diverse rules. The principal issue has to do with cleaning hands in a way different from the way in which other parts of the body and other unclean things are cleaned, which is in an immersion pool. Once we determine that hands are unclean when the rest of the body remains unaffected, then we have to find an appropriate analogy for the mode of purification herein under discussion. It is in the law, not of Miqvaot, which concerns undifferentiated purification, but of Parah.

The result is the strict requirement of the use of a utensil and of water drawn by man in a utensil, as against the conception of Miqvaot that we do not use water drawn in a utensil at all. The other aspect of the law is that two rinsings are required.

V. Purity in the Judaic System of the Dual Torah Viewed Whole

The Division of Purities presents a very simply system of three principal parts: sources of uncleanness, objects and substances susceptible to uncleanness, and modes of purification from uncleanness. So it tells the story of what makes what unclean and what makes it clean. The tractates on these several topics are as follows: (1) Sources of uncleanness – Ohalot, Negaim, Niddah, Makhshirin, Zabim, Tebul Yom; (2) Objects and substances susceptible to uncleanness – Kelim, Tohorot, Uqsin; and (3) Modes of purification – Parah, Miqvaot, Yadayim.

Viewed as a whole, the Division of Purities treats the interplay of persons, food, and liquids. Dry inanimate objects or food are not susceptible to uncleanness. What is wet is susceptible. So liquids activate the system. What is unclean, moreover, emerges from uncleanness through the operation of liquids, specifically, through immersion in fit water of requisite volume and in natural condition. Liquids thus deactivate the system. Thus, water in its natural condition is what concludes the process by removing uncleanness. Water in its unnatural condition, that is, deliberately affected by human agency, is what imparts susceptibility to uncleanness to begin with. The uncleanness of persons, furthermore, is signified by body liquids or flux in the case of the menstruating woman (Niddah) and the Zab (Zabim). Corpse uncleanness is conceived to be a kind of effluent, a viscous gas, which flows like a liquid. Utensils for their part receive uncleanness when they form receptacles able to contain liquid. In sum, we have a system in which the invisible flow of fluid-like substances or powers serves to put food, drink, and receptacles into the status of uncleanness and to remove those things from that status. Whether or not we call the system "metaphysical," it certainly has no material base but is conditioned upon highly abstract notions. Thus in material terms, the effect of liquid is upon food, drink, utensils, and man. The consequence has to do with who may eat and drink what food and liquid, and what food and drink may be consumed in which pots and pans. These loci are specified by tractates on utensils (Kelim) and on food and drink (Tohorot and Uqsin).

The human being is ambivalent. That is to say, persons fall in the middle, between sources and loci of uncleanness. They are both: they serve as sources of uncleanness; they also become unclean. The Zab, the menstruating woman, the woman after childbirth, the tebul yom, and the person afflicted with *nega'* – all are sources of uncleanness. But being unclean, they fall within the system's loci, its program of consequences. So they make other things unclean and are subject to penalties because they *are* unclean. Unambiguous sources of uncleanness never also constitute loci affected by uncleanness. They always are unclean and never can become clean: the corpse, the dead creeping thing, and things like them. Inanimate sources of uncleanness and inanimate objects are affected by uncleanness. Systemically unique man and liquids have the capacity to inaugurate the processes of uncleanness (as sources) and also are subject to those same processes (as objects of uncleanness).

What breaks established routine or what is broken out of established routine is what is subject to the fully articulated and extensive reflections of a whole Division of the Mishnah. What is unclean is abnormal and disruptive of the economy of nature, and what is clean is normal and constitutive of the economy and the wholeness of nature. The hermeneutic route to that conception is to be located to begin with in the way in which what is unclean is restored to a condition of cleanness. It is through the activity of nature, unimpeded by human intervention, in removing the uncleanness, through the natural force of water collected in its original state. Accordingly, if to be clean is normal, then it is that state of normality which is restored by natural processes themselves. It follows from the exegetical fulcrum of purification that to be unclean is abnormal and is the result of unnatural processes. The first of these is death, which disturbs the house of life by releasing, in quest of a new house, corpse uncleanness, to be defined as that which is released by death. Corpse uncleanness may be contained in a tent, which is a small enclosed space, in a broken utensil. Once corpse uncleanness finds that new home, its capacity for contamination ends. The second is menstrual blood, flux of blood outside of the menstrual cycle, and a flow from the penis outside of the normal reproductive process. Here, too, the source of uncleanness, in the case of the Zabah and the Zab, most certainly is constituted by that which functions contrary to nature or which disrupts what is deemed to be the normal course of nature.

The Mishnah's system of purities forms its meanings upon a two-dimensional grid. One is laid out so that the Temple stands in the middle, the world roundabout, with the sanctity of the Temple definitive of the potential sanctification of table and bed, the profane and unclean world outside. The other, superimposed upon the former, places man at one pole, nature at the other, each reciprocally complementing and completing the place and role of the other. Nature produces uncleanness and removes uncleanness. Man subjects food and utensils to uncleanness and, through his action, also imparts significance to the system as a whole. For in the end the question is, what can a man do, and the answer is, man stands at the center of this world's complementary loci of sanctification and uncleanness. The sustenance of is life and his reproductive activity form the focus of intense concentration. The life of man which is systemically central, the rhythm of his eating, drinking, and sexual activity, defines the working of he system, and the intention and will of man provide the key to the system. Without human will the system is inert. Utensils not useful to man are not susceptible. Vegetable matter and liquid not subject to human utilization are not going to be made unclean. Things which are dry are permanently clean. Only produce wet down deliberately and purposefully by man, therefore meant to serve his needs, is susceptible to uncleanness. What man does not do is equally decisive in the process of forming the principal means of purification. He does not intervene in nature's processes at the end of the system, just as he must determine to inaugurate the forces of uncleanness by deciding to use a utensil or to eat an apple. He cannot stimulate the bodily sources of uncleanness, for example, in the case of the Zab, all the more so in the case of the *nega'* or, under normal circumstances, in the case of the corpse. But he must impart purpose and significance to the things affected by those bodily sources of uncleanness. These facts have repeatedly come to the fore as we moved from one component of the system to the next.

When we describe the formation of the system, its comprehensive structure, we discover at its very foundations the definitive place of man. What the system proposes is to locate a place of critical importance in the unseen world of uncleanness and holiness, in the processes of the sanctification of this profane world in the model of the holy Temple's sanctity, for the activity and purpose of man. He is not helpless in the works of sanctification but, on the contrary, he the responsible, decisive figure, both in what he does deliberately and in what he sedulously refrains from doing. He is not a passive object of an independent process of material sanctification, begun and elected by heaven working solely through nature, but the principal subject in the contingent process of relative and circumstantial sanctification. And the arena for his activity is his own basic life's processes, eating food and so sustaining life, engaging in sexual relations and so maintaining life's continuity. Since the bodily function upon which emphasis is laid is nourishment, we must attempt to understand the principle of selection. Here the Scriptural heritage of the Priestly Code seems to me decisive: God is served meals of meat and meal, wine and oil, not holocausts of jewelry, not logs of wood, not perpetual fires, not mounds of ore, not fish or insects, and not ejaculations of semen. What sustains man nourishes God. What sustains God nourishes man. God is perceived to be isomorphic with man. In

God's image is man made and all of the circles of creation are concentric with the inner circle formed of man's creation.

This brings us, at the end, to the system's urgent question and self-evidently valid answer. It may be stated as a proposition: What can a human being do? And the answer is, by an act of will, a human being possesses the power of sanctification. What sustains man then is what the system proposes to sanctify. The purpose is that man, renewing life as God perpetually lives in the cult, may be formed and nourished by sustenance which is like God's, and so, in nature, become like supernature. To state the self-evidently valid answer to the urgent question in a simple way: by eating like God man becomes like God. And this "eating-like-God" is done naturally and routinely, in the context and course of ordinary life, with utensils available for any purpose, with food and drink, bed and chair, commonly used in the workaday world. Man at his most domestic and in his most natural context is susceptible to uncleanness and therefore potentially capable also of sanctification. What is unclean can be holy. What is most susceptible to uncleanness also is most available for sanctification (to turn on its head the rule of M. Toh. 2:3-7). For what does man do within the system? In a profound sense, he does perfectly routine, ordinary actions in a commonplace way. The system is remarkably lacking in specific cultic rituals or rites. The food is not subjected to blessing in order to become susceptible. The utensil is not made to pass through a rite, but is susceptible without prayer. The corpus of law lacks mythic expression. The laws are wholly descriptive of how things are, speaking of the natural course of events, not onetime actions. Eating takes place all the time. Utensils are always available for use. All things are neutral, except for human intervention.

What the man does is merely use things, not muttering incantations, blessings, prayers, or other sacred formulas or doing gestures analogous to those of the priests in the cult. He immerses in any suitable pond – so far as Miqvaot is concerned – without a word or deed of ritual concerning the pond or immersion therein. When the cow is burned and the ashes are collected and mixed with suitable water, not a word (excluding the confirmatory formulae or unnecessary action is prescribed. When the hands are rinsed two times, the name of heaven is not invoked, so far as Yadayim is concerned. Kelim speaks of the creation of ordinary objects for domestic use, Tohorot of ordinary olives and grapes, oil and wine for the workaday table. Ohalot, which proposes to describe now the economy of nature is restored when the body dies which has contained that which is emitted by the body at death, is remarkably reticent on the subject of funeral rites, of which it knows nothing. The several sources of uncleanness to which tractates are devoted, Negaim, Niddah, Zabim, Tebul Yom, sections of Ohalot – all represent the perfectly natural workings of the body in life or in death. Nothing man does brings uncleanness on himself. Constraint, intention, accident are explicitly excluded from effective causes of the bodily flows which contaminate. The natural character of the sources of uncleanness and the modes of its removal, on the one side, and the highly deliberate and conscious action of man required to subject food and drink, domestic utensils and objects, to the affect of the system, on the other, are complementary. The structure is formed of these two opposite elements: the availability of inert nature, the deliberation of man who forms intention and acts to effect it. So, to conclude, the Pentateuch's and the Mishnah's Purity laws are not discrete and unrelated rules but all together function as, and form, a whole and complete system: "A regularly interacting and interdependent group of rules forming a unified whole, an organized set of doctrines, ideas, and principles intended to explain the arrangement and working of a systematic whole."[2] Now to the details.

---

[2]Webster's *Seventh Collegiate Dictionary* (Springfield, 1965: G. C. Miriam Co.), s.v. "system."

Part One

SOURCES OF UNCLEANNESS AND
HOW THEY CONTAMINATE

2

Judaic Sources of Uncleanness

I. What Difference Uncleanness Makes:
The Sources of Uncleanness and Their Effects

The fluids and solids that sustain and create life – blood, semen, flesh – also form the sources of uncleanness. So, too, classes of food declared unclean for Israelites (as listed at Leviticus 11) also effect uncleanness. When in their natural condition, operating as nature's classifications dictate, these bring about life and mark the presence of life; when in unnatural condition, they represent death. Uncleanness forms a metaphor for death, cleanness, for its opposite, which is the condition of sanctification. The same thing then may be unclean or clean, stand for death or life. The creation myth of Genesis 1 which sets forth how God in the act of creation ordered all things, each in its proper category and classification, ends with the act of sanctification: all things properly ordered and classified. Then what violates the lines of order also contradicts that act and vitiates its effect: from sanctified to unclean: blood that does not sustain life; food that cannot be used to sustain life; semen that does not create life; skin that should be colored and healthy, marking life, but that has taken on the whiteness of death.

Corpse matter, menstrual blood, and fluid regarded as unnatural semen (flux in a woman, involuntary seminal emission in a man), living skin that looks like dead skin and its analogies (Leviticus Chapters 13 and 14) and unacceptable foods (inedible or dead of natural causes) therefore form principal sources of uncleanness; in fact there are no others that figure in the Judaic contexts – Pentateuchal and Mishnaic alike – in which the categories, clean and unclean, are invoked. Otherwise cleanness and uncleanness serve as metaphors bearing no material consequence. Gossip kills, but a gossip is not tried for murder. So too, a gossip is regarded as someone with an unclean mouth, but is not for that reason excluded from areas in which only clean persons may enter, for example, the Temple. When cleanness and uncleanness bear material and concrete consequences, therefore, it is in the specific setting of the Temple, on the one side, and the sustaining of life through the right kind of food and drink, on the other.

What this means is that uncleanness comes about through natural processes; its sources are unaffected by human will and not subject to culpability; uncleanness is not the result of voluntary action, therefore considerations of responsibility and blame do not enter, and moral judgments are not to be drawn because they are irrelevant. Uncleanness is an ontological taxon, not a moral one; it indicates what one may or may not do, where one may or may not go, but not what one is or is not, viewed under the aspect of righteousness and ethics. Nor is one more righteous by reason of being pure or clean of the kinds of uncleanness just now specified. A pilgrim to Jerusalem on the pilgrim festival must be clean; but such a person may have stolen a pair of shoes without being excluded from the Temple.

Now to elaborate on this point: the Judaic system of uncleanness set forth in the written and oral parts of the Torah, meaning, the Pentateuch and the Mishnah, focus upon bodily excretions or manifestations: the corpse, blood, semen, and skin that looks like that of a corpse being principal. The principal symbol and generative source of uncleanness is the corpse. Menstrual blood, on the one side, and flux (*zub*), meaning, semen produced by an other-than-erect penis, for males, or flow outside of the menstrual period, for females, are other principal sources. Unclean creatures, for example, a dead creeping thing, likewise produce uncleanness. The main account of sources of uncleanness is at Leviticus Chapters 11 through 15 and Numbers Chapter 19. To the data given in these passages, the Mishnah adds very little. So far as the specification of sources of uncleanness is concerned, pretty much the entire catalogue is contained within the Pentateuch.

That is not to imply that Mishnah stands wholly within the boundaries of the Scriptural system, resting entirely upon its foundations. That is not the case. Nor does the law of the Mishnah – here or at any other topic – derive by mere paraphrase from Scripture, rising in easy stages on an elevator of exegesis. Exegesis is undertaken only when attention has been drawn to specific Scriptural verses. The selection of verses for exegesis itself constitutes a major and innovative intellectual decision. The fact is, as Jonathan Z. Smith writes, "...Regardless of whether we are studying texts from literate or nonliterate cultures, we are dealing with historical processes of reinterpretation, with tradition.... For a given group at a given time to choose this or that mode of interpreting their tradition is to opt for a particular way of relating themselves to their historical past and social present."[1]

The interpretation of uncleanness in the Judaic system of the Pentateuch and the Mishnah therefore begins with the explanation of the principal of selection. If, as is the fact, the Mishnah identifies no source of uncleanness not specified by Scripture, though it deals with uncleanness in a variety of categories of its own, then the correct question is, so what? Attention then must focus upon how the Mishnah deals with the sources of uncleanness, the issues that it does or does not bring to bear upon that topic, the conclusions that it draws or refrains from drawing. These form critical components of the Mishnah's representation of the Judaic system of purity, beginning with the enumeration of the sources of uncleanness, and the context in which uncleanness makes a difference. The answer is, uncleanness matters invariably with respect to the classification of food and drink Israelites who wish to be pure may or may not eat, on the one side, and the classification of persons who may or may not participate in the Temple cult, on the other. It is a taxonomic category, a taxic indicator, bearing no moral implications whatsoever. And, it follows, one who attains purification is not a better, more moral, human being. Such a person enters the status in which he or she may have licit sexual relations, or may enter the Temple, or may consume food and drink that are to be utilized in conditions of cleanness. (And, it goes without saying, none of this has any bearing on hygienic cleanliness, which is an identified category without either ontic or moral implications of any kind.)

The context in which the language, clean or unclean, bears concrete consequence, for example, things one may or may not do on that account, shows what is at stake. When the Mishnah addresses uncleanness, beginning with its sources, it is concerned with a very specific matter, which has to do with food and drink, on the one side, and the cult, on the other. Scripture, for its part, uses the language of clean and unclean to refer to other matters in addition, for example, incestuous or otherwise genealogically improper marriage. These are not treated within the Division of Purities, and when they are discussed, the language of unclean and clean is not used. So, too, when priests are declared unsuited to participate in the cult for one reason or another, for example, being blemished, they are not called "unclean," even though excluded from the cult. The topic is treated in the Division of Holy Things, which concerns the cult in particular, and the priests who cannot serve are called unfit, not unclean. These two examples, among many, indicate

---

[1]Jonathan Z. Smith, *Map Is Not Territory: Studies in the History of Religion* (Leiden, 1977: E.J. Brill), p. xi.

that, when considering the Judaic system of uncleanness, beginning with its sources, we have to insert a consideration that the phenomenon, unclean or clean, would not invite. It is: Suitable or unsuitable, fit or unfit, clean or unclean – for what purpose? In what context? Something may be unsuitable, unfit, and unclean, but it is only in very specific contexts that, among the grounds for exclusion, the matter of uncleanness will be highlighted. When a priest is unclean, it means, he is suffering from contamination from a specified source of uncleanness and therefore cannot participate at that time in the cult; he may later on become suitable, meaning, clean. If that same priest has a physical deformity, for example, is left-handed, he also is unsuitable to participate in the cult, but he is not unclean. The same outcome therefore may be effected by more than a single cause. It follows that the categories clean and unclean effect a taxonomy only for a given purpose, in a specified context. Then the sources of uncleanness, consequently also their effects, are systemically relevant in very limited contexts. Uncleanness is not a general, and generic, condition; a person is unclean only for very specific purposes and in specified contexts. In other aspects, that same person is neutral, not distinguished from other persons.

The upshot is that when we know what one may or may not do – for example, eat, drink, what act one may or may not perform, where one may or may not go – by reason of context with a source of uncleanness, then we know the taxonomic power of that source of uncleanness. And, reversing matters, when we know what the source of uncleanness affects, we also know to what matter it is irrelevant. One important consequence concerns whether or not uncleanness is an ethical or moral category, as the use of the metaphor in prophetic literature suggests. While Isaiah says that he and his contemporaries have unclean lips, that does not mean (in the context of the priestly code) that he and they may not go to the Temple; if he were afflicted with the skin ailment of Leviticus 13 and 14, sara'at, by contrast, he could not go to the Temple, whatever the condition of his lips. So while cleanness or uncleanness serves as a metaphor for one's moral condition, in fact in a material, nonmetaphorical sense the same matter has concrete consequences; and when it comes to the Judaic system of cleanness, we deal solely with cleanness in a material and this-worldly, consequential context.

II. Uncleanness as an Ontological, Not a Moral, Category

That uncleanness produced by the specified sources of uncleanness addressed an issue quite distinct from a moral one therefore can be proven very simply. To identify the category of a conception, address to an authorship the challenge: state the opposite. The antonym tells us the category that guides thought. In the Essene Judaism of Qumran, uncleanness served as a metaphor of evil, and the opposite of unclean was virtuous, for example, one who disobeyed the rule was punished by being declared unclean for a given spell. In the Judaic system of the Mishnah, by contrast, the principal antonym of uncleanness is not only cleanness but holiness. Virtue and holiness constitute distinct classifications, the one having to do with morality, the other with ontology. To explain how uncleanness is an ontological, not a moral, category is very simple and may be presented with heavy emphasis: *To be able to become unclean formed a measure of the capacity to become holy, so that, the more susceptible to uncleanness, and the more differentiated the uncleanness to which susceptibility pertained, the more capable of becoming holy, and the more differentiated the layers and levels of holiness that entered consideration.* That fact will be spelled out later in this chapter.

It is important to say so at this point because we see that uncleanness or cleanness bears no implications whatever for whether or not an unclean person was a sinner, or a clean person not a sinner. For in the classification of uncleanness at hand, the opposite of unclean is holy, precisely as, throughout the priestly code, for example, the book of Leviticus, the antonym of unclean is holy, far more than it is merely clean (*tamé* vs. *qaddosh* appears far more regularly than *tamé* vs. *tahor*). But in the Mishnah, the more susceptible to uncleanness a person or an object, (for example, food,) is, the more layers or levels of sanctification that person or edible may attain. We think that to be "holier than thou" means to be more virtuous than the other. But in the context of the Mishnah's laws, we shall demonstrate at some length, to be "holier than thou," one has also to be more capable of becoming more unclean than thou, for example, to be more susceptible to uncleanness in more ways or at greater degrees of sensitivity to uncleanness, than whatever "thou" is at hand.

Throughout the Mishnah and much of its successor literature, "Israel," that is, the social entity of a Judaic system, is consistently represented as more susceptible to varieties and differentiated types of uncleanness than gentiles, and that forms, in a systemic context, an ontological judgment as to the ultimate being of that "Israel," and not a moral judgment as to the conduct and ethical character of Israelites or of "Israel," in general. That is why representing uncleanness as sin and a sign of wickedness for this Judaism is simply an error. By contrast, representing uncleanness as part of a hierarchical classification of social entities constitutes the correct systemic reading of the matter.

We emphasize this point because the Judaism we consider here contrasts in its uses of the theme of purity with the ways in which some of the important statements of nascent Christianity treat the same topic.

In the case at hand, the representation of uncleanness as a mark of sin or wickedness which requires eschatological purification through baptism constitutes Christianity's reading of uncleanness. The Christianity that deemed eschatological immersion for sin to relate to the category, uncleanness, made its statement of an eschatological system through that detail, as through other details, and the representation of uncleanness as a matter of sin formed a systemic statement of that Christianity, not a response to or a use of a fact of "Judaism." E.P. Sanders, in *Jesus and Judaism*, by contrast stresses that uncleanness in some instances in and of itself is a sin. In the Judaism put forth by the Pentateuch and the Mishnah, that is simply false. Accordingly, Sanders errs when he reads uncleanness as a moral category. It is worth dwelling on the case, because the error in the reading of this Judaism is commonplace because of the theology of cleanness as moral put forth by Christianity, and because Sanders's mistake is therefore routinely made in interpreting the meaning of the sources of uncleanness under consideration in this chapter.

Quite correctly, in describing the Old Testament account of uncleanness Sanders carefully stresses that "most impurities do not result from the transgression of a prohibition, although a few do."[2] He accurately emphasizes that an impure person is not a sinner; contact between an impure and a pure person is not ordinarily considered a sin. Once he has so represented biblical law, however, Sanders proceeds to allege the following:

> One should ask what was the situation of a person who disregarded the purity laws and did not use the immersion pool, but remained perpetually impure. Here it would be reasonable to equate being impure with being a "sinner" in the sense of "wicked," for such a person would have taken the position that the biblical laws need not be observed.[3]

That statement contradicts the judgments Sanders makes in his précis of the biblical representation of uncleanness, except for a single matter, which is sexual relations between husband and wife when the wife is menstruating. That is penalized by extirpation (Lev. 20:18), as Sanders says, and represents an exception, again explicitly specified by Sanders:

> But as a general rule, those who became impure...did not, as long as they lived their ordinary lives, sin. Normal human relations were not substantially affected.[4]

---

[2]E.P. Sanders, *Jesus and Judaism* (Philadelphia, 1985: Fortress), p. 183.
[3]Sanders, p. 184.
[4]Sanders, p. 183.

Now in order to harmonize the judgment made here with the position taken immediately following, Sanders gives an example, but, as we shall see, the example exemplifies only its own case:

> All the laws of purity and impurity are to be voluntarily observed. If, for example, a husband and wife agreed not to observe the prohibition of intercourse during menstruation, no one would ever know unless they announced the fact. If the woman never used the immersion pool, however, her neighbors would note that she was not observant.... Not intending to be observant is precisely what makes one "wicked"; but the wickedness comes not from impurity as such, but from the attitude that the commandments of the Bible need not be heeded.
>
> Thus these biblical purity laws, which most people seem to have observed, did not lead to a fixed view that the common people were sinners.[5]

In fact, the case exhausts the category; the only Old Testament purity law that affects conduct outside of the cult is the one that serves Sanders's claim that being impure may be equated with being a sinner in the sense of wicked.

Sanders's categorization of impurity as (sometimes) an issue of morality leaves open the question of how (at other times) we should classify the matter. The answer to that question will prove diverse, as we move from one Judaism to another. No one need doubt, for example, that Sanders's reading of uncleanness as sin will have found, in the Essene Judaism of Qumran, a broader scope than merely menstrual uncleanness, and eschatological immersion from sin, so prominent a motif in the description of John the Baptist, assuredly conforms to Sanders's view. But were we to interrogate the Judaism represented, as to its initial statement, by the Mishnah, we should come up with a quite different view of matters.

III. Uncleanness and the Ontology of the "Israel" of the Judaism of the Dual Torah

Let us start from the negative, which may be stated simply and categorically. *Not a single line in the entire Mishnah treats cultic uncleanness as in and of itself a representation of sin.* An unclean person is not a sinner, therefore not wicked. An unclean person cannot do things that a clean person can do. The sources of uncleanness we deal with here produce not moral turpitude but cultic uncleanness; not hygienic impurity; not physical uncleanliness at all. All of these classes and categories of uncleanness and cleanness are defined and placed into a single

---

[5]Sanders, p. 184-5. *Fathers According to Rabbi Nathan* Chapter 2 contains an explicit statement in accord with Sanders's example here, drawn from the privacy of marital relations.

continuum; there are not confused with one another but are carefully delineated. We find at Mishnah-tractate Sotah 9:15 the following:

> Heedfulness leads to physical cleanliness, cleanliness to levitical purity, purity to separateness, separateness to holiness, holiness to humility, humility to the shunning of sin, shunning of sin to saintliness, saintliness to the Holy Spirit, the Holy Spirit to the resurrection of the dead.

Clearly, the unclean person is not on that account wicked, and a polythetical taxonomic scheme does not permit the contrast only of uncleanness with morality.

How, then, does the Mishnah's treatment of uncleanness identify the correct classification or categorization of the matter? The answer is that, for the authorship of the Mishnah, uncleanness and cleanness form ontological, rather than moral categories. The capacity to become clean, a stage on the route to holiness as we saw, finds a counterpart in the capacity to become unclean; the more "holy" something may become, the more susceptible it is to uncleanness. Then to be susceptible to varieties and differentiated forms or sources of uncleanness is a mark not of sinfulness but of holiness. That conception finds no place in Sanders's representation of matters. And yet, as we shall now show in a very specific case, it is fundamental to the concrete legislation of the Mishnah's authorship, a position so profound in its implications as to mark as simply beside the point the allegation that an unclean person was, or could be construed as, a sinner or wicked.

Let us consider a concrete case that demonstrates the deep layers of thought on the hierarchization of uncleanness and holiness in the Mishnah's system. This case will show us two facts. First, that the opposite, for the authorship of the Mishnah, of unclean was not clean so much as holy. Second, that the synonym for unclean was not sinful or wicked but unfit or useless – something of an ontological, that is, in context, hierarchical, ordering of matters. That forms the key to the identification as ontological of the matter at hand, the conception that through capacity to become unclean, on the down side, and holy, on the up side, we hierarchize the entities before us, for example, gentiles and "Israel," or common food and food that has been designated as tithe, priestly rations ("heave-offering") and even Most Holy Things of the Temple altar itself. The case[6] derives from the very matter in which we

---

[6]At the end of this chapter we give a second such case, in the context of levels of cleanness and removes of uncleanness, that is, what happens if a generative source of uncleanness contacts something, which contacts something else, which contacts something else, for a sequence of removes. As we shall see later on, uncleanness proves affective at several stages removed from the original source

shall presently, in later writings of the same system, find a moral dimension, namely, "leprosy."

What we find here is a simple statement that the more susceptible a person to uncleanness, the more capable that person is of warding off the effects of uncleanness. The second case, offered in the next section, then will give us a richer perception of what is at stake in the simple assertion of correspondences with which we now deal. The reader will want to see the entire matter as it is set forth in the Mishnah and successor writings, even though the operative language is presented only in italics at the end. The version of the matter at Mishnah-tractate Negaim 13:10 is as follows:

F. If he [the leper] was standing inside and put his hand outside with his rings on this fingers, if he remained there a sufficient interval to eat a piece of bread, he is unclean.

G. [If] he was standing outside and put his hand inside with his rings on his fingers —

H. R. Judah declares [the ring] unclean forthwith.

I. And sages say, "Until he will remain long enough to eat a piece of bread."

J. They said to R. Judah, "Now if when his entire body is unclean, he has not made what is on him unclean until he remains a sufficient time to eat a piece of bread, when his entire body is not unclean, should he not render unclean that which is on him only after he remains a sufficient time to eat a piece of bread?" [M. Neg. 13:10]

To this point we have no account of Judah's thinking and therefore no reason to see the pertinence of the case to the principle we claim to locate here. To see what is at stake, we turn forthwith to the Tosefta's amplification of the matter.

Tosefta Negaim 7:9

K. Said to them R. Judah, "We find that the power of him who is unclean is stronger in affording protection than the power of him who is insusceptible to uncleanness.

L. "Israelites receive uncleanness and afford protection for clothing in the diseased house. The gentile and the beast, who do not receive uncleanness, also do not afford protection in the diseased house."

The Tosefta's authorship's amplification on Judah's reasoning provides the statement of correspondence and contrast, that is, of what is at stake, that we require. The reader will rightly ask why we maintain that the Tosefta's reading of the Mishnah's representation of Judah's view may be

---

of uncleanness, even a corpse, only in the case of things that also may be raised to higher levels of sanctification. That forms definitive proof of the proposition set forth here. But the case will prove of special interest only when we have examined the full range of exposition of the sources of uncleanness.

imputed to the Mishnah's authorship's conception, and the answer is, we can show that elsewhere, the Mishnah's authorship on its own presents precisely that view, only in a much more subtle and complex statement. Here the point is made in so many words: "Israelites receive uncleanness and afford protection for clothing in the diseased house. The gentile and the beast, who do not receive uncleanness, also do not afford protection in the diseased house."[7]

To this point, we have offered only a statement of the single proposition that the opposite of unclean is holy, and the synonym of unclean is not sinful but outsider or gentile. The entire composition as it is represented by the authorship of Sifra, which cites the Mishnah and the Tosefta verbatim and then joins the whole to an exegetical framework, makes that point explicit, since it introduces the beast and the gentile as operative categories, and neither the beast nor (by systemic analogy) the gentile forms a moral category, but only an ontological one. We give the Mishnah in boldface type and the Tosefta in italicized boldface type, to make clear the sequence of unfolding and underline still-later work of the authorship of Sifra:

Tosefta Negaim 7:9

A. Might one think that the beast and the gentile afford protection to garments in the diseased house?

B. Scripture says, "He will launder the garments" (Lev. 14:47) – as an inclusionary clause.

C. He whose clothing can be rendered unclean affords protection to clothing in the diseased house.

D. The beast and the gentile are excluded from the rule, for their clothing is not made unclean, and they do not afford protection for clothing in the diseased house.

E. In this connection sages have said:

F. **If he was standing inside and put his hand outside with his rings on this fingers, if he remained there a sufficient interval to eat a piece of bread, he is unclean.**

G. **[If] he was standing outside and put his hand inside with his rings on his fingers —**

H. **R. Judah declares [the ring] unclean forthwith.**

I. **And sages say, "Until he will remain long enough to eat a piece of bread."**

---

[7]Sanders's knowledge of the rabbinic sources is episodic and superficial, which is why, in his presentation of this matter, he shows himself ignorant of the details of the law that contain the systemic statement. He collects and arranges sayings, but he does not really understand the law; but it is in the law that the Judaism of the Dual Torah – Pentateuch and the Mishnah alike – makes its full statement on any given point. Everything Sanders has said about Judaism, based as it is on an insufficient knowledge of the details of the texts, has to be considered only with considerable caution.

J.   They said to R. Judah, "Now if when his entire body is unclean, he has not made what is on him unclean until he remains a sufficient time to eat a piece of bread, when his entire body is not unclean, should he not render unclean that which is on him only after he remains a sufficient time to eat a piece of bread" [M. Neg. 13:10]?

K.   *Said to them R. Judah, "We find that the power of him who is unclean is stronger in affording protection than the power of him who is insusceptible to uncleanness.*

L.   *"Israelites receive uncleanness and afford protection for clothing in the diseased house. The gentile and the beast, who do not receive uncleanness, also do not afford protection in the diseased house."*

Here we have a complete statement of the proposition in hand. Let us turn to what is at stake in what is clearly a set of ontological distinctions and points of differentiation. Judah's position is personal, hence not normative. But the principle that he expressed in finding a hierarchical relationship between the capacity to receive uncleanness and the capacity to afford protection presents a very important and explicit statement of the matter at hand. These are the conclusions necessary for an appreciation of the importance of the facts on the sources of uncleanness set forth in the Pentateuch and the Mishnah.

Now to review the main point: the most important language is Judah's assertion that a person who is more susceptible to uncleanness also affords greater protection from uncleanness than a person who is not. If Israelites are susceptible to uncleanness, they also can afford protection for clothing. Gentiles or beasts, insusceptible to the uncleanness of "leprosy," entering the afflicted house will forthwith produce contamination for garments or sandals which they may be wearing, even though they themselves are not susceptible to this form of uncleanness at all. What has all this to do with morality? Nothing whatsoever. The focus, the issue, these concern one's state or condition in an utterly abstract world of relationships that are intangible and unseen, yet, withal, critical. Later on in this chapter we shall consider further evidence that points to the same necessary conclusion.

IV. The Pentateuchal Statement of the Sources of Uncleanness

Let us now revert to the facts of the Pentateuchal and Mishnaic accounts of sources of uncleanness and state in general terms the principal components of the Scriptural system of cleanness, all of which derive from the priestly code.

I.   Sources of Uncleanness, Modes of Transfer in the Written Torah
  A. *Sources of Uncleanness*
     1. *Animals*
         Gen. 7:2: Seven pairs of all clean animals...and a pair of
      animals that are not clean (+ Gen. 7:8: Clean animals and
      birds sacrificed by Noah, Gen. 8:20).
         Lev. 11:24-46: And by these you shall become unclean,
      whoever touches their carcass shall be unclean until the
      evening.... + animals, swarming things (+ Lev. 11:39-40,
      Deut. 12:15, 14:3-21).
     2. *Living Persons*
         Lev. 12:1-8: Woman after childbirth is unclean as in
      menstrual period. Lev. 13:1-59: "Leper."[8]
         Lev. 15:1-15: The Zab, his spit, saddle.
         Lev. 15:16-18: Person who has had sexual intercourse or
      seminal emission (Deut. 23:10-11).
         Lev. 15 :19-24 (Lev. 20:18): Menstruating woman.
         Lev. 15:25-30: Woman who has discharge of blood many
      days outside of menstrual period (Zabah).
         Lev. 19:31: Mediums and wizards defile those who seek
      them out. Lev. 18:1-30: Various sexual taboos and how
      violating them defiles the land.
     3. *Inanimate Objects*
         Lev. 13:47-59: Leprous fabrics are deemed unclean and
      burned.
         Lev. 14:33-54: Leprous house makes person who enters it
      unclean.
         Num. 19:13: Corpse.

The "Zab," or "Zabah" (male, female) is then one afflicted with a flux
such as is defined in Leviticus 15; in the case of the male, it is flux of the
flaccid penis; in the case of the female, it is a flow other than during the
menstrual period. This flux or flow may be referred to in the Mishnah as
"*zob*," and for the flow not during the woman's menstrual period,
"*zibah*." The third component, of course, is introduced by the analogy
prevailing in context: *sara'at* and what is comparable thereto. The
priestly code specifies three types of sources of uncleanness: animals,
Leviticus Chapter 11; living people, Leviticus Chapters 12 through 15;

---

[8]The translation of *sara'at* as "leper" (= a victim of Hansen's Disease) is
indefensible, which is why I use quotation marks to signal the peculiarity of my
rendition; but it is familiar. To translate the Mishnah's *nega'* I use "plague,"
which is equally odd but perhaps serviceable.

and inanimate objects, in the case of leprous fabrics and the leprous house analogous to the leper, Leviticus Chapter 14, and, principally, the corpse, Numbers 19:13.

In addition, certain sexual taboos fall into the category constructed by the language of clean and unclean, as listed in Leviticus Chapter 18, but these play no role whatsoever in the consideration of sources of uncleanness in the Mishnah's reading of matters. The Mishnah receives these facts as givens and never treats as clean a source of uncleanness specified by Scripture. It does not, however, pay substantial attention to the pollution effected by violating sexual taboos, other than the menstrual one, and it is indifferent to the uncleanness created by consulting a wizard. The effects of violating sexual taboos (for example, mother-son sexual relations) are genealogical, and while the language of pollution is invoked, the effects are not to render such a person or the offspring of the union unclean in the way a corpse is unclean. So the use of "unclean" is metaphorical. The Mishnah does allude to the uncleanness of the idol and its appurtenances (for example, throughout Mishnah-tractate Abodah Zarah, cf. also T. Zab. 5:5-8). Uncleanness of unclean animals plays no significant role (M. Toh. Chapter 1), being treated in the context of the Division of Holy Things. The one important contribution of Leviticus Chapter 11 is the dead creeping thing, a recurrent theme; indeed, sources of uncleanness that figure most prominently in the Mishnah are, for food and drink, dead creeping things; for bodily uncleanness, the persons of Leviticus 15, and for utensils, the corpse.

V. Sources of Uncleanness in the Mishnah

If we ask, at what points do the emphases of Leviticus and Numbers and those of the Mishnah's Division of Purities come together, it is at Leviticus Chapters 12 through 15, which generate Mishnah-tractates Negaim (Lev. Chapters 13 and 14), Niddah (Lev. 15:25-30, and, by explicitly stated analogy, Lev. 12:1-8), and Zabim (Lev. 15:1-15, 19-24). Mishnah-tractate Ohalot (Chapters 1 through 3 and 16 through 18 rests upon Num. 19:13). The uncleanness of the seminal emission, Leviticus 15:16-18, receives some, if not sustained, attention (M. Nid. 7:1, T. 8:13C, M. Miq. 8:1-4/T. 6:1, 5-8, M. Zab. 1:2/T. Zab. 2:31/T.2:4).

Accordingly, there is no significant point in regard to sources of uncleanness at which the interests and emphases of the priestly code and those of our Division significantly diverge. What is important to the priestly code and other relevant passages of the Pentateuch is treated at length in the Mishnah. The tractates devoted to sources of uncleanness in general correspond to, and develop without innovation, the equivalent materials in the Written Torah, specifically Negaim, Niddah, Zabim, and the prologue and epilogue of Ohalot. (Omitted are Makhshirin and Tebul Yom).

For the Mishnah, the sources of uncleanness in particular are, first, menstrual blood and excretions deemed analogous to menstrual blood, for example, the flux of the Zab, and second, corpse uncleanness. These receive most attention. To the first century B.C.E. authorities, Hillel and Shammai, are attributed sayings[9] that take for granted that menstrual flow makes a woman unclean and dispute only about retroactive uncleanness (M. Nid. 1:1), that is to say, matters of doubt about the status of objects a woman touches before the onset of the menstrual flow has been confirmed. Shammai maintains that an object is unclean only from the time at which we know the flow has started. Hillel holds that we impute retroactive uncleanness, either for the period of twenty-four hours antecedent to the onset of the flow or to that point at which, before the woman knows her flow has started, the woman examined herself and found that she still had not had the flow of menstrual blood. Hillel's position of course imposes the stringent requirement. Shammai's and Hillel's disciples, called "the Houses" (of Shammai or of Hillel, respectively) further take for granted that sexual relations are prohibited during the menstrual period (M. Nid. 2:4). They also are in agreement that some sorts of blood are not unclean at all – for example, blood which is not red while others are (M. Nid. 2:5, 10:1). The rules assigned in Mishnah-tractate Niddah to Hillel, Shammai, and their Houses deal with three topics: (1) unclean fluids (colors of unclean blood, blood of the gentile woman, blood of the woman in labor, blood of the woman who dies in her period, hymeneal blood, blood of woman who has not immersed after childbirth); (2) the status of the woman in the days of her purifying (status as to Holy Things, blood of the woman who has not immersed after childbirth, does the woman after the days of purifying

---

[9]From this point forward, I shall omit the necessary qualifying language, "are attributed sayings...." The Mishnah and Tosefta contain numerous sayings assigned to authorities generally assumed to have lived between the first century B.C.E. and the early third century C.E., for example, Hillel and Shammai onward through Judah the Patriarch. We have no way of proving that what is attributed to an authority really was said by him. The sole facts we have in hand are those of attribution. On that basis, we cannot form a history of the law, only an account of how it is divided among a variety of authorities. The picture given here is not a historical but a phenomenological one, and therefore the historical question of whether a given authority made a statement assigned to him is irrelevant to the work of description, all the more so, analysis and interpretation as conducted here. For convenience's sake, therefore, we simply use the names as is, without taking a position on whether what is assigned to those names really was said by them, at a particular point in the historical unfolding of the law.

have to immerse?); (3) the issue of retroactive contamination, including the matter of examination. The third theme is secondary to the first, of course. I perceive no issue which Scripture has not generated. Whether or not contamination is retroactive is not distinctive to the facts of Niddah; it constitutes the first step beyond the facts laid forth in Scripture, thus the primary layer of developed law.

In respect to the Zab, whose uncleanness is equivalent to that of the menstruating woman, the Houses take for granted that flux and semen are analogous. They then investigate the status of a single appearance of flux. The Hillelites compare a man who has one to him who has had a seminal emission; the Shammaites, to a woman who awaits day against day, that is, to the prospective Zabah. Thus the issue is whether we treat a single flux – that is, the appearance of flux on a given day, or in a given time span – as equivalent to semen, or equivalent to the flux of the Zabah, and the larger issue is the governing analogy. The Houses further know that three issues of flux are required to establish the status as to uncleanness of the Zab (M. Zab. 1:1). The Houses, finally, take for granted that bits and pieces of a corpse contaminate in the tent as does the corpse as a whole (M. Zab. 2:2, 18:8). They assume that the corpse contamination flows through a passage of a specified size, a square handbreadth (M. Oh. 7:3), and that if there are various windows in a tent, one which is open draws the corpse contamination out, so that what is subject to the overshadowing of the others is not affected. The specification of the size of the passage way occurs at M. Oh. 11:1, M. Oh. 13:1, M. Oh. 13:4, and M. Oh. 15:8. Accordingly, the Houses know that a tent spreads contamination when it overshadows a corpse or things which derive from a corpse. A grave area is assumed to contain corpse matter, which may be removed. A gentile's dwelling in the Land of Israel is unclean.

A. Menstrual Blood

As we saw, the uncleanness of menstrual blood is specified by Lev. 15:19. The first question, in consequence, is the status of blood which comes prior to discharge; the second is the way in which we establish a regular period for discharge; the third is the status of the blood of a non-Israelite woman. With Shammai and Hillel, the analysis of the first question begins: How do we deal with a woman's status prior to the onset of her period? Shammai's view is that the woman is assumed clean until shown by her discharge to be unclean. It is Hillel who proposes to take into account the possibility of her having been unclean before she realizes that her period actually has already begun. A further, logical question is the status of the discharge if a menstruating woman dies. Is the discharge treated merely as an excretion of a corpse, or do we regard it as we should if the woman were still alive? The Houses take for granted, moreover, that hymeneal blood is not unclean, and this correlates with their view that some sorts of vaginal blood are unclean, some clean.

A further question raised by Scripture's rules concerns blood exuded not during the menstrual cycle, that specified in Lev. 15:25. The Houses assume that the blood of a woman who gives birth as a Zabah (that is, in the condition of producing a flow other than during her menstrual days) is unclean like that of a Zabah. They know that the woman who has given birth is deemed unclean "as at the time of her menstruation" (Lev. 12:2). They also know that a woman who is a Zabah is deemed unclean "as in the days of her menstrual period" (Lev. 15:25). There can, therefore, be no reason *not* to deem the woman who gives birth as a Zabah to produce unclean blood in the same status. If, however, the woman is not a Zabah and gives birth, the blood she produces is given the same status as blood after delivery. It is unclean as menstrual blood. This conception simply is based on the analogy between the status of blood produced after delivery and that of blood produced before then. The Zabah also is held to be able to contaminate one who has intercourse with her, just as does a menstruant. Since Scripture explicitly compares her to a menstruating woman, there is no reason to suppose the analogy far-fetched. Accordingly, all of the basic suppositions of the Houses derive from a careful, but not particularly acute, reading of Scripture, with stress upon carrying to their logical conclusions the analogies proposed by Scripture itself.

Scripture stands behind these further notions; first, the woman who bears a child is unclean seven or fourteen days: as at the time of her menstruation shall she be unclean (Lev. 12:2); second, after that time, she continues for thirty-three or sixty-six days in the blood of her purifying and shall not touch any holy thing or come into the sanctuary (Lev. 12:4); third, menstrual blood is unclean: when *a woman has a discharge of blood which is her regular discharge from her body, she shall be in her impurity for seven days, and whoever touches her shall be unclean until the evening* (Lev. 15:19), including the man who has intercourse with her, in which case he shares the status of menstrual uncleanness (Lev. 15:24); and, finally, the woman who has a discharge not during her menstrual period is unclean as a Zabah *so* long as the discharge continues: As in the days of her impurity shall she be unclean (Lev. 15:25).

B. The Zab

The Houses take for granted that three occurrences of flux confirm a man as a Zab. Lev. 15:2 contains no specification of the number of fluxes, or of days on which flux is to occur. But Lev. 15:25, referring to the

Zabah, speaks of a woman's having a discharge of blood "for many days, not at the time of her period." *Many days* then will be understood to mean a minimum of three days, the smallest simple plural (excluding the dual). It will follow that what is said of the Zabah by analogy is definitive of the Zab. But whether or not three fluxes must occur on three separate days or may occur on the same day is hardly settled either by Scripture or by the Houses. Once the analogy of the Zabah yields the notion that three issues of flux are required, the Houses' second point of interest is raised: the relationship between flux, which is assumed to be white, and semen. The analogy of Zab to Zabah should exclude the comparison of flux to semen. If a man produces semen in a normal act of intercourse, he is unclean during that day. The Houses' dispute concerns whether or not semen produced by a Zab is unclean *as if* it were flux. The Shammaites maintain that it is unclean as if it were flux, and the man loses the antecedent clean days, specified at Lev. 15:13. The Hillelites say the man is unclean on the day of semen, in line with Lev. 15:16-18, but not by reason of flux. These are secondary issues based upon Scripture's primary information.

C. Corpse Matter

As we noted, the contaminating effect of corpse matter is specified at Num. 19:11: "He who touches the dead body of any person shall be unclean seven days." The sole notion assumed by the Houses is that things which are derived from a corpse or deemed analogous to a corpse are unclean just like the corpse. Their dispute concerns the quantity of material deriving from a corpse which is to be deemed unclean like a whole corpse. They further assume that dirt from graves is unclean because it contains corpse matter, an assumption well attested, for the generality of Israelite religion, by Mt. 23:27's reference to whitewashed tombs and Lk. 11:44's reference to walking on unseen graves, with the implied supposition that said graves produce contamination. The reason that the gentile's dwelling in the Land of Israel is assumed to be unclean is not specified.

VI. The Insufficiently Observant Israelite *(Am Ha'ares)* in the System of Uncleanness

The taxonomic power of sources of uncleanness to differentiate Israel from the nations (gentiles being subject to an undifferentiated uncleanness and themselves constituting a source of uncleanness, Israelites being subject only to highly differentiated types of uncleanness, as we have already seen) serves yet another purpose. It is to differentiate among Israelites themselves, between those who observe the laws of cleanness to the fullest and those who keep those laws only with respect to the menstrual taboo, on the one hand, and the requirement to be cultically clean when going on a pilgrimage to Jerusalem and the Temple, on the other. The people who keep the cleanness rules only in the latter connection are classed as *am ha'ares,* which, in the Mishnah, refers to people who do not observe cleanness in eating everyday meals at home but only in eating cultic meals in Jerusalem; the same people do not keep all of the laws of tithing as defined by the sages, though they keep most of those laws.

While the Pentateuch knows nothing of this refinement in the differentiation of Israelites, the uncleanness of the *am ha'ares* is taken for granted in the Mishnah. The principal point of interest is in the conduct to be expected from the *am ha'ares.* Despite the presence of dissenting opinions, we gain the impression that the accepted view affirms the willingness of the *am ha'ares* to avoid contaminating what is not his. In connection with "heave-offering" – the portion of the crop that is designated as priestly rations and paid by all Israelites for the support of the priesthood – in particular, the *am ha'ares is* believed to take precautions. To be sure, the wife of the *am ha'ares* makes things unclean with midras uncleanness. But the second century authority, Yosé, at M. Toh. 10:1, makes it clear that that is a point of law about which the *am ha'ares* are assumed to be ignorant. The net result is that when they do know the law and understand its importance – as in regard to heave-offering – they will do nothing to effect contamination. Dosetai b. R. Yannai's version of the Houses' dispute (T. Toh. 8:10) leads us into the secondary development of the principle before us. When we deposit something with the *am ha'ares* then we place it in his charge, and he may well touch it. But when we merely leave an object with him, the *am ha'ares* will avoid contaminating it. The conception that the *am ha'ares* will respect the concern of the haber – the fully observant Israelite – to keep the rules of cleanness is thereby qualified. If property falls within the control or domain of the *am ha'ares* he will feel free to do as he likes with it. So, too, will his wife. Accordingly, what is within the domain of the *am ha'ares* will be regarded as contaminated, a severe limitation upon the first principle. The consideration under discussion is explicitly introduced in a number of paragraphs. As before, we have dissenting opinions, but these concern the full weight of our giving the *am ha'ares* charge of something. We agree that what he controls is unclean. But what is it that he controls? The key, or the whole house to which the key gives access? M. Toh. 8:5 shows how the two principles harmonize. The wife of the *am ha'ares* will not deliberately contaminate the house, because we have not placed the house in her charge. Accordingly, on the one hand, she respects the concern of the haber to keep the house clean; on the other, if we give her charge over the house, she will surely touch everything in it. Meir at M. Toh. 7:2 certainly takes a different view. Unsupervised, the *am ha'ares* left in a house will contaminate everything. Sages vis-à-vis Meir take a similarly negative view; the only reason the *am ha'ares* will not touch everything in the house is that he fears discovery, not that he respects the *haber's* obsessions. Here again, in detailed cases, the Mishnah makes its main point about the power of uncleanness to effect the taxonomy of holy Israel, between more holy and less holy, not between more virtuous and less virtuous; the consequences are cultic, not moral.

VII. Addressing a Common Agendum:
Uncleanness as a Moral Category in Later Canonical Writings
of the Judaism of the Dual Torah

Now that we have a clear picture of how uncleanness serves within the system of the Mishnah, namely, as an ontological category, an indicator of holiness, we return to the disposition of that same category in later stages of the same Judaic system. For, as time rendered still more remote the reality of the cult – which came to an end in 70 C.E. when the Romans destroyed the Temple and Jerusalem, and which definitively was closed off in 135 C.E., when the Romans forbade Jews to enter Jerusalem at all – and as the focus of thought within the unfolding system shifted to the governance, by sages, of that holy community that persisted beyond the end of the holy Temple, the ongoing system, as represented in successive writings, exhibited categorical reconstructions in diverse ways. And one of these ways, we think symptomatic of systemic changes in other categories also, represented uncleanness as not an ontological but a moral category. So while ontic and not moral (let alone eschatological) in the Pentateuch and the Mishnah, the sources of uncleanness were spiritualized and moralized in later writings, which we briefly survey.

The representation of levitical or cultic uncleanness as a matter of sin emerges, in the unfolding of the writings of the Judaism originally set forth in the Mishnah (a Judaism we call "the Judaism of the Dual Torah"), only in much later stages, in documents brought to closure long after the destruction of the Temple. Then uncleanness does serve as a metaphor for evil. A very rapid survey of the representations of uncleanness in successive documents, beyond the Mishnah, shows us that a contrast between uncleanness and morality was drawn by the authorship of the Tosefta, which condemned the view that "the uncleanness of the knife is more disturbing to Israel than the shedding of blood."[10]   Explicit statements that uncleanness forms an indicator of wickedness emerge in documents that first reached closure not before 300 C.E., and possibly considerably after that time.   Here is an explicit statement:

> R. Yosé the Galilean[11] says, "Come and see how strong is the power of sin, for before they put forth their hands in transgression, there were not found among [the Israelites] people unclean through having a discharge and lepers, but after they put forth their hands in transgression, there were among them people unclean through having a discharge and lepers...."[12]

True, no rabbi ever declared a sinner to be cultically unclean on that account, while in the Essene Judaism of Qumran, being impure is a sin, just as committing certain sins automatically imposed a period of uncleanness.   Still, we cannot doubt that, for the authorship that has included the saying attributed to Yosé, uncleanness marked a moral category.

A still more explicit statement of the same viewpoint, quite specific to a single, identified sin, maintains that the skin ailment describe at

---

[10]Tosefta Kippurim 1:12.

[11]It should be clear that the temporal assignment of sayings rests solely on the time of closure of the documents that contain those sayings, not on the attributions, which cannot be shown to go back to the time and person to whom the sayings are assigned.   Since the same saying can be given by diverse authorships and their documents to various authorities, and since no attribution can be shown to derive from first-hand evidence, for example, a book written by a named authority and preserved by his disciples in a chain of transmission we can trace as we can, for example, books by Philo, Josephus, Paul, Irenaeus, Justin, and other first and second (and later) century figures, there is no alternative for critical scholarship.   We therefore trace the canonical history of ideas, that is, the point, in the unfolding of the writings, at which a saying first occurs or an idea first makes its presence known.   The sequence of writings, first this, then that, is beyond serious doubt, since writings posterior to the Mishnah, such as the Tosefta, Sifra, and the two Sifrés, cite the Mishnah verbatim entirely outside the structure of their own discourse and comment on Mishnah passages.   The received conception of these writings as deriving from the first and second centuries, that is, the same time as the period of the formation of the Mishnah, and not from the third or fourth or still later times, rests upon the occurrence of the same names in both the Mishnah and the Tosefta or Sifra or the two Sifrés. That same theory assigns to the first or second centuries all sayings in the two Talmuds that appear bearing attributions of authorities who lived in those early times.   But absent the demonstration that that was so, we can no more assume that if the Tosefta or the Talmud of the Land of Israel or the Talmud of Babylonia assigns a saying to Yosé the Galilean, he really made that saying, than we can take for granted that Moses really said everything that the Pentateuchal authorships say he said.

[12]Sifré to Numbers Naso 2.

Leviticus 13 (wrongly translated "leprosy") is caused by a specific sin, namely, gossip. This view appears in Tosefta Negaim 6:7, Sifré to Deuteronomy 175, and Sifra Mesora Parashah 5:9, and is as follows:

A.   "Saying" (Lev. 14:35) –
B.   The priest will say to him words of reproach: "My son, plagues come only because of gossip [T. 6:7], as it is said, 'Take heed of the plague of leprosy to keep very much and to do, remember what the Lord God did to Miriam' (Deut. 24:8).
C.   "And what has one thing to do with the other?
D.   "But this teaches that she was punished only because of gossip.
E.   "And is it not an argument a fortiori?
F.   "If Miriam, who did not speak before Moses' presence, suffered so, one who speaks ill of his fellow in his very presence, how much the more so?"
G.   R. Simeon b. Eleazar says, "Also because of arrogance do plagues come, for so do we find concerning Uzziah,
H.   "as it is said, 'And he rebelled against the Lord his God and he came to the Temple of the Lord to offer on the altar incense and Azariah the Priest came after him and with him priests of the Lord, eighty strong men, and they stood against Uzziah and said to him, "It is not for you to do, Uzziah, to offer to the Lord, for only the priests the sons of Aaron who are sanctified do so. So forth from the sanctuary." And Uzziah was angry,' etc. (2 Chr. 26:16)" [T. Neg. 6:7H].

The same inquiry into the moral foundations of cultic uncleanness leads the authorship of Babylonian Talmud Niddah at 31b to attribute to Simeon b. Yohai the following explanation for the requirement that a woman after childbirth bring a sacrifice:

> When she kneels in bearing, she swears impetuously that she will have no intercourse with her husband. The Torah...ordained that she should bring a sacrifice.

But this does not encompass levitical uncleanness in particular. To summarize: the view that impurity is a sign of sin does not occur in the Mishnah. It does occur in the Tosefta in the specific allegation that leprosy is a sign that a person is guilty of having gossiped or is a sign of arrogance. Even in these passages, however, no concrete sanction or penalty of a moral order is invoked, as an explicit violation of the law would precipitate a concrete sanction. Sages do not leave a record of having imposed a penalty of uncleanness upon a gossip. So there is ample evidence that in the successor writings, after the Mishnah, the sources of uncleanness broadened to include sins of a social or moral character. But while the metaphorization of matters proceeded apace, the kinds of concrete consequences drawn by Scripture and the Mishnah from the presence of a source of uncleanness never were replicated.

What was metaphorized remained spiritual and without consequence in the workaday world.

VIII. Addressing a Common Agendum:
Sources of Uncleanness, Removes of Uncleanness, and
Levels of Sanctification. Unclean Versus Holy

To conclude, let us examine a clear statement of the proposition that the greater the capacity to receive uncleanness, the more holy a classification of persons or things is; the lesser the range of differentiation, the less holy is that same classification of persons or things. In this way we see conclusively how, in concrete, practical law, the conception of purity is set forth that purity forms a taxonomic and hierarchical indicator, defining who or what is holier or less holier than the other. What is undifferentiated as to uncleanness is also less capable of attaining the heights of sanctification; and what is more differentiated, therefore more susceptible, also is more capable of sanctification at a higher level. Susceptibility to uncleanness of more kinds at more removes is a mark of a higher level of sanctification, and so the sources of uncleanness we have specified deliver their systemic statement. It is that the fullest measure of life marks the highest status as to sanctification (and vice versa, the holier, the more alive). If what is a perversion of what creates or sustains life is unclean, then in the natural and rightful condition, what accords with the rules of life also marks the highest level of sanctification. The corpse therefore forms the generative metaphor for uncleanness, the high priest in the holy of holies, for cleanness. And everything else functions at the levels in between, classifying, and therefore, necessarily, also hierarchizing the steps and stages from death to life: the point at which we started.

In what follows we shall find a clear hierarchization of sanctification in terms of capacity to receive uncleanness, and the hierarchization is the premise of discourse, not the private opinion of one party, hence built into the normative structure of the legal theological system of the Mishnah. What we shall now see in a still less accessible case is that the greater one's susceptibility to uncleanness, the more exalted one's capacity for sanctification. To state the proposition in more abstract language, such as ontology demands: the greater the capacity for differentiation, the higher the potential of consecration. This fundamentally ontological principle of hierarchization is expressed in the detail of a legal case, and we shall have to work our way through the details of the case to see how profoundly embedded in the law is the conception of a hierarchical, or rather, hierarchizing, ontology that is fundamental to the system at hand. This case then will leave no doubt whatsoever that uncleanness for the system at hand, that is, the systemic statement of the Mishnah in particular, forms in no way a moral, but only an ontological category. The system as a whole, which proposes a hierarchizing ontology expressed through sanctification, then makes its statement here, as it will, uniformly, at all other relevant points. And to that system, the conception of uncleanness as a metaphor for evil, is simply beside the point, monumentally irrelevant.

We see this in a discussion of the several removes from a source of uncleanness and how they affect food in several degrees of consecration or sanctification. Once more we turn first to the text, then to the exposition, of Mishnah-tractate Tohorot 2:2-7.

Mishnah-tractate Tohorot 2:2

A.   R. Eliezer says, "(1) He who eats food unclean in the first remove is unclean in the second remove;
"(2) [he who eats] food unclean in the second remove is unclean in the second remove;
"(3) [he who eats] food unclean in the third remove is unclean in the third remove."

B.   R. Joshua says, "(1) He who eats food unclean in the first remove and food unclean in the second remove is unclean in the second remove.
"(2) [He who eats food] unclean in the third remove is unclean in the second remove so far as Holy Things are concerned,
"(3) and is not unclean in the second remove so far as heave-offering is concerned.

C.   "[We speak of] the case of unconsecrated food

D.   "which is prepared in conditions appropriate to heave-offering."

Mishnah-tractate Tohorot 2:3

A.   Unconsecrated food: In the first remove is unclean and renders unclean;

B.   in the second remove is unfit, but does not convey uncleanness;

C.   and in the third remove is eaten in the pottage of heave-offering.

Mishnah-tractate Tohorot 2:4

A.   *Heave-offering:*
In the first and in the second remove is unclean and renders unclean;

B.   in the third remove is unfit and does not convey uncleanness;

C.   and in the fourth remove is eaten in a pottage of Holy Things.

Mishnah-tractate Tohorot 2:5

A.   *Holy Things:*
In the first and the second and the third removes are susceptible to uncleanness and render unclean;

B.   and in the fourth remove are unfit and do not convey uncleanness;

C.   and in the fifth remove are eaten in a pottage of Holy Things.

Mishnah-tractate Tohorot 2:6

A. *Unconsecrated food:*
    In the second remove renders unconsecrated liquid unclean and renders food of heave-offering unfit.
B. *Heave-offering:*
    In the third remove renders unclean [the] liquid of Holy Things, and renders foods of Holy Things unfit,
C. if it [the heave-offering] was prepared in the condition of cleanness pertaining to Holy Things.
D. But if it was prepared in conditions pertaining to heave-offering, it renders unclean at two removes and renders unfit at one remove in reference to Holy Things.

Mishnah-tractate Tohorot 2:7

A. R. Eleazar says, "The three of them are equal:
B. *"Holy Things and heave-offering, and unconsecrated food:*
    "Which are at the first remove of uncleanness render unclean at two removes and unfit at one [further] remove in respect to Holy Things;
    "render unclean at one remove and spoil at one [further] remove in respect to heave-offering;
    "and spoil unconsecrated food.
C. "That which is unclean in the second remove in all of them renders unclean at one remove and unfit at one [further] remove in respect to Holy Things;
    "and renders liquid of unconsecrated food unclean;
    "and spoils foods of heave-offering.
D. "The third remove of uncleanness in all of them renders liquids of Holy Things unclean,
    "and spoils food of Holy Things."

Mishnah-tractate Tohorot 2:2-7 presupposes knowledge of the Mishnaic system of ritual purity. A review of some of its essential elements is necessary for an understanding of the arguments and analyses that follow. In the system, ritual impurity is acquired by contact with either a primary or a secondary source of uncleanness, called a "Father" or a "Child" (or "Offspring") of uncleanness, respectively. In the first category are contact with a corpse, a person suffering a flux, a leper, and the like. Objects made of metal, wood, leather, bone, cloth, or sacking become Fathers of uncleanness if they touch a corpse. Foodstuffs and liquids are susceptible to uncleanness, but will not render other foodstuffs unclean in the same degree or remove of uncleanness that they themselves suffer. Foodstuffs furthermore will not make vessels or utensils unclean. But liquids made unclean by a Father of uncleanness will do so if they touch the inner side of the vessel. That is, if they fall into the contained space of an earthenware vessel, they make the whole vessel unclean.

Food or liquid that touches a Father of uncleanness becomes unclean in the *first* remove. If food touches a person or vessel made unclean by a primary cause of uncleanness, it is unclean in the *second* remove. Food that touches *second-remove* uncleanness incurs *third-remove* uncleanness, and food that touches *third-remove* uncleanness incurs *fourth-remove* uncleanness, and so on. But liquids touching either a primary source of uncleanness (Father) or something unclean in the first or second remove (Offspring) are regarded as unclean in the first remove. They are able to make something else unclean. If, for example, the other side of a vessel is made unclean by a liquid – thus unclean in the second remove – and another liquid touches the outer side, the other liquid incurs not second, but first degree uncleanness.

Heave-offering (food raised up for priestly use only) unclean in the third remove of uncleanness, and Holy Things (that is, things belonging to the cult) unclean in the fourth remove, do not make other things, whether liquids or foods, unclean. The difference among removes of uncleanness is important. First-degree uncleanness in common food will convey uncleanness. But, although food unclean in the second remove will be unacceptable, it will not convey uncleanness, that is, third-degree uncleanness. But it will render heave-offering *unfit*. Further considerations apply to heave-offering and Holy Things. Heave-offering can be made unfit and unclean by a first, and unfit by a second, degree of uncleanness. If it touches something unclean in the third remove, it is made unfit, but itself will not impart fourth-degree uncleanness. A Holy Thing that suffers uncleanness in the first, second, or third remove is unclean and conveys uncleanness. If it is unclean in the fourth remove, it is invalid for the cult but does not convey uncleanness. It is much more susceptible than are noncultic things. Thus, common food that suffers second degree uncleanness will render heave-offering invalid. We already know that it makes liquid unclean in the first remove. Likewise, heave-offering unclean in the third remove will make Holy Things invalid and put them into a fourth remove of uncleanness. With these data firmly in hand, let us turn to a general discussion of M. Mishnah-tractate Tohorot 2:2-7.

Mishnah-tractate Tohorot 2:2 introduces the removes of uncleanness. Our interest is in the contaminating effect, upon a person, of eating unclean food. Does the food make the person unclean in the same remove of uncleanness as is borne by the food itself? Thus if one eats food unclean in the first remove, is he unclean in that same remove? This is the view of Eliezer. Joshua says he is unclean in the second remove. The dispute, Mishnah-tractate Tohorot 2:2A-B, at Mishnah-tractate Tohorot 2:2C-D is significantly glossed. The further consideration is introduced as to the sort of food under discussion. Joshua is made to say that there is a difference between the contaminating effects upon the one who eats heave-offering, on the one side, and unconsecrated food prepared in conditions of heave-offering, on the other. This matter, the status of unconsecrated food prepared as if it were heave-offering, or as if it were Holy Things, and heave-offering prepared as if it were Holy Things, forms a substratum of our chapter, added to several primary items and complicating the exegesis. Tosefta-Tractate Tohorot 2:1 confirms, however, that primary to the dispute between Eliezer and Joshua is simply the matter of the effects of food unclean in the first remove upon the person who eats such food. The gloss, Mishnah-tractate Tohorot 2:2C-D, forms a redactional thematic link between Joshua's opinion and the large construction of Mishnah-tractate Tohorot 2:3-7. Mishnah-tractate Tohorot 2:3-5, expanded and glossed by Mishnah-tractate Tohorot 2:6, follow a single and rather tight form. The sequence differentiates unconsecrated food, heave-offering, and Holy Things each at the several removes from the original source of uncleanness.

Eleazar at Mishnah-tractate Tohorot 2:7 insists that, at a given remove, all three are subject to the *same* rule. The contrary view, Mishnah-tractate Tohorot 2:3-6, is that unconsecrated food in the first remove makes heave-offering unclean and at the second remove spoils heave-offering; it does not enter a third remove and therefore has no effect upon Holy Things. Heave-offering at the first two removes may produce contaminating effects, and at the third remove spoils Holy Things, but is of no effect at the fourth. Holy Things in the first three removes produce uncleanness, and at the fourth impart unfitness to other Holy Things. Mishnah-tractate Tohorot 2:6 then goes over the ground of unconsecrated food at the second remove, and heave-offering at the third. The explanation of Mishnah-tractate Tohorot 2:6C is various; the simplest view is that the clause glosses Mishnah-tractate Tohorot 2:6B by insisting that the heave-offering to which we refer is prepared as if it were Holy Things, on which account, at the third remove, it can spoil Holy Things. At Mishnah-tractate Tohorot 2:7 Eleazar restates matters, treating all three – Holy Things, heave-offering, and unconsecrated food – as equivalent to one another at the first, second, and third removes, with the necessary qualification for unconsecrated food that it is like the other, consecrated foods in producing effects at the second and even the third removes. Commentators read *Eliezer.* They set the pericope up against Joshua's view at Mishnah-tractate Tohorot 2:2, assigning to Joshua Mishnah-tractate Tohorot 2:3ff. as well. To state the upshot simply: *So far as Eleazar is concerned, what is important is not the source of contamination – the unclean foods – but that which is contaminated, the unconsecrated food, heave-offering, and Holy Things.*

He could not state matters more clearly than he does when he says that the three of them are exactly equivalent. And they are, because the differentiations will emerge in the food affected, or contaminated, by the three. So at the root of the dispute is whether we gauge the contamination in accord with the source – unconsecrated food, or unconsecrated food prepared as if it were heave-offering, and so on – or whether the criterion is the food which is contaminated. Mishnah-tractate Tohorot 2:3-5 are all wrong, Eleazar states explicitly at Mishnah-tractate Tohorot 2:7A, because they differentiate among uncleanness imparted by unclean unconsecrated food, unclean heave-offering, and unclean Holy Things, and do not differentiate among the three sorts of food *to which* contamination is imparted. It is surely a logical position, for the three sorts of food do exhibit differentiated capacities to receive uncleanness; one sort *is* more contaminable than another.

And so, too, is the contrary view logical: *What is more sensitive to uncleanness also will have a greater capacity to impart uncleanness.* The subtle debate before us clearly is unknown to Eliezer and Joshua at Mishnah-tractate Tohorot 2:2. To them the operative categories are something unclean in first, second, or third *removes*, without distinction as to the relative sensitivities of the several types of food which may be unclean. The unfolding of the issue may be set forth very briefly by way of conclusion: the sequence thus begins with Eliezer and Joshua, who ask about the contaminating power of that which is unclean in the first and second removes, without regard to whether it is unconsecrated food, heave-offering, or Holy Things. To them, the distinction between the capacity to impart contamination, or to receive contamination, of the several sorts of food is unknown. Once, however, their question is raised – in such general terms – it will become natural to ask the next logical question, one which makes distinctions not only among the several removes of uncleanness, but also among the several sorts of food involved in the processes of contamination. So much for the sources of uncleanness and how they form part of a larger systemic statement.

Part Two

THE ARENA OF UNCLEANNESS:
EFFECTS OF POLLUTION

3

The Effects of Pollution in Judaism: How Uncleanness is Transmitted

I. The Pentateuchal Facts on How Uncleanness Is Transmitted

To understand uncleanness, we do best to resort to the metaphors of physics, whether or physical things or of intangible waves such as radiation or light. The basic conception of uncleanness is that we deal with a liquid that is physical and thus is transferred through direct contact; has or exerts weight, and thus is transferred not through direct contact but through weight bearing; but also is a kind of radiating, intangible wave, like radiation or light waves, effective in transferring uncleanness even though not to be weighed or measured as we weigh or measure physical properties of water or other liquids. Uncleanness flows, squishes, is contained, seeks its egress, and so on, much like liquid. But it also emanates the way (we now conceive) light does, that is, in waves of an other-than-material character, so that being in the same space, contained and cut off, as a certain kind of uncleanness will transfer uncleanness.

It follows that uncleanness bears material consequences, changing the status or use of persons or objects. But while it is conceived as being palpable, it exerts affect without direct contact of any kind. It functions like a thick liquid; if the weight of the liquid bears down on a person, that person is affected; if it what is unclean with said substance bears the weight of a clean person, it squishes and the clean person is unclean. That is, by being subject to the weight of that which is unclean, even without actual contact with the source of uncleanness itself, a person or object contracts uncleanness. And not only substantial weight, but the merest influence produces the same result. Thus being under the same roof ("tent") as a corpse inflicts uncleanness on objects in the same room; the qualification is, the contents of tightly sealed utensils are unaffected. So we have something like an invisible liquid, akin to radiation, which is not readily measured by physical traits, but which nonetheless produces very real physical consequences.

The principal media for the transmission of uncleanness are [1] direct contact; [2] indirect contact through weight bearing (reciprocal, as noted); and [3] containment in the same enclosed space. These are the pertinent references in Scripture:

Modes of Transfer of Uncleanness in the Pentateuch

Lev. 11:24: Touching (+ Lev. 15:5, 11, 12, 18, 21, 22, 27).

Lev. 11:25: Carrying (+ Lev. 15:1ff).

Lev. 11:32: And anything upon which any of them falls when they are dead shall be unclean....

Lev. 11:33: And if any of them falls into any earthen vessel, all that is in it shall be unclean.

Lev. 11:34: Any food in it...upon which water may come shall be unclean, and all drink; which may be drunk from such vessel shall be unclean. + Lev. 11:37: If any part of their carcass falls upon any seed for sowing..., it is clean. But if water be put on the seed, and any part of their carcass falls on it, it is unclean for you.

Lev. 13:4 6: He who enters a leprous house is unclean. He who lies down or eats therein washes his clothes.

Lev. 15:4: Every bed on which the Zab lies shall be unclean (+ Lev. 15:6, 9).

Lev. 15:20: Menstruant imparts uncleanness to bed and chair, and to one who has intercourse with her.

Lev. 15:26: Woman who has flow not in her period, as above, Lev. 15:20.

Num. 19:14 19: Being in the same tent with a corpse makes person unclean; also an open jar's contents are unclean. But a tight seal on a jar protects the jar's contents from uncleanness.

The matter of weight bearing is qualified in an interesting way. We introduce the consideration of natural use or designated purpose. If something is usually used for sitting of lying and is made unclean by a person with the capacity to impart uncleanness to such an object (for example, a menstruating woman, or a person afflicted with the flux uncleanness of Leviticus 15), then if a clean person sits or lies (that is, uses the object as it is ordinarily used), he contracts uncleanness. If, on the other hand, the object is not ordinarily used for sitting or lying, then a person who sits or lies there is unaffected. Accordingly, the natural or routine purpose of an object governs whether or not the fluid of uncleanness is contained within and squished out of the object; a menstruating woman who sits on a jar does not impart moshab uncleanness to the jar; a clean person who sits on said jar is unaffected by reason of his sitting. It follows that one very important point of differentiation among the modes of transfer of uncleanness is between that affecting objects used for sitting and lying, and the one affecting other objects. The former invariably is referred to as *midras* or pressure uncleanness, meaning, uncleanness imparted to an object that is susceptible to pressure uncleanness by a source of uncleanness that is transmitted through pressure. The object that is susceptible is one used for sitting or lying. The source of uncleanness that is transmitted in that way is a person afflicted with a kind of uncleanness that squishes out when said person exerts pressure, for example, through the weight of his or her body's pressing down on an object ordinarily meant to bear said weight. The distinction certainly may be generated in the rules of the menstruating woman (and the woman after childbirth, by analogy), the Zab, and the Zabah. Scripture is explicit that beds and chairs upon which the Zab and his fellows sit are made unclean. It also states that objects touched by the Zab are made unclean as well. Scripture therefore is understood to distinguish touching from exerting bodily pressure. Whether or not this was Scripture's original intent, the net result is the same. The distinction is clear, and Scripture's further specifications of the result certainly may be supposed to stand behind Mishnah's developments of the same matter. Carrying is referred to as a still further mode by which uncleanness is transferred.

The capacity of the inner, contained space of a clay utensil to receive uncleanness and to transfer it to the utensil itself is specified at Lev. 11:33. The specification that uncleanness is transferred to wet, not dry, food and seed is explicit at Lev. 11:34, 37. The transfer of corpse uncleanness through the affects of the tent is explicit at Num. 19:1-19. Accordingly, the concerns of the shank of Ohalot (Chapters 3 through 15) and of Makhshirin and the givens of Kelim, Negaim (principally Chapter 13), Zabim Chapter 5, find appropriate authority in Scripture. To be sure, the emphases of Scripture in these matters are not replicated in Mishnah. We should hardly expect an entire tractate to emerge from Lev. 11:34, 37, and much in Ohalot is distinct from the Priestly Code's conceptions. But the facts of the transfer of uncleanness upon which Mishnah works out its conceptions derive from Scripture. Not only so, but every mode of transfer of uncleanness that the Mishnah amplifies is to begin with set forth in Scripture. The Mishnah introduces a layer of meaning Scripture does not articulate, but no new facts.

II. Modes of Transfer of Uncleanness: The Mishnah's View

The Mishnah's treatment of modes of transfer of uncleanness encompasses pressure in the case of the menstrual woman's or the Zab's sitting on an chair or bed consistently given its own name *midras*, and through touching other objects, not used for lying or sitting. The distinction between *midras* uncleanness, which applies to an object used for sitting and lying, and corpse uncleanness, which applies to all other susceptible objects, is taken for granted by the Houses in particular at M. Kel. 20:2, 22:4, 26:5, 28:4, and M. Nid. 10:8.

A. The Distinction between Pressure and Touch

It follows that some objects are susceptible to uncleanness through pressure on the part of certain human sources of uncleanness, and others are not. Specifically, objects used for sitting and lying are susceptible to *midras* when a Zab, a menstruating woman, a Zabah, and their analogues sit or lie on said chair or bed. The issue before the Houses and their successors is the determination of the susceptibility of objects which may or may not serve for sitting and lying, sometimes being used for sitting and lying and sometimes not, and other gray areas awaiting elucidation. It follows that the established distinction is taken for granted as fact. And that fact immediately directs our attention to a second one, which is that some sources of uncleanness have the capacity to impart *midras* uncleanness to objects used for sitting and lying, and others do not. Accordingly, the presence of the notion of *midras* uncleanness signifies that, at the very beginning of the history of the Mishnaic system is a distinction of fundamental importance among both sources and modes of transfer of uncleanness. That distinction is clearly stated, in its effects, at Lev. 15:4 for the Zab, Lev. 15:20 for the menstruating woman, and Lev. 15:26 for the Zabah, and, by explicit analogy, at Lev. 12:2, for the woman who is unclean after childbirth.

In exactly the same context, moreover, Scripture makes clear a further set of considerations. A Zab and his fellows impart uncleanness that is to be transferred even to someone or something not in direct contact with him or not subject to his pressure at all. This is *midras* uncleanness. Lev. 15:4 specifies that objects used for lying or sitting on which a Zab lies or sits are unclean. Lev. 15:5 maintains that whoever touches an object made unclean by the Zab's lying or sitting shall wash his clothes. That means that the object has received the Zab's uncleanness indirectly, in such measure that said object, too, imparts uncleanness to the person, and, further, that the person made unclean by the Zab transmits uncleanness to his clothing. That latter uncleanness is the clear sense of Lev. 15:5: *And anyone who touches his bed shall wash his clothes and bathe himself in water.* Lev. 15:6 says the same of the Zab's chair, Lev. 15:7, of his body, Lev. 15:8, of his spit, Lev. 15:9, of his saddle.

The concept of *midras* early in the history of the law is joined by *maddaf.* That is the counterpart and complement to the notion of *midras* or pressure uncleanness. Just as a person afflicted with flux (and his counterparts) imparts pressure or *midras* uncleanness to objects located beneath him that are used for sitting and lying, so such a person imparts *maddaf* uncleanness to food and drink located above him, inclusive of objects not used for sitting or lying. We thus take account of the position, as well as the use, of objects in relationship to the person afflicted with flux. The twin concepts of *midras* and *maddaf* uncleanness carry to their logical conclusion the conception of uncleanness as a viscous fluid that cannot be seen. Such a fluid exudes from the unclean person, so that it forms a nimbus round about him or her. Things beneath, on which such a person might sit, upon which he or she imposes weight, are affected; things above, on which such a person might not sit, that come into nimbus of the person, are equivalently affected (though in a minor degree of uncleanness, as a matter of fact, the uncleanness being inflicted by the pressure of weight being far more severe than that inflicted by the emanating waves on their own).

Accordingly, the givenness of the concept of *midras* uncleanness requires us to extrapolate a number of other facts, which are required for a complete picture of the context and meaning of the first, and one, known fact, *midras*. These are, first, the distinction between objects susceptible to *midras* and those which are not (*maddaf*); second, the differentiation among modes of transfer of the Zab's uncleanness, for example, touching, sitting without touching but merely exerting pressure; third, the reckoning with removes of uncleanness, beginning with actual contact with, or subjection to, pressure of the Zab, then the result of such contact with, or subjection to, the pressure of the Zab after the contact is complete and after the pressure has ceased, and finally, the result of touching something or someone unclean by reason of the uncleanness at a second stage, that is, touching a person or sitting on a chair on which someone made unclean by touching a person or sitting on a chair has touched or sat.

This entire set of conceptions derives by a process of reasoning on the basis of the facts of Scripture itself. The process works itself out through a set of opposites: if A, then not B, if not B, then C, and so on. Take for example Lev. 15:10: *Whoever touches anything that was under him shall be unclean until the evening.* At first glance, this rule defines the status specified at the third remove from the original source of uncleanness, the Zab. But it contains a further implication, which is that *location* of an object used for sitting or lying in the area underneath a Zab, even though said chair or bed has not actually touched the Zab or been subjected to his pressure, produces uncleanness for the bed or chair. One who touches a bed or chair which has been located underneath a Zab is not so unclean as to have to wash his clothes. But he is unclean and has to bathe. Lev. 15:10b moreover specifies that one who carries an object which has been under a Zab does have to wash his clothes and bathe, so carrying in the specified context is still another mode of transfer of uncleanness. Obviously, Scripture can be read to yield such rules as the basic one, on *midras*. That conception clearly comes to the fore very early in the intellectual process which produced the ultimate laws of Mishnah. So too, the conception of uncleanness in varying measures – when in contact with the Zab and afterward, contact with someone after the person has been made unclean by the Zab – is generated by the facts of Scripture. That there are considerations of remove from the original source of uncleanness – the source, or Father of uncleanness, itself, then that which has touched the source, then that which has touched that, and so on outward in a chain of successive contacts – is clear in Scripture itself.

And that brings us back to the matter of *maddaf*, also taken for granted by authorities after 70 as a fact within the system of uncleanness. The notion of *maddaf* also is apt to form part of the ancient legacy. Once a man is in the status of the Zab, he imparts uncleanness (1) through diverse means of the transfer of uncleanness (2) to various objects: to man, to clay utensils, cleaned only through breakage, and utensils which are cleaned in an immersion pool and, by contrast to clay utensils, not solely by breaking; to utensils used for sitting and lying; and utensils not used for sitting and lying (*maddaf*) inclusive of food, and drink. Further, various body fluids are deemed equivalent to flux in their capacity to impart uncleanness, and others are not. Finally, the transfer of uncleanness is deemed to take place in two distinct aspects: (1) while a person or object actually is subject to the mode of transfer of uncleanness; (2) after a person or object has ceased to be subject to the mode of transfer of uncleanness. So much for the material character of the viscous fluid, uncleanness. What about the nimbus and its circulation – uncleanness as comparable (in our physics) to light waves?

B.   The Tent and the Squared Handbreadth

The Mishnah's most profound contribution to the theory of the transfer of uncleanness pertains to the transfer of corpse uncleanness to everything that is under the same tent, or roof, that is not tightly sealed. What the Mishnah's framers do – very early in the history of thought ultimately set down in the Mishnah's laws as a matter of fact – is to treat the "tent" as an analogy. Reducing the metaphor to its fact, they conclude that what is within contained space is affected by corpse uncleanness in said space. Then what is the "tent"? It is anything that is contained space sufficient to hold the corpse uncleanness's nimbus or radiation. If the contained space is too small, the radiation will spurt forth; if too large, the radiation will dissipate (though that concept is unexplored). The sages reached the measurement for said space in a simple way. They maintained that just as a human being measures three cubits, the soul or spirit of a human being measures a cubic handbreadth, that is, a space a handbreadth in height, breadth, and depth. This physical conception of the soul is joined by a more abstract theory, which is, a "tent" represents a dwelling for a soul, and any dwelling of the size of a soul's physical bulk then functions as a tent. So "tent" is not a physical thing at all, but a metaphor for contained space; and whatever functions like a tent has the effect of a tent.

These two conceptions – the metaphorization of "tent," the physicalization of "soul," go hand in hand. The handbreadth measurement is fundamental to the conception of the tent. A tent is a contained space that is, at a minimum, a handbreadth in height, breadth, and width, a measure taken for granted by the Houses of Shammai and Hillel. Then a primary aspect of the standard measurement of the tent – its metaphorization – concerns the ingress or egress of uncleanness. Corpse uncleanness is conceived as a kind of viscous gas, which cannot pass through a small space. For its passage (or containment) it requires, specifically, an open (or closed, contained) space of a handbreadth square. The Houses then assume that the corpse uncleanness certainly will seek out an exit, then bypass all those spaces which, if open, would also serve as an exit in favor of the one which actually is open, leaving the remaining exits uncontaminated. That conception clearly is an advance over the simple notion that corpse uncleanness passes through a space of a handbreadth, representing a development in theorizing about the passage of corpse contamination. A further assumed rule is that a tent must be a handbreadth above the ground, which is hardly surprising. The Houses thus expand the basic notion that the primary dimension of a tent is a handbreadth, that is, the tent must be at that height above the ground, or the tent must have at least that measure of egress for the effusion of uncleanness from within the tent.

While it is Scripture which declares the corpse to be a source of uncleanness, and analogical thinking which treats substances deriving from, or deemed similar to, a corpse (bones, decaying flesh, for instance) to be equivalently unclean, Scripture does not stand behind the conception that corpse uncleanness passes through, or is blocked by, a space of a handbreadth squared. That notion, fundamental to the conception of the transfer of corpse uncleanness, represents a radical redefinition of the meaning of "tent" in response to a distinctive notion of the essential character of corpse uncleanness. The Scriptural contribution to Mishnah's conception of corpse uncleanness therefore may be summarized as follows. The principle that corpses contaminate for seven days comes from *He who touches the dead body of any person shall be unclean for seven days.* The same verse, moreover, tells us that corpse contamination is conveyed through contact (touching). The person who touches the corpse is unclean with the seven days', or corpse, uncleanness. Contamination by the mode, or means, of tent or overshadowing a corpse is declared in Num. 19:14: *This is the law when a man dies in a tent: everyone who comes into the tent, and everyone who is in the tent, shall be unclean seven days.* Whatever is overshadowed by the tent is made unclean through overshadowing, the tent's effect, which is to spread the corpse uncleanness to all beneath its shadow, as if the person in the tent has touched the corpse itself. What about utensils in the tent? Num. 19:15 says, *And every open vessel which has no cover fastened upon it is unclean.* The contrary is that every closed and sealed vessel is clean. That can mean only, the contents of the vessel, not the outer surface. Num. 19:16 intends to tell us about a corpse not in a tent, *Whoever in the open field touches one who is slain with a sword or a dead body or a bone of a man or a grave shall be unclean seven days.* One would not have to be a very clever exegete to learn from this verse that things which are like the corpse or grave – the bone, the grave area itself – produce corpse contamination. Further, we learn that touching out of doors is equivalent to overshadowing in or by the tent. What about touching a utensil affected by a corpse? Num. 19:22 states, *But whatever the unclean person touches shall be unclean, and any one who touches it shall be unclean until the evening.* This verse surely meant in the first place that whatever object the person unclean with corpse uncleanness touches will be unclean in the same way as the person who has touched it. The converse – the rule about someone who touches that unclean object – is clearly stated.

To state the upshot of these rules, some Scripture, some secondary to Scripture: corpse uncleanness passes through a handbreadth of open space. Its passage may be prevented, therefore, by a handbreadth of closed space. What imposes that "measure" is the trait of corpse uncleanness, not of the tent. In no way is that concept related to Scripture. No exegete even tried to find some Scriptural foundation for it. What is at issue is not merely the measurement of a handbreadth, but all which is expressed by that simple measurement. For what the "handbreadth in breadth, depth, and height" means is that the Scriptural tent, a place where people live, obviously has been left far behind us. The tent at the earliest level of Mishnah, is anything but a place in which people dwell. The Mishnah to begin with speaks of a tent capable of containing that which exudes from the body at the moment of death, a tent which takes the place of the body. When, therefore, we say a tent must measure a handbreadth, either to prevent uncleanness from entering its enclosed space, or to keep uncleanness within its enclosed space, we do not refer to the body, for a whole body by definition is four times larger than a handbreadth, and therefore a body cannot be contained in a tent. What exudes from the body is an invisible, viscous gas which is uncleanness. It is everywhere taken for granted that uncleanness cannot penetrate a closed area of a handbreadth or less, on the one hand, or will be prevented from exuding by that same closed area, if it is enclosed by it.

Now we make the movement from the law to its metaphysics and then its theological anthropology. As to the metaphysics, a set of facts shows what is at stake. Corpse uncleanness is something which can be contained by a tent. A tent is something that can contain or interpose against corpse uncleanness. The one has – in the nature of things – to be defined in terms of the other. And this shades over into theological anthropology: the conception of the death of a human being. The conception of death is that at death something leaves, exudes from, the body. The tent serves as the functional equivalent to the body, or it is able to receive and contain that which exudes from the body. The tent is to be understood as a surrogate for the body, restoring the natural order that has been broken with the departure from the body of that which exudes from it. Death has released this effusion. The tent then contains it. We have avoided naming this thing which "exudes from the corpse at such a viscosity as to pass through an open space of a handbreadth or more, but no less." The facts now adduced justify our calling it the soul and alleging that the "uncleanness" of the corpse is the "soul" which is the "spirit" surviving after death and requiring a new locale.

When someone dies, therefore, a change affects the economy of nature. The body which has housed the person lies lifeless. Scripture is clear that that body produces "uncleanness," specifying the various ways in which the uncleanness is transferred and the things affected by it. That uncleanness now will find a new container, something which will keep and contain it as the body has done. What will do so is something a handbreadth in height, breadth, and depth, with adequate entry (thus: egress) for the effusion of the corpse to find a way in. This new "house," the "tent," takes the place of the old, thus restoring the natural economy and order. It may be envisioned as a house/tent, or it may be seen as something far more abstract, simply as that which will prevent the passage of uncleanness, keeping it in ("bringing the uncleanness") or preventing its entry ("interposing against the uncleanness"). The two processes, interposition or containment, are one and the same thing. The point of interest is in righting the imbalance caused by death, in explaining how the whole, complete division or economy of reality is to be conceived.

At the very foundations of the Mishnaic system we locate the striking conception that death upsets the economy of nature and that uncleanness, in this context, constitutes that which creates an imbalance in nature. The reason that that conception is important for the system is that that very same recurrent concern for balance, order, and the wholeness of nature, corresponding to an equivalent economy of supernature, at several other principal parts characterizes the Mishnaic system. Uncleanness, caused by an imbalance in nature, is removed by the natural working of water, unaffected by human intervention. That very fundamental conception of the process of purification, we shall see, correlates with, and completes, the one before us. Accordingly, the remarkable aspect of corpse uncleanness and its containment in a closed area measuring a cubic handbreadth is its systemically coherent character. What the system says about uncleanness in the case of the corpse is what it says about removing uncleanness in the case of the immersion pool. Just as each and every detail of the Zoroastrian system fits together into a cogent picture and expresses, in some small way, the still larger meaning created by the vast structure of which uncleanness is a part, so in the instance of the Mishnaic system of uncleanness, each principal part at the very outset originates in a complete and whole structure of meaning.

C.   How the Tent Transmits Uncleanness

The great innovation of the authorities before the turn of the first century therefore was to conceive of the tent of Scripture as something other than a real tent, a place where people live. This further yields the notion that what is important *about* the tent is not solely the fact of its physically overshadowing both a corpse and a utensil or a person, but also the function itself: overshadowing – even not by a real tent. Accordingly, the Scriptural tent not only is set aside by the principle of the square handbreadth through which uncleanness passes, but also is revised into a metaphor for any sort of overshadowing. In this second sense of tent – anything which shades both a corpse and some other object – diverse refinements and limitations are to be discovered. The first question is, is a tent, viewed functionally as anything which overshadows, to be inanimate, or may animate beings also function in the same way? And if they do serve as tents for overshadowing, can animate beings also interpose between a source of uncleanness and a utensil on their other side? Once we agree that a tent is not merely a building, but anything that overshadows, therefore, we ask whether a man or an animal may serve to bring uncleanness like a tent. The position of the House of Shammai is that men and utensils do not bring uncleanness and therefore they also cannot serve as a tent to contain or interpose against uncleanness. The House of Hillel maintain that they bring uncleanness but do not interpose (M. Oh. 11:3-6). The matter of the square handbreadth also is revised. May such a handbreadth be composed of juxtaposed spaces, or must it be wholly formed of a single open area not subdivided in any way? The Houses refine the matter of a hole sufficient to bring in corpse uncleanness. If we have grating or lattice work, do the holes join together? The Shammaites treat the several apertures as one, the Hillelites do not (M. Oh. 13:1, and compare M. Oh. 2:3).

The Shammaites further maintain that if a hole is deliberately made, then it brings uncleanness even if it is less than a square handbreadth (M. Oh. 13:4). If this ruling is properly to be attributed to them then their conception is that anything which functions as a hole for a particular purpose is deemed a sufficient area for the passage of corpse uncleanness. Then the square handbreadth measure is understood as a relative, not an absolute standard. What is important about that measure is that it is in general the sort of size used for routine purposes, not that it is a fixed measure.

Since the Houses agree that materials deriving from a corpse are analogous to the corpse, they refine the matter by asking how large a part of the corpse imparts uncleanness as the whole corpse does (M. Oh. 2:1, T. Ah. 3:5, M. Ed. 1:7). Accordingly, with respect to corpse matter, the Houses' shared presupposition of the uncleanness of materials only indirectly connected to the corpse – for example, dirt of various origins – produces some relatively minor disputes. For instance, a grave area is unclean, but does one such area produce another? How shall we gather grapes in such an area? The Houses take for granted that it is possible to gather grapes from a grave area and yet preserve the grapes in a state of cleanness (M. Oh. 18:1). They further agree that corpse matter may be found in the dwelling places of gentiles in the Land of Israel (M. Oh. 18:8). The continuity of these rulings with the details of the established system is self-evident.

Characteristic of materials attributed to the Houses, we recall, is concern for four fundamental themes: (1) materials which contaminate in a tent; (2) the measurements of a tent and of a space which will permit the passage of uncleanness; (3) the possibility of a man's and a utensil's serving as a tent; (4) the definition of the process for decontaminating a grave area and dwelling places of gentiles in the Land of Israel. It would be difficult to construct an agendum of simpler and more basic issues. When we come to the state of opinion toward the end of the first century, we find several secondary issues, for example, the capacity of limbs to produce uncleanness; combining, through the effect of a tent, several separate sources of uncleanness to make up a quantity sufficient for contamination; the definition of mixed blood. Earlier issues now carried forward include the matter of pots' protection when conjoined with the walls of tents; the issue of utensils and men (again); projections and other subdivisions of tents (tombs, a house); and similar matters. The conception that there are chains of contamination, with diminishing effects as one goes lower in the chain (M. Oh. 1:1-3) once more is congruent to the inquiry into removes of uncleanness. M. Oh 16:1 certainly carries forward the distinctions first recognized in the earlier stratum. Once we have distinguished carrying, contact, and tent, we then specify, as does Aqiba, the area required for contamination through the three modes.

A major issue at the end of the first century is how the tent functions, specifically, whether it joins together, under its own surface, quantities of contaminating material which, when not so joined together, under a tent would be insufficient by themselves to produce uncleanness. Aqiba (M. Oh. 2:2) stresses the role of the tent in effecting contamination, above and beyond what the specific source of uncleanness can accomplish on its own. Once stress is laid not on the *source* but on the *mode* of contamination (tent), we are apt later on to find further inquiry into the effects of combining other *modes* of contamination to produce uncleanness. Toward the middle of the second century, therefore, combining modes of uncleanness, not solely sources of uncleanness, came to the fore. The primary conception of Ohalot, the view of a tent as that which can contain what exudes or effuses from a corpse, stands behind Aqiba's view. The tent combines the contaminating effects of all that is in its shadow. Then Aqiba supplies to the tent an active role in the spreading of uncleanness, treating the tent as a positive, transitive force, which, as it were, takes over the effusion and shapes or moulds it (much as the body takes an active role in containing the soul). He penetrates the deepest implication of interpreting tent as the dimension of the standard measure, with all that that implies. The next stage is to attribute to the tent a formative force in the process of contamination.

With Aqiba what becomes important is the meaning of "tent" as active *overshadowing*, rather than as a merely passive object. That meaning imposes its own logic. Once something affirmatively acts by overshadowing, that active or transitive force dominates matters. The two names of the same tractate, the one in the Mishnah, the other in its complementary collection of rules called the Tosefta, namely, *Ohalot* and *Ahilot* – tents, overshadowings – therefore appear in retrospect to contain within themselves two large notions, the one, *tent* as a formal entity, the other *overshadowing* as process or function, or, more simply still, a noun as against a verb, a structure or thing as against a process. That will account for the two conceptions' existing side by side in the tractate, the one built upon the formal structure and traits of a building, with projections, flaps, and so forth, the other formed upon the way in which materials, however formed, either interpose against, or permit the transfer of, uncleanness.

Along the same lines, as noted, we may interpret Aqiba's reworking of the inherited dimensions (M. Oh. 16:1-2): movables contaminate through overshadowing if they are a handbreadth in size. That is, after all, what establishes the viability of a material for interposing or permitting the transfer of uncleanness. Movables become unclean whatever their size. That is, they are objects of uncleanness, not agents of contamination, by virtue of their status as utensils or objects. They serve to bring uncleanness on the person who carries them if they are as thick as an ox goad, an intermediate stage, depending upon a mode of uncleanness other than tent. The distinction underlying Aqiba's definition, therefore, is between carrying and tent. Contact is subsumed in the second dimension, "bring uncleanness on themselves through contact over any surface whatever." The combining of separate sources of uncleanness therefore derives directly from Aqiba's conception of the tent.

D. The Transfer of Uncleanness by a Menstruating Woman

The principal concern of the Mishnah authorities has to do with matters of doubt. A menstruating woman is unclean from the moment at which she sees the first drop of blood. But we do not know that that first drop of blood really is the first blood to exude; hence if a woman does not have a fixed period, we have to take account of the possibility that she has contaminated objects that she has touched during some indeterminate period prior to the onset of her menstrual blood. How long a period is subject to consideration? It may be decided in various ways.

At T. Nid. 9:5 sages rule that a woman who sees blood imparts uncleanness to objects she has touched during the preceding twenty-four hours, specifically, food, drink, chairs and beds, but not to the person with whom she had intercourse. Aqiba maintains that she imparts uncleanness to the man with whom she has had intercourse in the stated period. But she counts seven days only from the moment of discovering the blood, not from the time of the beginning of retroactive contamination. Accordingly, retroactive uncleanness does not change the fact that the period is counted only from the discovery of blood. This is another clear-cut development of the principle of retroactive contamination. Aqiba takes a view consistent with that principle. Since the woman imparts uncleanness, the uncleanness also affects her husband.

Yet all parties are clear that the beginning of the counting of seven unclean days is solely from the time of the discovery of the blood, not from the time that retroactive contamination is imputed to objects touched by the woman. The question now to be investigated is whether we include bloodstains in the matter. There is, therefore, a clear distinction between imputing uncleanness retroactively, on the one side, and deeming the period actually to have begun, on the other. Accordingly, the difference between Aqiba and sages is not so great as it seems. Both agree that the period only begins from the point that the blood is found. Aqiba nonetheless treats the imputation of uncleanness consistently: since other things the woman has touched are deemed unclean, why not the husband? Sages understand that the uncleanness imparted to the husband is exactly that of the menstrual period, and they therefore maintain that, since the period begins only at the discovery of blood, the husband is affected only at that time and thereafter. Only one question remains: Do we include bloodstains in the matter of doubt and retroactive contamination? The second century authorities will take up that question.

The same matter – resolving matters of doubt – draws attention to the analogous source of uncleanness, flux. Flux is marked as unclean if it appears on three successive days. Then a person who has suffered that involuntary excretion has to count seven "clean days," that is, days on which there is no such flow of semen through a flaccid penis. What happens if the Zab or Zabah is mindless and does not inspect the sexual parts on one of the intermediate days between the first and the seventh clean days? Do we assume that the Zab or Zabah has suffered no flux on that day on which there was no inspection, by analogy to the days fore and aft? The dispute among Eliezer, Joshua, and Aqiba at M. Nid. 10:3 concerns whether we impute cleanness, in the Zab's counting of seven clean days, to days on which there was no examination. Eliezer holds that we do.

Questions of doubt about menstrual uncleanness tend at the end of the first century to raise issues secondary to those advanced in the antecedent period. We know, for example, that an examination is required by the woman and those like her, for instance, the Zab. What if an unclean person (here: the Zab) examines himself at the start and at the end of a period of uncleanness, but not in the intervening days? Do we regard the status at the end as determinative, retroactively, of the status during the days on which no examination has taken place? This obviously is a refinement of the principle of retroactivity. The bloodstain on a garment, the origin of which may or may not be menstrual, may or may not be blood. If it is blood, it may or may not be unclean blood. That is, we do not know whether a bloodstain derives from menstrual blood, therefore is unclean, or from some other, clean source of blood. That has to be sorted out.

Both Eliezer and Joshua know that if a child is delivered forthwith upon labor, then the blood is not deemed blood of *Zibah* but is attributed to the labor. The woman is clean so far as *Zibah* is concerned. But now it is necessary to ask, What about a delivery not of a live child but of a dead one? And, more serious still, what if that which emerges is an abortion of some sort? Do we then hold that the woman is nonetheless clean so far as *Zibah* is concerned? Joshua limits the matter to the delivery of a child, not specifying whether it is live or stillborn. Sages hold that any sort of abortion invokes the principle that the woman is subject to the laws of childbirth. They obviously will regard a stillborn child as equivalent to a live birth. Thus the woman also is subject to their leniencies. Among these, the pertinent one is that the blood of travail is attributed to labor and not to *Zibah*.

III. Liquids in the System of Uncleanness

Thought on the role of liquids in the system of uncleanness is remarkably cogent. There are three aspects of the matter. Liquids have the capacity to impart susceptibility to uncleanness only if they are wanted, serve a human purpose, or otherwise are drawn with approval. They exercise that capacity only when put on the dry produce intentionally and not accidentally. And, further, that portion of liquid which intentionally is used to wet down an object imparts susceptibility to uncleanness, and that portion which is not does not impart susceptibility. What one has wet down is wet down with approval, and what incidentally is wet down is not susceptible at all. These three wholly correlative conceptions will be vastly expanded by second century authorities, but the intellectual structure and problematic of Makhshirin are complete by the end of the end of first century times.

While in the Mishnaic stratum of purity law, we identify secondary expansion of the Pentateuchal rules, we also find the reframing of rules that Scripture has yielded. These are now made to express considerations critical to the authorities of the Mishnah but not attested in the Pentateuchal rules, and the transforming considerations bear a distinctly philosophical character, concerned as they are with such issues as causation, the relationship of what is potential to what is actual, the power of intentionality to affect a situation, hence the issue of cause and blame. These questions, familiar to philosophy in philosophical and abstract language, come to expression in the Mishnaic treatment of the arcane matter of uncleanness. One profound concern addresses the power of intentionality and its effects. For what I want to have happen I bear responsibility, therefore blame; so intentionality forms a subdivision of thought on the character and classification of causality. At the same time, the issue of intentionality will define debate in its own terms. The way in which causation and intentionality intersect with purity (as with nearly every other chapter of the law of Judaism) is shown at the reading of a particular rule.

Specifically, Lev. 11:34, 37 are read to mean that produce that is dry is insusceptible to uncleanness, but, when wet down, it is susceptible. The theme of Mishnah-tractate Makhshirin is liquids which impart to dry produce susceptibility to uncleanness. The problematic is the role of human intention in the application of said liquids so that they function to render produce susceptible, and, secondarily, the role of human intention in the definition of affective liquids. The working out of the problematic is in terms of the interplay between what a person wants to do and what he actually does. That is the point at which intentionality intersects with causality and blame. One possible position is that we interpret the effects of what is done in terms of what is intended. A second and opposite position is that we define what is intended in terms of the ultimate result. A third is that we balance the one with the other, thus interpreting intention in terms of result, but also result in terms of prior intention. These are three possible positions yielded by the logical requirements of the problematic. There are no others. The determinative problematic, whether or not liquids are applied intentionally, thus is itself redefined in terms of a still more profound and fundamental question.

The process begins in Aqiba's position that we take account only of water which has actually conformed to a person's original intent, ignoring the presence of water which is peripheral to the accomplishment of one's purpose. The process then is completed by the inquiry into Aqiba's position, specifically the meaning of intent; the limitations upon the capacity of water to impart susceptibility imposed by one's original intent in drawing the water. The structure is articulated in terms of the view that water intrinsic to one's purpose is detached with approval, while that which is not essential to one's original intent is not able to impart susceptibility. If water applied with approval can impart susceptibility, then, as I said, only that part of the water which is essential to one's accomplishment of his original intent imparts susceptibility. It is at this point that the question is raised about the relationship between intention and deed. First, intention to do something governs the effect of one's action, even though one's action has produced a different effect from his original intention. Or, second, one's consequent action revises the original definition, therefore the effects, of his prior intention. That is, what happens is retrospectively deemed to define what one wanted to happen. Or, third, as I noted above, what one wanted to make happen affects the assessment of what actually has happened. There are no other logical possibilities contained within the original problematic. All of this is worked out in Mishnah-tractate Makhshirin.

The place of Makhshirin, at the inauguration of the system of intention, raises the question of its relationship to Kelim. Both tractates wish in essence to say the same thing. For liquids and for food as for utensils – that is, for all constituents of the system's entire realm of susceptibility to uncleanness – man must deliberately do something to bring the system into operation. He must complete an object, regard it as a utensil. He must deem food to be edible, liquid to be drawn with approval or otherwise useful, take dry, insusceptible produce and wet it down, with an eye to making use of the produce. Accordingly, no component of the multidimensional locus of uncleanness – utensils, food (produce), and drink – is exempt from the requirement that human deliberation play the principal and definitive role. It is man who creates the entire locus of uncleanness by introducing into that locus – rendering susceptible to uncleanness – the several materials which form its components. While Kelim, Makhshirin, and the relevant units of Tohorot fully work out their respective problematic, each one moreover finds completion and fulfillment in the provision of the corresponding and reciprocally pertinent tractate. Each says concerning its own topic what all of them say in common about the shared theme. This brings us to the fundamental pericope at M. Makh. 5:4:

A.   He who measures the cistern –
B .   "whether for depth or for breadth –
C.   "lo, this [water which is on the measuring rod] is under the law, 'If water be put,'" the words of R. Tarfon.
D.   R. Aqiba says, "[If he measured it] for depth, [the water on the measuring rod] is under the law, 'If water be put.' And [if he measured it] for breadth, [the water on the measuring rod] is not under the law, 'If water be put.'"

Since it is not possible to get at the water without getting the rope wet, Aqiba, maintains that what is essential is subject to the law, If water be put. What is not essential or necessary is not subject to the law, If water be put. But Tarfon makes no such distinction. So far as he is concerned, once one deliberately puts a rod into the water to measure the water's depth, whether lengthwise or breadthwise, he has wanted the water and what falls on the produce makes it susceptible to uncleanness.

The interesting side therefore is the criterion for the definition of liquids which do or do not impart susceptibility to uncleanness: ordinary usefulness or desirability. The specified liquids all are deemed edible or useful, flowing with approval. This paramount criterion is clear at M. Makh. 6:5F, 6:7M, N, which distinguish wanted, from unwanted, blood. The former is blood which flows because of an action aimed at serving human needs, for example, slaughtering clean animals or drawing blood for drink. And this criterion further is blatant at M. Makh. 6:8 where Aqiba and sages dispute about whether or not cow's milk imparts susceptibility to uncleanness when it is not drawn intentionally or with approval. This means, then, that first century authorities around Aqiba – but not Eliezer – conceive the matter of capacity to impart susceptibility to be affected by one's attitude not only toward the application of the liquid, but even toward the liquid itself. Liquids which one cannot possibly desire, for example, sweat or pus, do not fall within the system of contamination, whereas those which people do want to use and do produce by intent (as against sweat) have the capacity to impart susceptibility to uncleanness. Accordingly, the system flowing from Aqiba's notion is whole and harmonious: the liquid itself must be wanted by man or useful to man; and the liquid, furthermore, must be applied intentionally and not accidentally or under constraint or in a way peripheral to one's principal purpose.

Let us now turn to the matter of purposeful application of liquid. At M. Makh. 1:3, Joshua states in the name of Abba Yosé, "Be surprised if there is a liquid in the Torah which is unclean before a person actually intends to put it on dry produce." At the foundations of Makhshirin is the view expressed here. Abba Yosé wishes to say that, if produce is wet down unintentionally, it is not made susceptible to uncleanness. Virtually every pertinent ruling assigned to a subsequent authority is intended to refine and expand his conception. But, as we already have seen, liquid itself has the capacity to impart susceptibility to uncleanness only if produced with approval or serves a human purpose – a notion contained within the distinction, attested by Aqiba, between blood produced by slaughter of a clean animal and blood produced by slaughter of an unclean one, or between mother's milk and cow's milk. Once we insist that liquid only imparts susceptibility when applied by intention, we then ask whether the liquid itself, before application and without regard to application, is intrinsically able to impart susceptibility to uncleanness.

The second century materials of Makhshirin form a large essay on the interplay between intention and action. Two antecedent items assume a fundamental role. First, Abba Yosé's saying self-evidently supplies the agendum. Water which is not applied intentionally does not impart susceptibility to uncleanness. A secondary and derivative rule, Aqiba's distinction, then comes into play: water intrinsic to one's purpose is detached with approval, but that which is not essential in accomplishing one's primary purpose is not under the law, If water be put. What Aqiba has done is to carry to its logical next stage the generative principle. If water applied with approval can impart susceptibility to uncleanness, then, it follows, only that part of the detached and applied water which is essential to one's intention is subject to the law, If water be put. Second century items which develop Aqiba's improvement of Abba Yosé's principle raise an interesting question: What is the relationship between intention and action? Does intention to do something govern the decision, even though one's action has produced a different effect? For example, if I intend to wet down only part of an object, or make use of only part of a body of water, but then wet down the whole or dispose of the whole, is the whole deemed susceptible? Does my consequent action revise the original and limited effects of my intention? Judah and his son, Yosé, take up the position that ultimate deed or result is definitive of intention. What happens retrospectively is deemed what one wanted to happen. Others, Yosé in particular, maintain the view that, while consequence plays a role in the determination of intention, it is not exclusive and definitive. What one wanted to make happen affects the assessment of what actually has happened. Both Yosé b. R. Judah and Yosé furthermore assign their conceptions to the Houses and define the Houses' dispute in terms of their own highly subtle conceptions of the interplay between intention and action, will and result.

Judah's view (M. Makh. 3:5) is that the man's intention is not fully revealed and effective until he does a deed to carry out his intention. Attitude does not constitute effective intention, because one may always change his mind. Judah's ruling is not intrinsic to the data of Makhshirin, but a general conception applicable to any appropriate case. On the surface Judah's reason is that, since the person's attitude in the specific case is unavoidable, he cannot be adjudged except by what he does actually to carry out, and thus give concrete expression to, that attitude. But underneath his ruling is the realistic notion that a person changes his mind, and we therefore adjudge a case solely by what he does and not by what he says he will do, intends or has intended to do.

This notion, while secondary to Makhshirin, forms an apt introduction to the other pertinent rulings, because, if we turn Judah's statement around, we come up with the conception predominant throughout: a case is judged in terms solely of what the person does. If he puts on water, that water in particular which he has deliberately applied imparts susceptibility to uncleanness. If he removes water, only that water which he actually removes imparts susceptibility to uncleanness, but water which he intends to remove but which is not actually removed is not deemed subject to the person's original intention. And, it is fair to add, we know it is not subject to the original intention, because the person's action has not accomplished the original intention or has placed limits upon the original intention. What is done is wholly determinative of what is originally intended, and that is the case whether the result is that the water is deemed capable or incapable of imparting susceptibility to uncleanness.

Here is a brief survey of the main second century expansions on the law at hand: Yosé at M. Makh. 1:5 maintains that water which has been wiped off a leek is detached with approval. But water which has remained on the leek has not conformed to the man's intention, and that intention is shown by what the man has actually done. Accordingly, the water remaining on the leek is not subject to the law, If water be put. The main point of M. Makh. 1:6 is that liquid which is not essential in accomplishing one's purpose is not taken into account and does not come under the law, If water be put. Why not? Because water is held to be applied with approval when it serves a specific purpose. That water which is incidental has not been subjected to the man's wishes and therefore does not impart susceptibility to uncleanness. M. Makh. 3:5-7 raises the problem of dampening wheat with wet clay. Simeon rules that if there is dripping moisture on the wheat, it is deemed to have been wet down with approval. The man's original intention was to wet down the wheat, and the wheat has been wet down. Accordingly, Simeon wants to know whether there is dripping moisture in the clay. If there is, then the facts of the case self-evidently conform to the man's intention. If there is no water, then the man's intention cannot have been to wet down the grain. In any event he has accomplished nothing. At M. Makh. 5:3 Simeon holds that, since one has wet down the formerly dry fruit, it has been made susceptible to uncleanness, even though one intended ultimately to dry the entire quantity of fruit. Sages hold that, since one's ultimate purpose was to dry the whole, the means used to reach that end are interpreted in the light of the end. We clearly do not distinguish between original intention and ultimate deed. If the ultimate purpose in detaching and using the water was not to wet down the wheat but to wash down the floor of the house, then do we hold that the wheat which is placed in the house thereafter has been wet down not with approval? No, we deem that it has been wet down with approval. Why? Because the result of our deed is before us: the wheat is wet. Therefore we say that, at this point in the process, the water has been used with approval, even though, at the outset, it was not our original intention to use the water for the purpose which it ultimately served.

IV. Addressing a Common Agendum:
The Systemic Statement Made through the Rules of
the Transmission of Uncleanness

The framers of the Mishnah speak of the physics of mixtures, conflicts of principles which must be sorted out, areas of doubt generated by confusion. The detritus of a world seeking order but suffering chaos now is reduced to the construction of intellect. As in the case just now examined, the persistent answer to confusion is to appeal to human intentionality. In treating this topic as many others, the Mishnah's authors lay out roads to guide people by ranges of permissible doubt. Consequently, the Mishnah's mode of control over the chaos of conflicting principles, the confusion of doubt, the improbabilities of a world out of alignment, is to delimit and demarcate, always by appealing to the power of a human being to decide things. By exploring the range of interstitial conflict through its ubiquitous disputes, the Mishnah keeps conflict under control. It so preserves that larger range of agreement, that pervasive and shared conviction, which is never expressed, which is always instantiated, and which, above all, is forever taken for granted. The Mishnah's deepest convictions about what lies beyond confusion and conflict are never spelled out; they lie in the preliminary, unstated exercise prior to the commencement of a sustained exercise of inquiry, a tractate. They are the things we know before we take up that exercise and study that tractate.

What causes and resolves confusion and chaos is the power of the Israelite's will. As is said in the context of measurements for minimum quantities to be subject to uncleanness, "All accords with the measure of the man" (M. Kel. 17:11). The Mishnah's principal message in working out confusion and doubt, on the one side, and classifying all things, on the other, is that Israelite man is at the center of creation, the head of all creatures upon earth, corresponding to God in heaven, in whose image man is made. The way in which the Mishnah makes this simple and fundamental statement is to impute power to the Israelite to inaugurate and initiate those corresponding processes, sanctification and uncleanness, which play so critical a role in the Mishnah's account of reality. The will of man, expressed through the deed of man, is the active power in the world. Will and deed – these constitute those actors of creation which work upon neutral realms, subject to either sanctification or uncleanness: the Temple and table, the field and family, the altar and hearth, woman, time, space, transactions in the material world and in the world above as well. An object, a substance, a transaction, even a phrase or a sentence, is inert but may be made holy, when the interplay of the will and deed of man arouses and generates its potential to be sanctified.

Each may be treated as ordinary or (where relevant) made unclean by neglect of the will and inattentive act of man. Just as the entire system of uncleanness and holiness awaits the intervention of man, which imparts the capacity to become unclean upon what was formerly inert, or which removes the capacity to impart cleanness from what was formerly in its natural and puissant condition, so in the other ranges of reality, man is at the center on earth, just as is God in heaven. Man is counterpart and partner in creation, in that, like God he has power over the status and condition of creation, putting everything in its proper place, calling everything by its rightful name.

So, stated briefly, the question taken up by the Mishnah is, What can a man do? And the answer laid down by the Mishnah is, Man, through will and deed, is master of this world, the measure of all things. Since when the Mishnah thinks of man, it means the Israelite, who is the subject and actor of its system, the statement is clear. This man is Israel, who can do what he wills. In the aftermath of the two wars, with the destruction of Jerusalem in 70 and its definitive closure to Israel in 135, the message of the Mishnah cannot have proved more pertinent – or poignant and tragic. The principal message of the Mishnah is that the will of man affects the material reality of the world and governs the working of those forces, visible or not, which express and effect the sanctification of creation and of Israel alike. This message comes to the surface in countless ways. At the outset a simple example of the supernatural power of man's intention suffices to show the basic power of the Israelite's will to change concrete, tangible facts. This we saw in the case of the effect on the status of water that is brought about by a person's intentionality in respect to the use of the water. But the power of the human will is nowhere more effective than in the cult, where, under certain circumstances, what a person is thinking is more important than what he does.

But the entirety of the law of the Mishnah goes over the same few propositions. So we move beyond the limits of the law of purity to find the same conception. The basic point in the matter of the sanctification of a beast for use on the altar is that if an animal is designated for a given purpose, but the priest prepares the animal with the thought in mind that the beast serves some other sacrificial purpose, then, in some instances, in particular involving a sin-offering and a Passover on the fourteenth of Nisan, the sacrifice is ruined. In this matter of preparation of the animal, moreover, are involved the deeds of slaughtering the beast, collecting, conveying, and tossing the blood on the altar, that is, the principal priestly deeds of sacrifice. Again, if the priest has in mind, when doing these deeds, to offer up the parts to be offered up on the altar, or to eat the parts to be eaten by the priest, in some location other than the proper one (the altar, the courtyard, respectively), or at some time other than the requisite one (the next few hours), the rite is spoiled, the meat must be thrown out. Now that is the case, even if the priest did not do what he was thinking of doing. Here again we have a testimony to the fundamental importance imputed to what a person is thinking, even over what he actually does, in critical aspects of the holy life (M. Zeb. 1:1-4:6, Men. 1:1-4:5).

Once man wants something, a system of the law begins to function. Intention has the power, in particular, to initiate the processes of sanctification. So the moment at which something becomes sacred and so falls under a range of severe penalties for misappropriation or requires a range of strict modes of attentiveness and protection for the preservation of cleanness is defined by the human will. Stated simply: at the center of the Mishnaic system is the notion that man has the power to inaugurate the work of sanctification, and the Mishnaic system states and restates that power. So, too, man has the power to trigger the working of the system of uncleanness, rendering something susceptible to uncleanness that, without the human will, is simply inert. This assessment of the positive power of the human will begins with the matter of uncleanness, one antonym of sanctification or holiness. Man alone has the power to inaugurate the system of uncleanness.

From the power of man to introduce an object or substance into the processes of uncleanness, we turn to the corresponding power of man to sanctify an object or a substance. This is a much more subtle matter, but it also is more striking. It is the act of designation by a human being which "activates" that holiness inherent in crops from which no tithes have yet been set aside and removed. Once the human being has designated what is holy within the larger crop, then that designated portion of the crop gathers within itself the formerly diffused holiness and becomes holy, set aside for the use and benefit of the priest to whom it is given. So it is the interplay between the will of the farmer, who owns the crop, and the sanctity inherent in the whole batch of the crop itself, which is required for the processes of sanctification to work themselves out.

In addition to the power to initiate the process of sanctification and the system of uncleanness and cleanness, man has the power, through the working of his will, to differentiate one thing from another. The fundamental category into which an entity, which may be this or that, is to be placed is decided by the human will for that entity. Man exercises the power of categorization, so ends confusion. Once more, the consequence will be that, what man decides. Heaven confirms or ratifies. Once man determines that something falls into one category and not another, the interest of heaven is provoked. Then misuse of that thing invokes heavenly penalties. So man's will has the capacity so to work as to engage the ratifying power of heaven. Let us take up first of all the most striking example, the deed itself. It would be difficult to doubt that what one does determines the effect of what one does. But that position is rejected. The very valence and result of a deed depend, to begin with, on one's prior intent. The intent which leads a person to do a deed governs the culpability of the deed. There is no intrinsic weight to the deed itself. Human will not only is definitive. It also provides the criterion for differentiation in cases of uncertainty or doubt. This is an overriding fact. That is why I insist that the principal range of questions addressed by the Mishnah – areas of doubt and uncertainty about status or taxonomy – provokes an encompassing response. This response, it now is clear, in the deep conviction of the Mishnaic law, present at the deepest structures of the law, is that what man wills or thinks decides all issues of taxonomy.

The characteristic mode of thought of the Mishnah thus is to try to sort things out, exploring the limits of conflict and the range of consensus. The one thing which the Mishnah's framers predictably want to know concerns what falls between two established categories or rules, the gray area of the law, the excluded middle among entities, whether persons, places, or things. This obsession with the liminal or marginal comes to its climax and fulfillment in the remarkably wide-ranging inquiry into the nature of mixtures, whether these are mixtures of substance in a concrete framework or of principles and rules in an abstract one. So the question is fully phrased by both the style of the Mishnaic discourse and its rhetoric. It then is fully answered. The question of how we know what something is, the way in which we assign to its proper frame and category what crosses the lines between categories, is settled by what Israelite man wants, thinks, hopes, believes, and how he so acts as to indicate his attitude. With the question properly phrased in the style and mode of Mishnaic thought and discourse, the answer is not difficult to express. What makes the difference, what sets things into their proper category and resolves those gray areas of confusion and conflict formed when simple principles intersect and produce dispute, is man's will. Israel's despair or hope is the definitive and differentiating criterion.

Passionate concern for order and stability, for sorting things out and resolving confusion, ambiguity, and doubt – these characterize the deepest concerns of a people deeply tired of war and its dislocation, profoundly distrustful of messiahs and their dangerous promises. These concerns speak to folk aching for a stable and predictable world in which to tend their crops and herds, feed their families and workers, keep to the natural rhythms of the seasons and the lunar cycles, and, in all, live out their lives within strong and secure boundaries, on earth and in heaven. The philosophers of Israelite society speak of location but to an Israel that has none. This locative polity is built upon utopia: no one place. The ultimate act of will is forming a locative system in no particular place, speaking nowhere about somewhere, concretely specifying utopia. This is done – in context – because Israel wills it. Here, there, and everywhere in the Mishnaic representation of the Pentateuchal system comes a single statement: all depends upon Israel's will. It is not surprising that even the power of water to impart the capacity to receive uncleanness depends not on the physical presence of water, but on the intentionality of the person who has poured out the water. With that point, the matter of uncleanness leaves the world of the physical altogether and becomes a taxic indicator, a matter of classifying things without regard to their intrinsic properties: all things become relative to one fixed fact: Israel's will.

4

The Loci of Uncleanness in Judaism

I. The Pentateuchal Facts on What is Affected by Uncleanness

Both the Pentateuch and the Mishnah understand the loci of
uncleanness to encompass both the altar and the home, though the
principal concerns of the Pentateuch pertain to the altar, the priesthood,
and the food provided to God and to the priesthood, while the much of
the purity law of the Mishnah concerns the domestic setting.
Considerations of cleanness and uncleanness affect the cult and the
home. In the cult the altar and space around it, utensils used in its
connection, animals, grain, wine, and oil presented in it, male persons in
charge of it – all must be kept clean of the sources of uncleanness
transmitted in the manner Leviticus and Numbers describe. Food priests
are given as their rations ("heave-offering") and other offerings assigned
to them likewise have to protected from uncleanness and may not be
eaten if the priest or a family member is in a state of uncleanness.
Affirming all of these facts, the Mishnah's authorities invoke the analogy
between the table of the Lord in the Temple and the table of the Israelite
in the home, placing the latter into a continuum with the former. The
distinction is therefore made between unclean and clean food, the latter
of which must be protected from uncleanness and eaten in a condition of
cleanness. That is in addition to the distinction between unclean and
clean food made at Leviticus Chapter 11. The utensils of the home, as
much as those of the Temple altar, likewise are subject to uncleanness
and must be kept cultically clean. The Pentateuch further knows about
the uncleanness of persons, as we have seen, and makes it clear that
certain actions, for example, sexual relations, are not to be carried on
with such persons (with a woman in her menstrual period).

Administrators of the Cult and of the Law of Uncleanness

Lev. 10:10: Sons of Aaron are to distinguish between holy and common, unclean and clean (+ Ezek. 44:23).

Lev. 13:2 3: The priest examines the diseased spot and determines its status (+ Lev. 13:5, 6, etc.).

Negaim explicitly concurs on Lev. 13:2-3.

The Cult

Gen. 8:20: Noah offers up clean animals.

Lev. 7 :19-21: Flesh that touches any unclean thing shall not be eaten.... All who are clean may eat flesh. But the person who eats of the flesh of the sacrifice of the Lord's peace-offerings while an uncleanness is upon him shall be cut off from his people. And if any one touches an unclean thing...and then eats of the flesh of the sacrifice of the Lord's peace-offerings – that person shall be cut off....

Lev. 10:12-14: Priests are to eat in a clean place the cereal-offering and breast that is waved and thigh.

Lev. 12:4: Woman after childbirth for a specified period shall not touch any holy thing or come to the sanctuary.

Lev. 13:46: Leper remains outside the camp.

Lev. 15:31: Thus you shall keep the children of Israel separate from their uncleanness, lest they die in their uncleanness by defiling my tabernacle that is in their midst.

Lev. 16:16: Thus he shall make atonement for the holy place, because of the uncleanness of the people of Israel...and so shall he do for the tent of meeting, which abides with them in the midst of their uncleanness.... And he shall hallow it from the uncleannesses of the people of Israel.

Lev. 21:1: Priests are not to defile themselves for the dead, except for near relatives..."for they offer offerings by fire to the Lord...." Chief priest is not to leave the sanctuary at all, so as to preserve cleanness.

Lev. 22:3: Priests are to preserve cleanness of holy things, not to approach them while unclean, or as a leper or a Zab. None of the line of Aaron who is a leper or suffers a discharge may eat of holy things.... Whoever touches anything unclean through contact with the dead or a man who has had an emission of semen, and whoever touches a creeping thing by which he may be made unclean or a man from whom he may take uncleanness, whatever his uncleanness may be – the person who touches any such shall be unclean until evening and shall not eat of holy things unless he has bathed his body in water....

Num. 5:1-4: Lepers, Zabs, those unclean by corpse uncleanness, are put outside the camp, "that they may not defile their camp, in the midst of which I dwell" (+ Ezek. 44:25).

Num. 8:5-13: Levites are purified for cultic service.

Num. 19:20: Man who is unclean and does not cleanse himself is cut off..., since he has defiled the sanctuary of the Lord.

Uncleanness Outside of the Cult

Lev. 5:2: If any one touches an unclean thing – whether carcass of an unclean beast or cattle or swarming things, and it is hidden from him and he has become unclean, he shall be guilty.

Lev. 5:3: Human uncleanness.

Lev. 5:5: When a man is guilty in any of these, he shall confess the sin and bring his guilt-offering....

Lev. 11:32: And anything upon which any of them falls shall be unclean, whether it is an article of wood or a garment or a skin or a sack, any vessel that is used for any purpose....

Lev. 11:43: You shall not defile yourselves with swarming things lest you become unclean. For I am the Lord...consecrate yourselves and be holy, for I am holy. You shall not defile yourselves with any swarming thing. For I am the Lord who brought you up out of the Land of Egypt, to be your God. You shall therefore be holy, for I am holy.

Lev. 13:47-59: Leprous fabrics are burned.

Lev. 14:33-54: Leprous house is torn down and the stones thrown outside of the city.

Lev. 15:1-15: Zab is unclean.

Lev. 15:16-18: One who has emission of semen, sexual relations, is unclean.

Lev. 15 :19-25: Menstruant is unclean, and he who has sexual relations with her is unclean (+ Lev. 18:19, 21:18).

Lev. 18:24-5: Do not defile yourselves in sexual uncleanness, for by all these the nations I am casting out before you defiled themselves, and the land became defiled, so that I punished its iniquity and the land vomited out its inhabitants (Lev. 19:29).

Lev. 20:25-26: You shall therefore make a distinction between clean beast and unclean.... You shall be holy to me, for I the Lord...have separated you from the people, that you should be mine.

Num. 6:1-12: Nazir is to keep self clean of corpse uncleanness.

(Num 9: 9-14: Passover kept in uncleanness.)

(Deut. 12:22: Unclean and clean people may eat meat.)

The loci of uncleanness, moreover, are specified in so many words, for the priestly code is rich in references to why one should be clean, to places and circumstances and objects to be kept clean. Let us state its view of cleanness in respect to the cult:

1. The cult is to be carried on in conditions of cleanness.
2. Only clean animals are to be used in the cult.
3. A priest is to be clean when he consumes the cultic perquisites.
4. The woman after childbirth (therefore also the menstruant) is not to come to the sanctuary.
5. The leper is not to come to the camp.
6. The people are to be clean so as not to defile the Tabernacle; Whether or not this means they should be clean at all times is not specified.
7. If the holy place is made unclean, atonement must be effected.
8. Priests are to remain clean, therefore are not to contract corpse uncleanness.
9. Priests are not to come into contact with unclean things or persons, and, if they do or if they suffer such uncleanness, are not to consume holy things.
10. Lepers, Zabs, and those unclean by corpse uncleanness are sent away so that they do not defile the camp, in which God lives.
11. A person who contracts corpse uncleanness must be clean so as not to defile the sanctuary.

There can be no doubt that one principal conception of the locus of cleanness is that the cult and everyone and everything pertaining to it must be clean. There are two consequences. First, a priest who has contracted uncleanness may not carry out rites. Second, a priest or dependent who has contracted uncleanness may not eat priestly rations.

But that is not to suggest that, so far as the Pentateuch is concerned, cleanness is a matter only for the cult and the priesthood, for there is a second set of propositions which suggest an other than cultic locus of cleanness:

1. A person who becomes unclean by reason of touching unclean food is guilty. It is a sin to become unclean.
2. The objects specified at Lev. 11:32 are not explicitly designated for use in the cult.
3. The people are to be clean and are not to become unclean, because God is holy.
4. Leprous fabrics and a leprous house are to be disposed of, with no connection whatsoever to the cult.

5.   The persons who are unclean, the Zab, the one who emits semen, the menstruant, and so on, are unclean without regard to the cult. Not only so, but the menstruant may not have sexual relations, and that prohibition bears no explicit relationship to the cult.

6.   The people are to be clean of violation of sexual taboos because the land is holy and should not be made unclean.

7.   The people are to be clean because God has separated them.

Clearly, the holiness of the cult is not the sole concern in regard to the preservation of cleanness. But Leviticus is explicit that the people and the land are deemed analogous to the cult. This will account for the requirement that cleanness be preserved and uncleanness be removed from the holy people who dwell in the holy land. Standing by themselves, the several references to personal uncleanness nonetheless bear no relationship to the cult. The various unclean people, in particular, produce consequences outside of the cult, principally in respect to the prohibition of sexual relations.

Yet the priestly code's generative motive to keep clean is because of the cult. This is expressed in two ways. First, when penalties actually are stated with reference to violation of cleanness, it invariably is in the context of the cult. When, by contrast, people not involved in priestly activities are declared unclean, the consequence is not specified. It simply is that they are unclean. Thus we know why we must distinguish clean from unclean animals, why a priest is to be clean, what is the consequence of the uncleanness of the woman after childbirth, the effect of the leper's uncleanness, why the people are to be clean, what happens if the holy place becomes unclean, why lepers, Zabs, and those unclean by reason of corpse uncleanness are sent away, and so on. *The reason in all instances is that the cult must be protected from uncleanness.* On the other hand, as I said, when we refer to these same sources of uncleanness *not* in a cultic context, we ignore both the reason not to become unclean and the consequence of being unclean. None is specified, save in the case of the menstruant. In this regard, the contrast between treatment of the leper, the Zab, and other unclean persons in Lev. 22:3 and Num. 5:1-4 and that at Leviticus Chapters 13 through 15 could not be drawn more clearly. The former, taking for granted the specifications of the latter, makes explicit the purpose of the designation of the uncleanness of these parties.

The sequence of references, invariably in a redactional context, to keeping the people and the land clean so as to preserve their holiness, contradicts the substance of the rules. Uncleanness is uncleanness – even outside of the cult. But it is the cult which is made central by Lev. 15:31, and which blatantly marks the conclusion to the discussion inaugurated at Lev. 12:1, a clearly unitary sequence of rules: "Thus you shall keep the people of Israel separate from their uncleanness, lest they die in their uncleanness by defiling my Tabernacle that is in their midst." There is therefore no way to distinguish cult from people and land, and the cleanness of the latter is directly and repeatedly related to the preservation of the holiness of the former. That seems to me the indubitable requirement of the priestly code. Leviticus also insists that, because the cult must be kept clean, the land and the people also must be kept clean. That point is unambiguous and explicit.

If we have to specify the point of correspondence between cult and world, it is in the conduct of sexual relationships. That is where the pollution of the land is made specific (Leviticus Chapter 18). It also is the one point at which the penalty for personal uncleanness is specified: the menstruant is not to have sexual relations. Sexual uncleanness makes the land unclean, and the land is the locus of the Temple. Sexual uncleanness, further, is the way in which the people itself becomes unclean, contaminates itself. Accordingly, the opposite of cleanness in the cult is contamination in the bed. The latter affects people and land, just as the former is indicative of the condition and character of the people and the land. Sexual uncleanness contrasts with cultic cleanness, and the two complement one another. The cleanness of domestic utensils and foods does not receive equivalent emphasis. The Mishnah's tractates devoted to loci of uncleanness are curiously silent on this very matter. They treat as central the table, not the bed – utensils used in cooking and eating (Kelim) and the cleanness of foods (Tohorot, Makhshirin, Uqsin). The taboo against sexual relations during the menstrual period is treated mainly in terms of situations of doubt; it generates no independent problematic of its own in tractate Niddah. The contrast with Makhshirin is readily drawn.

II. The Mishnah's Account of What is Affected by Uncleanness

In addition to the Temple cult, the Mishnaic law prescribes to two other important aspects of Israelite life the status of cleanness and prohibits uncleanness: food and sex, sustaining and creating life. The former matter may be explained very simply: just as the table of the Lord in the Temple is kept clean, so the table of the Israelite at home is to be kept clean. Life is sustained through nourishment, carried on in exactly the conditions under which, in the cult, God's food is laid forth. *Eating like God so that a person may become like God* – a conception of the incarnation wholly congruent to the priestly myth of creation which, to begin with, specifies that man is made in God's image. What is it that man does in a way like God's? The priestly code describes in detail how God's food is prepared, and, it follows for those who create the system before us, man's food, too, is to be prepared and consumed in a state of cultic cleanness. The analogical mode of thought by which details of the system are spun out also guides the formation of the system as a whole. Life, as I said, is created and sustained in a state of cultic cleanness. Since the food taboos of Leviticus 11 refer to no specific locus (Temple/home) but only to Israel, the people, in general, the conception of the Mishnah will have presented no surprises to the framers of the priestly code.

This brings us to the cessation of sexual relations during the menstrual period, the point at which life is not going to be created. The rule on menstrual uncleanness, so that the woman will not engage in sexual activities during her menstrual period, is in Scripture. Lev. 18:19 is explicit: *You shall not approach a woman to uncover her nakedness while she is in her menstrual uncleanness.* (Lev. 15:24 is curiously silent in this regard). This prohibition is not linked to attendance in cultic activities. So far as it is set into a context, it is that of the holiness of the land, as Lev. 18:24-28 make explicit, and the holiness of the people, Lev. 24:29, both of which are linked to the holiness of God, Lev. 24:30. By contrast Lev. Chapter 15, which deals with the Zab, the menstruating woman, and the Zabah invokes the holiness of the Temple, so Lev. 15:31: *Thus you shall keep the people of Israel separate from their uncleanness lest they die in their uncleanness by defiling my Tabernacle that is in their midst.* In any event observance of the menstrual taboo in no way is unique to the authorities who stand behind Mishnah, nor is a distinctive worldview revealed merely by their interest in the matter. Implicit in the rules governing the uncleanness of a menstrual woman is that utensils she touches, beds and chairs on which she sits, and the like all contract uncleanness from her; but the menstruating woman is not on that account required to take up residence away from her family for a week out of each month; presumably she is careful about what she touches and where she sits; she will sleep in a separate bed (a requirement that is well documented indeed); but no isolation is otherwise prescribed for her.

III. Uncleanness Affecting Ordinary Food, Not Deriving from the Cult

The principle, however, that ordinary meals, not composed of food which has been sanctified for priestly or Levitical or cultic use, are to be eaten in a state of cleanness certainly can have been generated by the reading of Scripture. Leviticus Chapter 11 speaks of animals which may or may not be eaten. The language of cleanness is extensively employed in naming said animals. The clear implication of the chapter is that a person is made unclean by eating what is unclean: *These are living things which you may eat...* (Lev. 11:2), and uncleanness is invoked in exactly the same context (Lev. 11:8): *Of their flesh you shall not eat, and their carcasses you shall not touch; they are unclean for you* (Lev. 11:8). Lev. 11:24 further specifies, *And by these you shall become unclean; whoever touches their carcass shall be unclean until the evening, and whoever carries any part of their carcass shall wash his clothes.* And with respect to swarming things, Lev. 11:29 states: *And these are unclean to you among the swarming things...,* concluding (Lev. 11:31): *These are unclean to you among all that swarm; whoever touches them when they are dead shall be unclean until the evening.* The chapter in no way refers to the cult, although it clearly implies that what is suitable for the altar is suitable for the table, and what is unclean for the altar makes the Israelite unclean.

In context, therefore, how does cleanness of animals, fish, fowl, and winged insects affect the domestic meal, and, it will follow, how is cleanness of utensils of concern at home as much as in the sanctuary? The answer is that all of these rules against defiling oneself conclude, *...lest you become unclean. For I am the Lord your God. Consecrate yourselves therefore and do not become unclean. For I am the Lord your God: consecrate yourselves therefore and be holy, for I am holy. You shall not defile yourselves with any swarming thing that swarms upon the earth. For I am the Lord your God who brought you up out of the land of Egypt to be your God; you shall therefore be holy, for I am holy. This is the Torah pertaining to beast and bird and every living creature that moves through the waters and every creature that swarms upon the earth, to make a distinction between the unclean and the clean, and between the living creature that may be eaten and the living creature that may not be eaten* (Lev. 11: 43-47).

Scripture self-evidently does not explicitly state that one must eat clean animals and avoid unclean ones, or that one must preserve a state of cleanness in ordinary meals. But the various Scriptures do say that *if* one eats such unclean food, he becomes unclean, and that if he wants to become holy, he will preserve cleanness. The use of clean and unclean in this context, the further explicit statement that to be holy, one must be clean and not defile himself, and, still further, the distinction between clean and unclean, parallel to that between what may be eaten and what may not be eaten – all of these propositions hardly leave doubt, at least to one who asks about the matter to begin with, that eating must be done in a state of cleanness. One eats clean animals and food. To avoid contaminating them one must himself be clean. That, in point of fact, is simply the reverse of Leviticus Chapter 11's stress that if one eats unclean animals, he becomes unclean. All we know is that if one is unclean, he makes his food unclean. And one should *be* clean for eating and also should *eat* clean food so that he may be holy. Accordingly, from the Scriptural rule that one should avoid unclean foods so as not to become unclean, and one should avoid being unclean because he cannot be holy if he is unclean, it is a very small step indeed to the conclusion concerning the cleanness of domestic meals that the Mishnah's rules take for granted is the requirement of the law.

Of special interest is the uncleanness attaching to olives and grapes, which, when dry, are insusceptible, but when purposely wet down, are susceptible to uncleanness. M. Toh. 9:1, 9:2-3, and 10:4 represent the Houses as debating when olives and grapes become susceptible to uncleanness. While in their present formulation, the disputes make the point that liquid which is desired renders produce susceptible to uncleanness, and that which is not desired does not, the primitive version of the dispute need not be interpreted to deal with that principle. If we had no idea that the major issue of the units before us is the desirability of liquid, how should we have interpreted the materials attributed to the Houses? M. Toh. 9:1 gives several answers to the question, When do olives receive uncleanness? The Shammaites say this comes when the olives in the vat have exuded slime or sweat. The Hillelites simply say that this comes when three olives stick together, whether or not this takes place in the vat. The Houses differ on the location of the olives when the exuded liquid is taken into account. Do olives stick together before they go into the vat? Of course they do – in the basket. This definition, on the face of it, has nothing to do with one's attitude toward the exuded liquid. The Houses differ on the issue of the location of the olives when they become susceptible, as I said: vat, not basket, then, even basket. The Houses differ on whether during the process of cutting the olives, before the olives are brought to the vat, the work must be done in a state of cleanness. The Hillelites' position yields the rule that work must be done in a state of cleanness. The Shammaites will allow the work to be done in a state of uncleanness until the olives are actually in the vat. This brings us to the story about Shammai and Hillel on this very question:

> He who cuts grapes for the vat –
> Shammai says, "It is made susceptible to uncleanness."
> Hillel says, "It is not made susceptible to uncleanness."
> b. Shab. 15a/17a

> Said Hillel to Shammai: "Why do they put grapes for the vat in purity but not gather olives in purity?"
> He said to him, "If you anger me, I shall decree susceptibility to uncleanness even on the process of gathering olives."
> b. Shab. 17a

Both authorities hold that when olives are being cut down and prepared for the vat, they are not susceptible to uncleanness. The Houses' dispute concerns the point at which the process of gathering olives is complete. Since we know the process may be done in a state of uncleanness, we have to place a limit on it. The limit is after the olives have been in the vat, not after they have been in the basket, so the House of Shammai. The House of Hillel hold that at the point at which olives, in the basket, exude moisture and stick together, the work of gathering is complete, the work of producing the oil begins.

M. Toh. 10:4 brings us to the dispute of Shammai and Hillel. Shammai is clear that he who cuts grapes for the vat has rendered them susceptible; Hillel holds that he has not rendered them susceptible to uncleanness. What about cutting grapes not for the vat, but for eating? Grapes stored in the sort of baskets which do not hold in the liquid and spread out on the ground are eating grapes, not for vintaging. The House of Shammai hold that these grapes, too, are susceptible to uncleanness. The House of Hillel say that these grapes are not susceptible. This is a refinement of the protasis of the dispute between Shammai and Hillel: *He who cuts grapes for the vat.* What about him who cuts grapes *not for the vat?* This, too, is to be understood as referring to grapes cut for the vat, the liquid of which naturally is preserved, as against grapes cut for eating, which are spread out to dry. The issue of liquid obviously may be invoked in the interpretation of the dispute. But the dispute, without the matter of intention, is perfectly clear. Accordingly, the earliest problem at the Mishnah's level of the exposition of the system is to work out the implication of the distinction between the harvesting of grapes, which requires cleanness, and olives, which does not. The secondary issue of the intention of the owner in regard to the liquid is not essential in the interpretation of the primary stratum of the Houses' dispute.

Accordingly, the principal interest of the Houses is when olives and grapes become susceptible to uncleanness. Their presupposition is that there is a point at which olives and grapes are not susceptible, and another at which they become so. It follows that the Houses take for granted that food at some time in its preparation does not enter the system of uncleanness, and that means that an act of man, or his intention, is required to subject food – in the present instance, olives or grapes – to the working of the system as a whole. We shall see later on that that same conception of man's instrumental importance in inaugurating the function of the system of uncleanness applies also to utensils. The two principal loci of uncleanness – food and cooking utensils – therefore are treated in exactly the same way.

IV. Removes of Uncleanness and Levels of Sanctification of Food and Drink

We have already considered (in Chapter Four) the question of the interrelationships between removes of uncleanness and levels of sanctification. That matter forms a central consideration in the analysis of the uncleanness of food and drink. We recall that there are two separate, but interrelated problems. One has to do with the removes, or sequences of contacts, with the original source of uncleanness. Solid food which touches a Father of uncleanness falls into the first remove. That which touches food in the first remove falls into the second. That which touches food in the second remove falls into the third, and so on, theoretically, to infinity. But that progress is limited by a second set of conceptions. We distinguish among foods at various levels of sanctification. That which is unconsecrated is susceptible to uncleanness at fewer removes from the Father of uncleanness than is heave-offering, and heave-offering is less sensitive to contamination at several removes from the original source of contamination than are Holy Things. The combination of these two data produces a major conflict. Do we assess the effects of removes of uncleanness upon food in terms of that which is made unclean, that is, by reference to the levels of sanctification of the food? Or do we take account of that which produces the uncleanness, by reference to the levels of contamination of the food which imparts contamination? This is the complex interweaving of separate, yet reciprocally influential, principles. Readers interested in reviewing the details of this matter are referred to Chapter Four.

We turn directly to the second century authorities' expansion of the rule of levels of sanctification. Unconsecrated food (M. Toh. 2:2C-D) in ordinary circumstances does not produce a third remove. But if it is prepared within the discipline applying to heave-offering, it produces the effects, in further contacts, of heave-offering, thus a third remove. If heave-offering is prepared as if it were Holy Things, it will be able to produce the number of effective removes of Holy Things. Common food prepared as if it were Holy Things nonetheless does not produce contamination at the third remove, for there is nothing that can impart fourth grade uncleanness to Holy Things save only that which has itself been hallowed. The issue obviously is secondary to M. Toh. 2:2-6. That is, are we able to raise to a higher degree of capacity to impart contamination unconsecrated food and heave-offering (priestly rations)? We can indeed raise something by one remove, unconsecrated food to the status of heave-offering, heave-offering to the status of Holy Things. But we cannot raise something – the issue now concerns only unconsecrated food – by two removes. Eleazar b. R. Sadoq says that, while that is the case, we still can raise unconsecrated food by one remove. He would argue that, if we can raise unconsecrated food to the status of heave-offering – so far as its capacity to impart contamination is concerned – why should we not produce the same effect upon the unconsecrated food if we treat it in accord with a still more stringent corpus of rules? It is clear, moreover, that the supposition of this entire set is the same as that of M. Toh. 2:3-6, namely, we differentiate in accord with that which imparts contamination, not in accord with that to which contamination is imparted. M. Toh. 2:2C-D thus depend upon the late first century authorities' problems faced at M. Toh. 2:3-7/M. Sot. 5:2. Once we have raised the late first century authorities' question, we ask the one attested at the middle of the second century: How do we regard unconsecrated food prepared as if it were heave-offering, or heave-offering as if it were Holy Things? Before we have differentiated among unconsecrated food, heave-offering, and Holy Things, there is hardly reason to ask about the first named when it is treated as if it were the second.

V. Utensils Used in the Home, Not in the Temple

The matter of utensils is still more clearly related to Scripture. Beginning at that point, the Houses know two facts. First, clay utensils are not made unclean when touched on their outer parts by a source of uncleanness. Second, uncleanness affects them only through their inner sides. They limit that rule to clay utensils, with the status of utensils of analogous materials, particularly alum crystal, being subject to dispute. (This will, in time, yield the notion that diverse substances bear various traits as to uncleanness). The division of utensils is further attested by Hezekiah's saying before Gamaliel and by Mt. 23:25-6 and Lk. 11:38-41. Let us now ask, What is the origin of the twin notions that utensils are deemed divided into inside and outer side so far as being affected by uncleanness, and that clay utensils in particular are subject to said definition? The answer is obvious.

Lev. 11:33 states: *And if any of them falls into any earthen vessel, all that is in it shall be unclean, and you shall break it.* Let us first read the neighboring verse: *And anything upon which any of them falls when they are dead shall be unclean, whether it is an article of food or a garment or a skin or a sack, any vessel that is used for any purpose.* Accordingly, Lev. 11:33 refers explicitly to a clay utensil. Lev. 11:32 refers to other than clay utensils. Second, we notice the contrast between Lev. 11:32's reference to anything upon which any of them falls and Lev. 11:33's specification, *And if any of them falls into any earthen vessel.* It is hardly a considerable imposition on one's exegetical imagination – the contrastive mode of thought being invoked – to come to the conclusion that (1) if a dead creeping thing falls upon a wooden object, the object is unclean: but if it falls *upon* a clay object, it is not. On the other hand, (2) if it falls *into* the clay object, that is, into its contained airspace, then the object is unclean. Accordingly, in the case of the clay utensil, uncleanness is received from or at the inner part. And, it follows, first, that uncleanness is not received from contact with a dead creeping thing on the utensil's outer part, and, second, that we distinguish the inner part, which is susceptible to uncleanness, from the outer part, which is not.

In this same context, moreover, we learn that diverse materials will bear various traits as to the receiving of uncleanness and that distinctions, in particular, between clay and nonclay objects are to be drawn. Accordingly, an important concept is that utensils are regarded as divided into their inside or inner part and their outside or outer part. The first implication of that division is that something which has a 'midst' or an inner part or a receptacle is susceptible to uncleanness, and something which does not – which is flat – is insusceptible. Lev. 11:33 readily generated that concept. To be sure, that Scripture in the first place need not have brought the idea into mind. The importance of a receptacle in containing uncleanness may have derived from the larger notion of uncleanness. If one conceives uncleanness as a kind of gas of heavy viscosity, which will flow every which way unless it is contained within some receptacle – a utensil or a tent – but which then will be kept in that one place, then the importance of the receptacle depends not upon Lev. 11:33 but upon a quite separate conception of the material qualities of uncleanness. Accordingly, the first major development in the formation of the law of the susceptibility of domestic utensils stresses the presence of a receptacle or contained space as the requisite for the containment of uncleanness.

This bring us to the matter of nails. The Houses argue about whether or not they are deemed susceptible to uncleanness. The principle agreed upon by the Houses is that objects bearing some distinctive character or serving some distinctive purpose are susceptible, and those which do not are not susceptible. The basis for that principle is before us at Lev. 11:32: *And anything upon which any of them falls...shall be unclean, whether it is an article of wood...any vessel that is used for any purpose.* The concluding clause tells us that an unformed object, not a vessel, is not susceptible; and that it is the availability of a formed object for the service of some distinctive (human) purpose which denotes susceptibility to uncleanness. Let us now examine this proposition in greater detail. The one specific concept characteristic of the Mishnaic law of Kelim, beginning with the Houses, is that a utensil which is susceptible to uncleanness is one which is whole, complete, useful – normal. That notion is to be discovered in Scripture.

Leviticus 11:33 tells us that to clean an unclean clay utensil, one has to break it, make it useless. Then a utensil which can become unclean is one which is not broken, but which is useful. The same exegete can have understood a utensil – a KLY – to be deemed in the same place, "Every KLY made of any material" refers to anything at all; "any KLY used for any purpose" limits the foregoing to useful objects only. Autonomy, distinctiveness follow in the wake of purpose. At Lev. 11:32 we find: "Any vessel that is used for any purpose," KL KLY 'SR Y'SH ML'KH BHM.

The point is that, since there are some objects, also referred to as KLY, which are not "used for any purpose," after listing various materials, Scripture adds, "every utensil." This must function as an inclusionary phrase, followed by "used for any purpose," a limiting one – and the rest follows. That very simple process of reasoning, governing the answer to the question, "When is a KLY a utensil?" begins in a not very close reading of Scripture. So much for an object as utensil, that is, as something useful. Now let us ask about autonomy and distinctiveness. These, I think, are the clear intent of the construction in inclusionary, then exclusionary, clauses: "Every KLY made of any material" will include any object whatsoever. Then, "any KLY used for any purpose" excludes the just stated proposition, for we no longer have in mind *any* KLY, meaning any object, but now refer explicitly to any KLY, meaning any *useful* object. In other words, as soon as we refer to use, autonomy and distinctiveness will, in the nature of the Scripture, follow in its wake. Indeed, it is entirely possible that the categories of autonomy and distinctiveness ("having a name of its own") are Mishnaic ways of rephrasing the primary Scriptural statement, "with which work is done." Once more we conclude that, as soon as it gets underway, the Mishnaic system turns naturally to Scripture and elicits its most fundamental, factual data through a close reading of Scriptural passages deemed relevant to the question which, to begin with, Mishnah asks.

When we turn to the principles which underlie or seem to underlie, the many specific rulings, matters are simple. We are able to isolate a very few generalizations available before 70 to account for and organize all details:

1.   A receptacle is susceptible.
2.   A utensil to be susceptible must be fully processed and available for routine use.
3.   To be susceptible, an object must have a distinctive and permanent character, shape, or purpose. It must be designated for that distinctive function.

4. An object which is attached to the earth or which functions so that it is connected to the ground is clean.

All four data of the late first century rulings are familiar, and the first three certainly derive, to begin with, from Scriptural exegesis.

The single most important aspect of the law of utensils concerns the susceptibility of materials in general and of specific objects in particular. In respect to the susceptibility of materials and objects we find the second century authorities interested in traits of materials not under consideration among the late first century authorities' group, in particular, cloth, sacking, and especially, leather and wood. The second century authorities' capacity for sophisticated revisions of the law is most clearly seen in M. Kel. 11:3, which deals with a subtle issue: How do we assess the status of a mixture of materials? The matter is treated elsewhere in accord with the view that we follow the status of the material which predominates, and the late first century authorities probably would have agreed. But that obvious point is revised by the second century authorities, who ask not only, which material predominates? but also, which material is itself subject to the more stringent rules? That is, which is more sensitive to uncleanness to begin with? That consideration sets aside the question about which material predominates and demands a more complex answer, another case of the second century authorities' capacity for raising profound considerations in matters settled by late first century authorities in a simple manner.

I see no ways in which the lists of specific objects composed by the second century authorities differ from those of the late first century authorities. Both tend to deal with a myriad of specific objects. It seems likely that to both were available substantial traditions on the susceptibility of discrete utensils – odds and ends – and both took as their task the organization of these traditions into meaningful and principled groups. But the principles behind the second century authorities' rulings go beyond those sensible to the late first century authorities. Let us now list these principles:

1. Granted that a receptacle will be susceptible, what about a receptacle which serves only imperfectly? If a receptacle lets out a small part of its contents, or if it holds its contents only for a limited time, it will (or, will not) be susceptible.
2. Granted that an object must have a distinctive and permanent character, shape, or purpose and that it must be so designated, what about the parts of a utensil? Are they deemed distinctive if they function in a clear-cut way, or are they treated as part of a larger, insusceptible object?

3.   Granted that an object must serve man, must it serve man all the
     time? What about an object which is useful only part of the
     time?
4.   Granted that an object must be autonomous, what makes it so?
     Is reprocessing or adaptation required to impart that distinctive
     quality?
5.   Granted that an object must be "useful," how do we answer the
     primary question, What constitutes a sign that something is of
     use? Do we take account of the manufacturer's original
     intention? Since, for instance, he made an object very large, he
     must have intended it for some useful purpose, despite its large
     size and immobility.
6.   Granted that an object not used at random for a number of
     purposes is unclean, what will mark it as distinctive? Is it a
     formal trait imparted to the utensil, or is it the use to which the
     utensil is subjected? A flat object, without particular traits,
     when adapted for a single function, is susceptible.
7.   What is the relationship between form and function? Do we
     take account only of the presence of handles, or do the handles
     have actually to function normally?
8.   If something functions for a stated purpose, even though of
     normally insufficient size, is it susceptible? If something is
     suitable for a child but not for an adult, is it susceptible?
9.   Granted that two materials mixed together will follow the status
     of the primary one, how do we know which is primary? The
     answer is, that part of the utensil which carries out the function
     of the whole is primary, and the material of which that part is
     composed therefore determines the susceptibility of the whole.

Along with these new or better developed principles, moreover, we
find the considerations important to the late first century authorities:
normal use, presence of a receptacle, routine availability for a given
purpose, and so on. Some of the late first century authorities' principles
are refined at the middle of the second century; some continue without
modification; and the second century authorities introduce new ideas as
well.

Further questions of refinement have to do with the parts of utensils.
Having considered the susceptibility of utensils as a whole, we come to
the interrelated problems of the parts of utensils: What about handles
and other extrusions from the basic tool? To what degree do they share
in the uncleanness of the primary object? What about fringes, extensions,
and similar secondary extensions? How shall we know whether they are
treated as integral or separate? What is striking in the second century

authorities' stratum is the very quantity of rulings on the matter of connection. The provision of measurements of specific lengths of materials or extrusions of objects regarded as connected to the primary utensil is almost certainly absent among late first century authorities. But not only are the formal rulings greatly augmented. The principles by which the rulings are made also are vastly refined. The matter of connection is tied to the issue of function. This seems, at best, adumbrated among the late first century authorities. To the second century authorities it is made explicit and everywhere operative.

The issue of whether an attached object is movable is made articulate. The connector must not interfere with the normal functioning of the object. An extension which interferes and will be chopped off is treated as already disconnected, even though at the moment the owner does not plan to chop off the extrusion. This is parallel to the view that what is going to happen is treated as if it has already happened. Eliezer b. Jacob proposes a striking innovation in theory: connection is not a two way process. If the primary object is unclean, so is the connector; but if the attached part is made unclean, the primary object is unaffected. Eliezer's principle, if adopted, would have resulted in a vast profusion of new rules; as it is, it is rejected and stands by itself. Since connection is not formal at all but is determined solely by function, we do not take into consideration only whether the connected item interferes with the normal working of the utensil. We also ask, Does the connected item make possible the normal working of the tool? If it is extrinsic, though attached, it is not regarded as connected for the purposes of conveying uncleanness to the primary utensil. Eliezer b. Jacob follows this conception, for he holds that we distinguish among the functions of the primary object.

What is serviceable when an object is used in one way is connected, but when the object is used in another way, at which point, for example, an attached rope serves no purpose, said rope is now regarded as not part of the primary net. M. Kel. 20:3, which holds that if an attachment is not routinely available for use, it is not connected, accords with late first century authorities' ideas. But in this instance (M. Kel. 22:4), the issue is not phrased in terms of connection at all. It concerns the autonomy and serviceability of the utensil. So we cannot clearly distinguish between the aspect of connection and the issue of susceptibility in respect to dividing utensils; the only new case is in M. Kel. 5:6. We treat a utensil as divided only when it is so manufactured as to take account of the division. What is important to the second century authorities is simply whether and how a clay utensil is divided for purposes of uncleanness; the matter of the inside, outside, and holding place does not appear. The question of whether a minor element of an oven is treated as inside or outside hardly marks a theoretical departure. At M. Kel. 25:1-5, the issue of division is interpreted in terms of form or function. If there is a formal differentiation between inner and outer part, then we make the distinction for purposes of assessing uncleanness. The other view is that if one part of the object carries out the object's primary function, then that part is regarded as "inner," so the meaning of "inside" and "outside" is greatly revised.

VI. Resolving Matters of Doubt Concerning What Is Unclean

The middle of the second century produces a sizable number of principles for reckoning with matters of doubt in connection with uncleanness, all occurring in Mishnah-tractate Tohorot. These may be briefly catalogued. The first principle is that we settle matters of doubt by reference to the situation prevailing when the doubt is discovered or uncovered. Entirely separate is the view that, when we have a doubt, we refer to the condition prevailing among the majority. And alongside comes the contrary principle that, even if there is only one unclean thing mixed with many clean things, in a matter of doubt we rule that the unclean things' presence determines our decision in favor of uncleanness. We do not follow the status of the majority. The third principle is that, when we have the opportunity to interrogate someone in a situation of doubt, we deem the doubt to be unclean. When we do not have the possibility of interrogation, for example, when we deal with doubt about utensils or about minors, then we rule that the doubt is clean. Once more what is defined is the limits of doubts. Doubts indeed are deemed to be clean – but our state of ignorance must be complete.

A small but interesting set distinguishes one sort of action from another. If one is in doubt about having touched something, the matter of doubt is deemed unclean. If we are in doubt about having walked somewhere, the matter of doubt is deemed clean. Yosé's position at M. Toh. 5:2 is that, if the man did an act which may lead to uncleanness, he is unclean in a case of doubt. But if he merely walked in a path, it is a doubt which is deemed clean. Why? Because this is not an unusual action.

A further principle is that, if something unclean is in transit, matters of doubt are deemed clean. But if it has a place in which to come to rest, they are deemed unclean. Why? Because what goes up does come down, and if we know where the unclean thing is apt to come down, we assume it has indeed effected contamination. M. Toh. 4:7 refers to "doubt about liquids," glossing with, "to be made unclean – unclean, and to impart uncleanness – clean." The articulation of the saying indicates that the second century authorities have in hand nothing more than a saying that "doubts about liquids – clean," which then has to be worked out in detail and produces several quite distinct conceptions of the sorts of doubts regarding liquids to be regarded as clean. The saying, *doubt about liquids – unclean*, produces the explanation that we deal with an illustration of M. Toh. 4:1, throwing an unclean loaf of bread, and of M. Toh. 7:1, interrogation; and further yields the distinction between utensils and food, the new point. The second century authorities intertwine principles, explaining given cases or problems in diverse ways in accord with distinct general rules. Yosé and Simeon make the really new point that if we have a doubt about liquids in respect to utensils, the utensils are deemed clean, and if the doubt concerns food, the food is deemed unclean. Meir's view is that the phrase is interpreted in terms of the distinction between "to be made unclean/unclean; to be made clean/clean," thus, for example, if we do not know whether liquids are unclean, we hold that they are unclean; and if the doubt is whether they are clean they are clean. M. Toh. 4:8 presents another sort of doubt about liquids, this time, uncleanness floating on water. Now the distinction is made between liquids in utensils and liquids lying on the ground; or between descending into and ascending from liquids – cases totally unrelated to one another.

Doubt about the actual uncleanness of the source of uncleanness is a separate matter. The problems derive from other tractates, for example, the probable but not definite uncleanness of dirt in a grave area. The doubt is not whether the heave-offering (priestly rations) has touched that dirt, but whether the dirt is unclean. The doubt at M. Toh. 4:5 in some instances is not whether there has been contact between the heave-offering and the source of uncleanness, but whether the source of uncleanness in fact is indubitably unclean. In others, for example, concerning the *am ha'ares*, whose utensils or spittles which were found, the doubt is whether or not the heave-offering has touched the source of uncleanness – which is indubitably unclean. Yosé then introduces the matter of private domain. If there is doubt about having touched the unclean things in private domain, the heave-offering is burned. Sages hold that if the doubt affects private domain, the heave-offering is left in suspense; if it involves public domain, the heave-offering is clean.

Resolving doubts has still another angle: if we settle the status of one of two items whose situation is in doubt, we thereby "prove" the contrary status of the other of the two items. (That is the familiar matter of the excluded middle.) If in a case of doubt about two things, we treat one of them as if it is definitely unclean, then the second is treated as clean – its status being proved, by the treatment accorded to the first, to be contrary to that of the first. The principle of M. Toh. 5:3-4 is simply

that what we do to one of the two items has its affect upon the status of
the other.

Clearly, the late first century authorities knew the view that doubts
in public domain are deemed clean, private, unclean. That in sum and
substance constitutes the late first century authorities' stratum. In
addition to refining that item in some trivial ways and employing it in
new circumstances, second century authorities contribute the following
additional principles.

1.   We resolve doubt in matters of uncleanness in terms of the
     situation before us when the doubt arises;
2.   We follow the status either of the majority or of even a single
     unclean thing among a hundred clean ones;
3.   If we have doubt and can interrogate someone about it, matters
     of doubt are deemed unclean; if there is no possibility of
     interrogation matters of doubt are deemed clean;
4.   A doubt concerning touching is unclean, a doubt concerning
     walking is clean;
5.   A matter of doubt concerning an unclean thing which is at rest
     is unclean, a matter of doubt concerning an unclean thing which
     is in transit is clean;
6.   Doubts about liquids (various definitions);
7.   Doubt about the uncleanness of the source of uncleanness itself
     (with special reference to heave-offering);
8.   Settling doubts retrospectively.

What seems to have happened is that, receiving the principle that in
resolving doubts about matters of uncleanness, we impose a given
distinction, second century authorities determined both to propose
further differentiating principles and to explore the potentialities of the
inherited distinction when measured against others. The model of
private and public domain serves to generate the further distinction
between the possibility of interrogation and the absence of that
possibility. Problems of law in other connections entirely, for example,
ritual slaughter and plagues, supply the issue of whether we follow the
condition of the majority or decree that if there is a single unclean thing
mixed with a hundred clean ones, the whole is unclean, a notion which
will not have surprised the authorities behind M. Neg. 11:12. The
distinction between one sort of action and another depends upon one's
assessment of whether a deed is common or uncommon, and upon the
further consideration of whether we impose a negative evaluation or a
positive one on what is common or uncommon. Rules of testimony come
to bear. Yet, throughout, there is the unstated principle which,
imprecisely to be sure, we might call 'Common sense': if we have a doubt

which is no doubt at all, for example, if contamination simply has to have taken place, or if we cannot testify that there are solid grounds for doubt at all, then we rule the object to be unclean.

VII. Addressing a Common Agendum: History and the Loci of Purity

From these details concerning the loci of uncleanness, let us move to more general questions about the meaning of the system as a whole. The loci of the system are held in exquisite stasis in a system resting upon eternally recurrent natural forces and one that, at its essence, is above the realm of historical event and action. What is unclean is abnormal and disruptive of the economy of nature, and what is clean is normal and constitutive of the economy and the wholeness of nature. The hermeneutic route to that conception is to be located, to begin with, in the way in which what is unclean is restored to a condition of cleanness, to which we shall turn in the final part of this exposition. Purity, as we shall see presently, is restored through the activity of nature – unimpeded by human intervention in removing the uncleanness – through the natural force of water collected in its original state. Accordingly, if to be clean is normal, then it is that state of normality which is restored by natural processes themselves. It follows from the exegetical fulcrum of purification that to be unclean is abnormal and is the result of unnatural processes. We have already noted the counterpart and complementary conception concerning the sources of uncleanness, and our consideration of the loci of uncleanness has now completed the picture.

The system takes shape, therefore, through the confluence and contrast of opposites perpetually moving from the one side to the other – from the clean to the unclean, from the unclean to the clean. It is remarkably stable and unchanging. Death happens constantly. Water flows regularly from heaven to earth. The source of menstrual uncleanness is as regular as the rain. And the similar uncleanness of the Zab and Zabah through analogy attains regularity through that same source. Meals happen day by day, and if, for the Israelite within the system, the table is a regular resort, so, too, is the bed. The system therefore creates an unchanging rhythm of its own. It is based on recurrent natural sources of uncleanness and perpetual sources of cleanness, and it focuses upon the loci of ordinary life in which people, whatever else they do, invariably and always are going to be engaged: nourishment and reproduction – *the sustenance of life and the creation of life.*

And that brings us to the question of time, change, history – which is omitted from the picture altogether. When we glance at the loci of cleanness and uncleanness, we see that there is scarcely room for history, which above all is disruptive and disintegrative. Only when the symbolic perfection of the cult's perpetuity is shattered by events will a place have to be made for history. But at that point the cultic system, including uncleanness, is made subordinate to some other system and no longer serves as the principal focus and pivot of the system. Then uncleanness and all that goes with it become conditions for the expression of some further, now deeper, ontology, rather than the a priori ontological and mythopoeic reality. History, in the form of perceived disruption of the Temple. whether through destruction and cessation of the cult at Jerusalem or through the conviction of the cult's desecration by its own practitioners, transforms what is primary and uncontingent into something contingent and secondary. That we have seen in our examination of the topic of how water affects the susceptibility of objects; there we move from the physical to the relative; water by itself is null. Only when human will intervenes do the physical property of water prove effective. The upshot is that, with the destruction of the Temple, the authorities of the second century find that some systemic element in the available symbolic repertoire other than Temple and cult, for instance, Land and People, comes to the center.

The argument that at the core of the system is the conviction that what is normal is clean and what is abnormal or disruptive is unclean, is powerfully supported by the convictions of the priestly code on why Israel should keep clean and normally is clean. It is because the opposite of *unclean* is *holy*. Israel's natural condition, pertinent to the three dimensions of life – Land, people, and cult – is holiness. God's people is to be like God in order to have ultimate access to him. Accordingly, it is what causes Israel to cease to be holy, in the present context uncleanness, which is abnormal, and, to state the reverse, what is abnormal is unclean. Cleanness thus is a this-worldly expression of the mythic conception of the holiness and the set apartness of all three – people, Land, and cult. By keeping oneself apart from what affects and afflicts other lands, peoples, and cults ("the Canaanites who were here before you"), the Israelite attains that separateness which is expressive of holiness and reaches the holiness which is definitive also of the natural condition of Israel. The processes of nature correspond to those of supernature, restoring in this world the datum to which this world corresponds. The disruptive sources of uncleanness – unclean foods and dead creeping things, persons who depart from their natural condition in sexual and reproductive organs (or, later on, in their skin condition and physical appearance), and the corpse – all of these affect Israel and necessitate restorative natural processes.

To gain perspective on the purity system of the Judaism of the Dual Torah, we turn to the Dead Sea Library, which tells us about the viewpoint of the group that valued the library, commonly held to be Essenes. What is the place of the system of cleanness in the larger structure of which it is part? For the Essene community at Qumran the answer is not difficult to find. The community treated cleanness as vital at its chief group activity, the meal, because it saw itself as a sacred community assembled at a meal, the cleanness of which both expressed the holiness of the group and replicated the holiness of the Temple. Of still greater interest, cleanness is a precondition of participation in the eschatological war which loomed on the community's horizon and for which it proposed to prepare carefully, in part through perpetual cultic cleanness. After the war the soldiers were to restore their status of cleanness and that of the Jerusalem Temple, presumably because of the contamination of the corpses they would make in battle. It follows that cleanness is understood as a precondition of holiness; and holiness, of the messianic eschaton. Cleanness for the Essenes therefore constitutes not an abiding status, a permanent process outside of history. It is a necessary step in the historical process itself; the condition of the eschatological war which leads to the end of history.

The Essene community at Qumran, after all, conceived that a world historical event had already intruded into the realm of cleanness. Jerusalem and its Temple were hopelessly contaminated at the hands of willfully unclean people, people who had sexual relations in the Temple or the city and thereby contaminated both. Accordingly, the eternal and recurrent system of cleanness *already* had been disrupted. That is, in part, why the Essene community found it necessary at a given point in time to establish a realm of holiness, and therefore of cleanness, on its own and outside of the Temple. But the original breaking of the system out of its eternal cycle once and for all time introduced into the system a historical eschatological concern. Cleanness now is not natural to Israel but only to that segment of Israel assembled in the community. Cleanness is to be restored through the activity of that saving, pure, and purifying remnant. Provisional for now, cleanness will be made permanent only at the end of time and the conclusion of history.

The endless cycle, once removed from the eternity of the holy Temple which had been desecrated, could be restored to its perfect cyclicality only when history itself could for all time be brought to a final conclusion by the anointed Messiah and the holy warriors, at which time the holiness and cleanness of the Temple would be restored. Cleanness is a precondition of the end of days, which at the table of Qumran can be foreshadowed and adumbrated. But cleanness also, for its perfection, now depends upon the coming of the end of days. It is, therefore, an accident of history, not an element of a system essentially immune to history. Once historicized, cleanness and the system of which it is part never cease to be, not subjects and actors, but objects of social and metaphysical reality. Perfection once was and once more can be attained. But those for whom the Temple had been desecrated and was as good as destroyed conceived that what should not be subject to the vagaries of historical disaster indeed had been destroyed. It is only through the introduction into historical processes of the sacred community that cleanness would regain the perfect locus it had lost. In the meantime, cleanness would, at best, contingently serve as a precondition of the end and as a definition of the commune aiming at the end. The unarticulated system of the Essenes, remarkably congruent in its skeletal characteristics to that of the earliest sages of Mishnah, therefore locates cleanness within the scheme of history in the interim and not as essential to an eternally recurring cycle in an unchanging natural economy.

The Mishnaic system at its origins, by contrast, hardly leaves space for change. Its cogency and capacity to function as a system depend upon the opposite of change. We refer once more to the way in which uncleanness is removed, for that is the path into the center of the system. The system itself exhibits two fixed and static dimensions which correspond to and complement one another: nature and supernature. Omitted from the system is what is not natural but man-made. The intervention of man interrupts the process of purification and renders water incapable of effecting uncleanness. By definition, water drawn by man is unsuitable. Thus, the one point when human intervention is possible is the point which explicitly secures human exclusion from the system. Man of course does not bring about the uncleanness of the sources of uncleanness. But what the Mishnaic system at the outset chooses to say about that matter is insufficiently distinctive to produce a contrary expectation. Man is the locus of uncleanness. The ways in which human beings sustain and create life define the foci and the loci of the system. But in these matters, too, human intervention is secondary. Man cannot clean food but must choose clean food and protect its cleanness. Human beings must refrain from sexual relations at certain times. Their unnatural condition with respect to their sexual organs makes them vehicles for the imposition of uncleanness on objects they use in ordinary life – beds and chairs. That means everywhere they stand or sit or lie can be made unclean by them. But, as I said, the one point at which human volition enters the system, the choice to remove uncleanness, permits no role whatsoever to the human being. A person can enter the system by inadvertence. A person cannot leave it by conscious creation of means of purification. That pair of opposites is excluded.

If human action is systematically excluded, what about the complex of human actions which constitutes history? Obviously, human beings may desecrate not only themselves, but their tables and beds, and the cult and Temple as well. But, for the Pharisees, the Temple has not been desecrated. Everything we know about them suggests that, to the contrary, the cult is as it always was from the moment God ordained it: a locus of sanctity, a place of cleanness. So far as the cult defines the being of Israel, so long as the enduring conduct of its affairs in cleanness and holiness shapes the fundamental ontological situation of Israel, Israel – Land, cult, and people alike – is beyond history. Or, to put it differently, while things happen, history does not. The first destruction and the subsequent restoration of the Temple testify to the permanence of that system of permanent normality of which the center is the cult, the setting is the Land, the actors are the priests and people – all of them holy and set apart, above all, from history.

To ask further about the role of history in the Mishnah's system of uncleanness, we return to our observation that, for the Essenes, the lines of structure delineated by uncleanness shift, along with the point of centrality, the locus of the system's interest. At the Essene community of Qumran uncleanness served to exclude and cleanness to include, therefore defining the periphery of the commune. Cleanness performed a social and sectarian function. The center from which lines of structure go forth is reached by following those lines back to the locus defined by them. It thereby becomes clear that cult is replaced at the center by society, the Essene society in particular. The cult of Jerusalem has been rejected at one specific time. From that moment what happens perpetually is made contingent upon what has happened at some point. Ontological reality now is defined not in eternal, recurrent, and unchanging patterns of being. Once something has happened, then happenings, events of the life of the commune, disrupt the old eternal patterns. The community itself perceives just that and focuses its attention on what is to come in the eschaton. It follows that the vehicle, the locus, of meaning is that one thing which moves from the old mode of permanence to the new: the community itself, which in the interim is all there is to bear the burden of the sacred. That is why, I think, the focus of uncleanness shifts from cult which is reduced to a mere metaphor, to community which is served by, and also generative of, the said metaphor.

The Two Systems Compared

If this is a sound observation, then what do we learn about Mishnah's equivalent focus of uncleanness and the point of origin of lines of structure signified thereby in the context of history? What place is there for transience and historical movement in the earliest system of uncleanness contained within Mishnah? The answer to the question of who is excluded by uncleanness and included by cleanness must lie in exactly the same datum as has just now come under discussion. What is permitted and prohibited? We begin with the negative observation that, while in the laws of the Dead Sea Scrolls Library, one is unclean who violates the norms of the community; in early and late Mishnaic law one is unclean who is made unclean only and solely by those sources of uncleanness specified in Scripture or generated by analogy to those of Scripture. The contrast of the Essene community yields the fact that the Mishnaic system at its foundations presents no element of a societal revision of the locus of uncleanness, for there is none in the definition of the sources of uncleanness. The locus remains in the cult, where it was, but the periphery is extended to include the table. Keeping clean does not define one's membership in a sect, so far as Mishnah is concerned. The very tight adherence in Mishnah's fundamental stratum to Scripture and its explicit rules, both by interpreting them literally (as was done at Qumran) and by exegetically expanding them by analogy – treating the table like the table of the Lord in the Temple and the bed like the bed which in Canaanite times polluted the land, shows that no shift whatsoever had taken place in the point from which the lines of structure, delineated by uncleanness, go forth.

The Temple is uncontingent. The extension of the Temple's rules outside is secondary and contingent. The bed and table depend for meaning and significance upon the cult. Life is to be created and sustained in accord with the rules definitive of the world which is the center of life: the holy altar. Nothing has effected a shift in focus, from the enduring, real Temple of Jerusalem, either exclusively or even primarily to the community which keeps the cleanness laws and defines itself in terms of those laws. What is prohibited by uncleanness is entry into the Temple and analogous commensality at any table, anywhere. What is permitted is nurture and creation of human life everywhere. Israel remains whole, and uncleanness and cleanness do not effect social differentiation within it. If the law is not made to define a sect but to establish the rules by which common actions may be carried out, then for those who shape the world (in part) through the system under examination, nothing has happened to reshape the locus of the rules and disrupt their linear relationship to their enduring center. To state matters bluntly: for the Mishnaic system history has not (yet) happened.

The cult ordained by God goes on above, not through, time. For the Mishnaic system at its origins, no shift has taken place in the patterns of the lines of structure. The table and the bed are at the periphery and conduct at the one and in the other depends, as it always has, on the model by which rules of conduct are framed. Since the Temple in all its holiness endures, no other locus comes into view. The community formed by those who keep the laws in just the right way is not distinct from the world of those who do not, and indeed does not constitute a community at all; Israel remains Israel in all its full, old sense. The Land is wholly holy, not only that part of it consecrated by the life of the holy community thereon. Nothing has changed in the age-old ontology which defines being and discovers reality in order, permanence, recurrence, and the eternal, enduring passage of time. The sacrifice still marks and differentiates the days and months and seasons and links them into a larger pattern. Time's passage depends upon it. The cult still stands at the pivot, the spatial center of the Land, still forms the nexus between heaven and earth. The people, the whole people, still performs regular and holy actions through the priesthood which is at its center. Those who then eat their meals as if they are priests know they are not priests but aspire to the priestly sanctity. They do not claim to be the new priests or the only true and right ones.

If, as seems clear, nothing has changed, then the reason is that nothing has happened. It follows that cleanness is not a precondition of the eschaton, and uncleanness is not a function of history. That result, set forth in Chapter Four, is now to be reaffirmed. Cleanness is attained now where it always has been attained and uncleanness now is definitive of the locus of cleanness as it has always defined the locus of cleanness. The Temple remains, depriving of consequence what happens around and outside it. If we are unable to discern either a place for history in the uncleanness law, or a role in history for that law, the reason is apt to be that there is none.

It follows that, within the system at hand, with its powerful affirmation of eternity in time, sanctification in the here and now of everyday Israel, the destruction of the Temple cannot be presented as the principal cause of the several important shifts in the Mishnaic system of uncleanness which took place in the late first century authorities' period. The lines of development in many important components of the system are continuous with the character of the law before 70. Whether or not the Temple was destroyed, it was inevitable that these areas would develop within the as yet unanswered questions – the logical tensions implicit in their earliest structure. The profound thought of Makhshirin and Kelim on the role of man in inaugurating the working of the system responds to the conception of Miqvaot of the role of nature in bringing the process to a conclusion and restoring the economy of nature. Internal systemic considerations, imbedded in the logic of the law, account even for the transformation of what had been an undifferentiated metaphor into a fact. A single continuum now joins the table at home to the altar. Cleanness of the domestic table is not merely *like* cleanness of the Temple altar but stands in a single concrete line which ascends from the former, via the cleanness of the priest's heave-offering, to the latter. What formerly was compared to something else now is placed into material relationship with that other thing.

While we cannot ask how the destruction of the Temple affected the Mishnaic system of uncleanness, we do ask how the development of the system after 70 is congruent with the effects of the Temple's destruction. The answer is obvious. First, the destruction radically revises the institutional context for the priestly government of surviving Israel. New sorts of leaders emerge, one of which is the sage, qualified because he is expert "in them and in their names." Mishnah-tractate Negaim testifies to that fact and to the further and still more important fact that Aqiba in particular proposes to investigate the deep implications of the rise of the sage for a law to the working of which the priest is essential. The catastrophe raises the question of whether or not people bear responsibility for what has happened. If they do, they take on a heavy burden of guilt. If they do not, however, they face an equally paralyzing fact: their own powerlessness to shape their fate. The issue is resolved by stress upon the responsibility of Israel for its own fate, a painful conclusion made ineluctable by the whole of the scriptural heritage of Leviticus, Deuteronomy, and the prophetic literature. But Scripture is clear that those who have brought disaster by their deeds also can overcome it. Reversion to the right way will produce inexorable redemption. If people are not helpless, then their deeds and their intentions matter very much. The catastrophe provides an occasion for reflection on the interplay between action and intention, in the established supposition that what people propose to do and actually do are their own responsibility. And, as we have seen, the central issue – the fate and focus of the sacred – is faced head-on.

The loci defined by the Mishnaic system of uncleanness after 70 contain developments remarkably congruent to the institutional, psychological, and metaphysical crisis precipitated by the destruction of the Temple. The systemic message is clear. The sages will lead Israel to the restoration of the world destroyed by Israel's own deeds. They will do so through the reformation of attitudes and motives, which will lead to right action with the result that, even now, the remnants of holiness may be protected from the power of uncleanness. The holy priesthood and people, which endure and which are all that endure after the cultic holocaust of 70, form the last, if diminished, sanctuary of the sacred. In domestic life, at table, the processes of life are nurtured and so shaped as to preserve and express that remnant of the sacred which remains in this world. The net result of the late first century authorities' stage in the law's unfolding is that history – the world shattering events of the day – is kept at a distance from the center of life. The system of sustaining life shaped essentially within an ahistorical, indeed antihistorical, ontology goes forward in its own path, a way above history.

Yet the facts of history are otherwise. The people as a whole can hardly be said to have accepted the ahistorical ontology framed by the sages and in part expressed by the system of uncleanness. They followed the path of Bar Kokhba and took the road to war once more. When three generations had passed after the destruction and the historical occasion for restoration through historical – political and military – action came to fulfillment, the great war of 132-35 broke forth. A view of being in which people were seen to be moving toward some point within time, the fulfillment and the end of history as it was known, clearly shaped the ontological consciousness of Israel after 70 just as had been the case in the decades before 70. So if to the sages of our system, history and the end of history were essentially beside the point and pivot, the construction of a world of cyclic eternities being the purpose and center, and the conduct of humble things like eating and drinking the paramount and decisive focus of the sacred, others saw things differently. To those who hoped and therefore fought, life had some other meanings entirely. The second war proved still more calamitous than the first. In 70 the Temple was lost and in 135, even access to the city. In 70 the people, though suffering grievous losses, endured more or less intact. In 135 the land of Judah, surely the holiest part of the holy Land, evidently lost the bulk of its Jewish population. Temple, Land, people – all were gone in the forms in which they had been known. In the generation following the calamity of Bar Kokhba, what would be the effect upon the system of uncleanness?

The answer is predictable: there would be no effect whatsoever. The system would go on pretty much as before, generating its second and third-level questions as if nothing had happened. For a brief, unreal twilight, the old pretense of a life beyond history and a system untouched by dynamics of time and change would be attempted. The result, in the history of the Mishnaic system of uncleanness, would be the hour of systemic fulfillment, the moment of the richest conceptual, dialectical achievement, a bright and brilliant time in which 200 (or more) years of thought would come to ultimate incandescence. And, at the end, Our Holy Rabbi (Judah the Patriarch) would capture the light in permanent utensils of unbreakable language. But pretense that nothing had happened, or could happen, does not make history. Things *had* happened. The system of uncleanness, unfolding beyond time and change, now complete and whole in flawless intellectual and literary structures, is set aside at the time of its perfection. In the two Talmuds, the Division of Purities that formed the Mishnah's largest and most profound statement was ignored, except for the tractate on Menstrual

Uncleanness. The system which had denied an end time and constructed a world without end itself would fall into desuetude. History would give it its place on the crowded shelf of unused utensils, each containing its true, but implausible truths.

Part Three

THE RESOLUTION OF UNCLEANNESS:
REMOVAL AND PURIFICATION

5

Rites of Purification in Judaism

The theory of purification – mainly in an immersion pool, composed of still, not running water; water that has collected naturally, not been drawn – expresses the larger systemic view of the Judaism of the Dual Torah that the profound issue facing people is the working of eternity in time, sanctification in the here and now of Israel's common life. Here too, the choice is time moving toward an end, or eternity realized in sanctification. The case at hand yields a contrast. In an age in which men and women immersed themselves in spring-fed lakes and rushing rivers, in moving water washing away their sins in preparation for the end of days, the founders of the Mishnaic system took a different view. They observed regularities and orderly processes, the passing of the seasons, which go onward through time, the coming of rain in due season, for which they prayed; so they preferred purification effected through immersing in the still, collected water which falls from heaven. They bathed not in running water, water going somewhere; the moving water stood for the movement of time, in the anticipation of the end of days and for the sake of eschatological purity. They preferred to immerse for the purification from uncleanness, rather, in still water, to attain the cleanness appropriate to the eternal Temple, the cycle of cleanness, and the perpetual sacrifice.

They removed the uncleanness defined by the Written Torah for the holy altar, because of the conviction that the hearth and home, table and bed, going onward through ages without end, also must and can be cleaned, in particular, through the rain: the living water from heaven, falling in its perpetual seasons, trickling down the hills and naturally gathering in ponds, ditches, and caverns, for time immemorial. This brings us back to concern for sunset as the completion of the rite. As sun sets, bringing purification for the Temple, so rain falls, bringing purification for the table. It should be clear, therefore, that the Mishnaic conception of the immersion pool bears no relationship to baptism for the removal of sins, and lustration for cultic purity at table is totally irrelevant to the washing away of sin. This fact underlines the observation, stated above, that for the Mishnaic system, cleanness and uncleanness bear no metaphorical valence in an ethical, let alone historical eschatological, framework, but are addressed to a quite distinctive ontology. The system takes shape in two interrelated, but not wholly congruent, stages.

I. Modes of Purification in the Pentateuch

Uncleanness is removed by a variety of processes, including the use of water (still or running), the passage of time, breakage, burning, and so on, depending upon the source of uncleanness and the character of what has contracted uncleanness. Scripture knows a two-stage process for objects other than clay, immersion in water (the character of which is unspecified), followed by the passage of time to sunset; sunset completes the process of purification. Once more, uncleanness seems conceived as a fluid or substantive radiation, which is then washed away by appropriate fluid, but then affected by the passage of time, perhaps dried up. Breaking a clay utensil, meaning, rendering it useless for its former purpose, so changing its character, likewise dissipates the uncleanness that has taken hold of it. Fire serves to purify what is forged in flames. Finally, corpse uncleanness is removed by purification water, which is a mixture of water and the ashes of a red cow that has been burned up (Numbers Chapter 19). The main Scriptural references to rites of purification other than for corpse uncleanness are as follows:

> Lev. 11:32: And it shall be put into water and it shall be unclean until the evening. Then it shall be clean. (+ Lev. 11:25, 28, 40, 14:8, 9, 16, 24, 15:5-8, 10, 11, 16, 18, 19, 21, 22, 23, 27, 16:28, 17:16, 22:6-7, Num. 19:7, 8, 10, 19, 21 [Num. 31:24]. + Deut. 23:10 11.)
>
> Lev. 11:34: And you shall break it [= an earthen vessel which is made unclean] (+ Lev. 11: 35: Everything upon which any part of their carcass falls...whether oven or stove – it shall be broken in pieces... + Lev. 15:12).
>
> Lev. 11:36: Nevertheless a spring or cistern holding water shall be clean....
>
> Lev. 14:47: He who lies down in a leprous house shall wash his clothes. Lev. 15:2: Every vessel of wood shall be rinsed in water.
>
> Lev. 15:13: Zab bathes his body in running water.

> Lev. 15:16: If a man has emission of semen, he shall bathe in water and be unclean until evening (+ 15:17, 18).
>
> Num. 31:22: Fire purifies gold, silver, bronze, iron, tin, lead.

Scripture knows that water mixed with blood or with ash effects purification. An earthen vessel which becomes unclean is to be broken. That should mean it cannot be cleaned. A spring or cistern into which a dead creeping thing falls is not made unclean thereby. The spring or cistern, however, does not effect purification. Running water does, and so does fire. Accordingly the priestly code is remarkably indifferent to the purificatory capacity of ordinary water, which is at the center of Mishnah's system of purification, in tractates Miqvaot and Yadayim, and which necessitates the rules of Tebul Yom as well. We shall return to these facts of Scripture in due course.

II. Modes of Purification in the Mishnah

In the Mishnah it is taken for granted that purification is effected through washing in water, on the one side, and through breakage of a clay object, on the other. The fact that utensils are cleaned through rinsing in water is taken for granted at T. Kel. B.Q. 2:1. A principal interest concerns the point at which an object is useless, therefore insusceptible, corresponding to the discussions of when an object serves for its intended purpose, therefore is susceptible to uncleanness. Even at the earliest stages of the Mishnah's treatment of the subject, therefore, other than physical or material considerations enter in; the status of objects is settled by the intentionality or attitude affecting them, not only the physical substances that have been in contact with them, either to impart uncleanness or to remove it. This concern for the point at which objects are insusceptible by reason of uselessness and therefore clean comes to expression at a variety of points.

For one example, the Houses dispute about the point at which a metal siphon placed on the head of a staff or on a door becomes clean. The Shammaites hold that it is after the object is damaged, at which point it is insusceptible: breaking is cleaning. The Hillelites say that it is after the object is permanently affixed to the door: what is attached to the ground is insusceptible (M. Kel. 14:2, 20:6, T. Kel. B.B. 5:7-8). The Houses further assume that one must wash hands before eating a meal (M. Ber. 8:2).

The Shammaite position, moreover, maintains that a dry object is insusceptible. A wet utensil is susceptible. If unwashed hands touch a wet utensil, the hands impart uncleanness to the water on the utensil. The water falls in the first remove of uncleanness and therefore imparts uncleanness to the utensil when it enters its inner parts. At M. Ber. 8:3, moreover, the Houses take for granted that unclean hands are in the second remove of uncleanness and do not impart uncleanness to food. The Houses take for granted that water purifies, and also that water can become unclean. The supposition of their dispute (M, Miq. 1:5) is that rain water, in particular, is the material used for purification. That is water in its natural condition, still, on the one side, not drawn by man, on the other. The meaning of *purification* in this context is, become suitable for use for immersion. The Houses further dispute whether or not one may immerse in a rain stream (M. Miq. 5:6, 10:6, M. Ed. 4:6B). The issue at hand flows from the common supposition. At M. Miq. 4:6B/M. Miq. 10:6 the dispute on whether or not the immersion pool produces intermingling of unclean and clean water if the two sorts of water are not of the same temperature and character yields the supposition that water is cleaned in an immersion pool. Shammai and Hillel, finally, are in agreement that drawn water is unsuitable for immersion and furthermore spoils a collection of water which is not drawn. Their dispute (M. Ed. 1:3) concerns the volume of drawn water which spoils the pool. Purification water which has served its purpose is deemed by the House of Shammai to be clean, by the House of Hillel to be unclean. The supposition of the argument is that the status of said water is not settled by Scripture (M. Ed. 5:3).

Let us now consider how these various propositions originated beginning with Scripture and its views of the same matters. The ways in which contamination is prevented or removed rest on the principle that something or someone need not remain unclean and can emerge from uncleanness. That notion, of course, is explicit at Num. 19:15 and at the numerous passages in Leviticus at which a mode of purification is specified. The system does not imagine that what is unclean remains forever unclean. Uncleanness can be washed away, dried up in fire, removed by special mixtures, and evaporate with the passage of time, marked by sunset. Uncleanness, moreover, is relative to cleanness, and cleanness to uncleanness. The system is one of correlated opposites, and attains wholeness through the balance of opposites.

Accordingly, at the beginning of the system is a balanced set of mutually responsive distinctions on purifying objects, on the one side, and diverse modes not only of prophylaxis but of purification, on the other. The purification of clay objects by breaking and of other objects by immersion is derived from the now familiar contrast between Lev. 11:32 and Lev. 11:33. Lev. 11:32 states, *And anything upon which any of them falls when they are dead shall be unclean, whether it is an article of wood or a garment or a skin or a sack, any vessel that is used for any purpose; it must be put into water and it shall be unclean until the evening. Then it shall be clean.* It follows that utensils made of wood, fabric, skin, or sacking are to be cleaned by the processes of immersion and sunset. By contrast Lev. 11:33 specifies that an earthen vessel is not cleaned in water but by breaking: *And if any of them falls into any earthen vessel, all that is in it shall be unclean; you shall break it.* The breaking is read in Lev. 11:33 as the counterpart of immersion in Lev. 11:32. That means, therefore, that clay utensils are cleaned by breaking – being rendered no longer useful for any purpose. The matter of food and drink is dealt with in Lev. 11:34. There no provision whatsoever is made for purification, with the concomitant notion that in no way are these to be purified: *Any food in it which may be eaten upon which water may come shall be unclean and all drink which may be drunk from every such vessel shall be unclean.* Accordingly, Scripture is read to yield the three fundamental rules of purification as these apply to rinsable utensils, clay utensils, and food and drink, respectively.

Since Scripture does not specify metal objects at Lev. 11:32, there is room for inquiry. The purification of metal objects in the Mishnaic law is through immersion, of course. But Scripture itself is clear at Num. 31:22 that it is through fire: *Only the gold, the silver, the bronze, the iron, the tin, and the lead – everything that can stand the fire you shall pass through the fire and it shall be clean.* Omission of purification by fire is evidence that Scripture by itself does not generate the system before us. For what is neglected, not subjected to exegetical processes and taken into the system, is as significant as what is developed. The position of the Hillelites takes for granted that there is no mode of purification for metal objects. They know nothing of its immersion, therefore treat metal as equivalent to food and drink. That of the Shammaites maintains that metal objects are cleaned in some suitable manner. They therefore take account of a purificatory rite, though whether it is through fire or immersion in water is not specified.

III. The Immersion Pool

The single most important medium of purification of things that can be purified, inclusive of persons, is the immersion pool: a pool of still water, that has naturally collected; not been drawn by human intervention; not running water. The priestly code makes no provision for the purifying power of a "gathering of water" or an immersion pool. The Scripture which is evoked in this regard in the later exegetical compilations is Lev. 11:36. The context is the effects of dead creeping things on various objects and substances: utensils of wood and the like (Lev. 11:32), utensils of clay (Lev. 11:33), food and drink (Lev. 11:34), an oven or a stove (Lev. 11:35). The meaning can only be that if a dead creeping thing falls into a spring or a cistern which contains water, the spring or the cistern is not contaminated thereby. Yet it is certainly possible to propose an exegesis of the verse to prove that a spring or cistern then does effect contamination. How so? We have seen how the system of uncleanness operates through the setting up of correlated and reciprocally contingent opposites, beginning with the clean and the unclean. What is not unclean is clean; what is not clean is unclean. There is no neutral ground, for, as I have stressed, the one both completes, and is completed by, the other. Accordingly, if a spring or a cistern holding water is not made unclean by a dead creeping thing, the reason must be that said spring or cistern itself is not going to become unclean at all. If that is so, then the spring or cistern is an agent of cleanness and effects purification.

Scripture knows nothing of the immersion pool which has collected naturally and not by human agency – or, consequently, of the distinction between still and running water. The priestly code does not imagine such a thing as an immersion pool formed by rain water which has collected and lies still on the ground. It knows only that when one is contaminated, he or she is to wash in water, the location, character, and volume of which are not specified. Why not? Because in any case the water does not accomplish purification. Water at best removes material contamination. Sunset, not water, effects systemic purification, so far as the priestly code is concerned. The priestly code's modes of purification are blood, spring water – not still water collected naturally – and spring water mixed with another substance, blood or cow ash, and, finally, sunset. Washing in water explicitly is said to leave a person or object *unclean until sunset.* The survey of pertinent Scriptures leaves no doubt whatsoever of the state of affairs. The priestly code does differentiate among words for washing, bathing, and laundering. The generative distinction is the character of the object to be put into water. People bathe. Clothes are laundered. Objects are put in water, and so on. But when the context is attaining cleanness from uncleanness in particular, the Code time and again specifies that once an object or person has been washed, laundered, or put in water, the object or person is *unclean until sunset.*

Thus still water is distinguished from spring, or living, water. Still water is not understood as a substance able to purify anything from uncleanness. The reason that the traits of the "gathering of water" are not specified is that such a gathering of water – while itself not made unclean by the dead creeping thing of Lev. 11:36 – in any event does not effect purification. The fact that the one who has immersed but awaits sunset is deemed not unclean as he was before is a datum of Tebul Yom, the one unclean after immersion until sunset, that is, at a diminished level of uncleanness but still unclean. Accordingly, the Mishnah in its most basic conceptual stratum certainly does assume what Scripture nowhere recognizes, which is that immersion in the still water of a pool, collected naturally on the ground and without human intervention, effects purification. The one who has immersed and awaits sunset is clean, yet, to be sure, not wholly so. Scripture knows a person in that status to be unclean until sunset. The Tebul Yom in the Mishnah will be a category deemed wholly and solely in response to the prior conception that the immersion pool effects purification.

The concept that water in an immersion pool has the power of removing uncleanness, which for the Mishnah is the same thing as effecting cleanness, is at the very foundation of the opinions of the Houses and their fathers and certainly is to be assigned, at the latest, to the period before they come along, which is to say, at the latest, the first century B.C.E. Clearly some time between the conclusion of the priestly code, in the sixth century B.C.E., and the end of the first century B.C.E., a shift has taken place in conceptions of purification. The shift is that while for the priestly code blood and living water (spring water), not still water, purify, in the earliest conception of the Mishnah's law on the same subject, still water accomplishes purification, even in the absence of blood for the cult or living water for persons. That is why water must be preserved in its natural state, like spring water, and the analogy to the spring is so vital. For spring water does purify, in the Scriptural view. Accordingly, the blood which accomplishes purification at the altar and the water which accomplishes purification in the immersion pool act in analogous ways, and the living water, which flows like blood but which is water, like still water, forms the analogical nexus.

Yet that is not the whole story. The Houses do know the flowing spring. They take for granted, that, because the stream is flowing, a specific volume of water will not be collected together in any one place, which accounts for their dispute. The system *ab origine* thus sets up the *miqveh*, the immersion pool of forty seahs as a contrast: the spring flows, the immersion pool is still. The spring may purify in any volume whatever, while the immersion pool requires the requisite volume. Yet since the spring derives from natural, not artificial, sources, and is not made by means of human agency, in this respect, the pool is exactly alike. Accordingly, the rules of the Mishnah for the immersion pool begin in the analogy between the spring and the pool. The spring and pool are alike in that neither is subject to human agency. Both accomplish purification through natural means. That is appropriate, since bodily uncleanness derives from natural, not self-inducted action, for example, menstruation, seminal emission, flux, and the like. The spring and the immersion pool, however, do differ in their basic definition, therefore use. They are different solely in the obvious fact that spring water flows, and the "gathering of water" which is the immersion pool is still water.

What seems to lie at the base, from the viewpoint of exegesis, is that the conception of the still pool that purifies has been attached to the Scriptures which speak merely of washing in water. Yet the essential trait of the still pool is exactly the opposite of that of the spring: its water is still, not flowing. Accordingly, from their viewpoint at the basis of the capacity of the immersion pool to effect purification is the notion that spring water, deriving from the earth, and immersion pool water, deriving from heaven, are equivalent in their purificatory power, *so long as they are preserved in their equivalent, natural, form.* So long as rain water is unaffected by human agency, it is equivalent to spring water, flowing naturally. But just as rain water is spoiled when it is drawn, so spring water is spoiled when it is collected in a utensil, which water, indeed, diminishes in its puissance as it is allowed to cease its flow and dammed up in a pool. The upshot is simple. The main point of the priestly code is that for cultic purposes purification is attained through the application of blood or through immersion in living water, or through sunset. But for purification our system begins in immersion in the appropriate pool, or, self evidently, a flowing stream. Immersion takes place in a pool of water, the natural properties of which have not been affected by human agency. Since the purpose of immersion is the attainment of cultic purity, this is a position quite outside that imagined in Scripture.

The Mishnaic system, to begin with, thus provides a mode of purification different from that specified in the Written Torah for the Temple, but analogous to that suitable for the Temple. Still water serves for the table, living water cleans the zab, and, when mixed with blood or ashes, the leper and the person unclean by reason of touching a corpse. All those other things cleaned by the setting of the sun, the passage of time, in the Mishnaic system are cleaned in still water, gathered in the ground, in the rains which know no time, but only the eternal seasons. What is at stake in the distinction between one and the other media for purification, still water and running water? To understand the difference we remember that baptism for the eschatological forgiveness of sin, such as was practiced by John the Baptist, took place in running water, as did other forms of purification of other-than-routine conditions of uncleanness. So the contrast between running and still water bears metaphorical meaning.

This brings us to some of the details on purification processes, most of them – predictably – having to do with the character of the water that is to be used. On the process of purification through water, the Houses once more explore the role of the utensil. Specifically, they take up the notion that drawn water spoils the pool and conclude that if water merely passes through a utensil, it is deemed drawn water. We begin with the matter of drawn water itself to see how the role of utensils in particular enters the system. Hillel and Shammai are the earliest authorities to whom materials pertinent to the immersion pool are assigned. Their pericope takes for granted that drawn water is not to be used in the immersion pool. But they are alleged to have disagreed about the invalidating volume. Since Eliezer later on wishes to make a distinction between the situation before any water at all is in the pool, at which point a quarter-qab of drawn water spoils the pool, and that prevailing after there is some water in the pool, at which point the larger volume specified by Shemaiah and Abtalyon is invoked, there seems to me clear evidence of a progression of problems in logical sequence, as follows:

1. Drawn water prohibited;
2. Volume of drawn water specified;
3. Application of the requisite volume of drawn clarified (ab initio/post facto).

The successive logical stages in the unfolding of the law are assigned to people who, it is generally assumed, lived in exactly the same chronological relationship to one another.

There is a quite separate tradition on the prohibition of drawn water, but it has nothing to do with the immersion pool. To the Houses is attributed the view that a person on whose body and head drawn water is poured or a person who enters into that sort of water, is deemed unclean in respect to heave-offering. The relevant pericope is as follows:

> M. Shab. 1:4: And these are among the laws which they stated in the upper chamber of Hananiah, etc.
> B. Shab. 13b: What are the eighteen measures?...The following render heave-offering unfit:...one whose head and the greater part of whose body enter into (three logs of) drawn water; a clean person upon whose head and the greater part of whose body (three logs of) drawn water have fallen....

The primary tradition on the prohibition of drawn water has nothing whatever to do with immersion, a matter introduced only in the later exegesis. The linking of the prohibition of drawn water to the invalidation of the immersion pool certainly derives from the period before 70. The evidence is very strong that at that time drawn water was deemed to spoil the immersion pool. It remains to observe that the language that speaks of drawn water as spoiling the immersion pool does not specify that the immersion pool which is subject to invalidation is one which lacks the requisite volume of forty seahs, and that the immersion pool which contains that volume absorbs any volume of drawn water or other unacceptable substance without invalidation. Use of utensils to draw the water spoils the water, the Houses agree, and mere passage of water through utensils renders it drawn water. The Houses take for granted (M. Miq. 4:1) that water which flows into utensils is spoiled by them. The substance of the case concerns water collected in utensils under the water spout. The view that utensils have the effect of turning water into drawn water derives from the principle, prior to the Houses, that drawn water spoils the pool. Since water is drawn in utensils, it will follow that the use of presence in utensils is prima facie evidence that water has been drawn.

At M. Miq. 5:6 the Houses debate whether or not one may immerse in a rain stream. The Hillelites maintain that one does not do so. They agree that if one dams the stream with utensils, he may dip in it, although the utensils themselves are not thereby purified. The Shammaite position is that if in the entire flow of the rain stream we have the requisite volume, one may immerse in the stream, even though in the particular place in which one immerses are not the forty seahs which are required. Accordingly, dripping water purifies when it is flowing. The Hillelites want forty seahs of still rain water, all in one place.

At M. Miq. 10:6 the House of Shammai maintain that people do not immerse one sort of water in another sort of water, for example, hot in cold, fresh in foul. The House of Hillel say that they do. The Shammaite position is that we do not have intermingling of water unless the water which is to be purified is of the same character, for example, hot in hot, as that of the pool with which it is to be mingled and thereby purified. One therefore may not immerse unclean hot water in clean cold water and so forth. The pericope involves two problems, first intermingling, second, and, consequently, interposition. If the water does not intermingle, then, it follows, one sort of water interposes between the purification water and the object which is immersed. That is, both Houses clearly agree that water mingles, and, while the Hillelites hold that various kinds of water are deemed to unite with one another, they do not add that all sorts of liquid do so. The primary concern, the question of whether various sorts of water are deemed to intermingle, should not be neglected. It involves several elements. First and most important, it is taken for granted that water can be cleaned in an immersion pool. Why? Because if that were not the case then why discuss whether one immerses hot and cold, and so on? It will follow that other liquids cannot be cleaned in an immersion pool, by the same reasoning as is just now laid forth. Second, the question of whether we distinguish among kinds of water in various conditions, for example, hot and cool, simply refines this basic matter.

The law of making an immersion pool unfolds in a single line from its earliest suppositions. In summary, its primary concerns are these:

1. An immersion pool is formed by rain water, which is still and not flowing, and which contrasts to Scripture's spring, which is flowing. (A corollary, which I cannot satisfactorily locate before Usha, is that the pool must contain forty seahs of water, while spring water purifies in any [appropriate] amount.)

2. Drawn water spoils the pool, and water becomes drawn water by passing through a utensil. Drawn water can be removed or purified.

3. Water mingles and takes on the character of the predominant element of a mixture. Unsuitable water mingles with an immersion pool and takes on the purificatory puissance of the pool.

Clearly, a small but weighty corpus of conceptions is taken for granted even at the earliest stages of the law. First, rain water purifies. Second, rain water is not to be gathered by human agency, that is, it is not to be drawn from a well. Third, utensils are not to be used in this connection, a repetition and refinement of the foregoing. Fourth, water is purified in the immersion pool (but other liquids are not). The development of these conceptions is not inconsiderable, but it also is not innovative.

The late first century contribution to the amplification of the principles and rules of the immersion pool takes up the definition of decidedly secondary matters. We know that a pool must contain a given volume of water which is not drawn. But what sort of water, not drawn in utensils, is to be used? At M. Miq. 7:1-2 opinions are given on the sorts of liquids which raise the immersion pool to requisite volume and which, if they fall into it in a utensil, thus as drawn water, will not invalidate the pool; liquids which will invalidate it but not raise its level to requisite volume; liquids which will neither raise it to requisite volume and not invalid it. Eliezer (M. Miq. 2:10) accepts pure water and only that. Joshua, by contrast, admits mud, that is, water mixed with dirt but still sufficiently liquid to allow for immersion. Along the lines of his view, water in solid form remains water and serves for filling the pool. That is fundamental to the list of things which raise the immersion pool to requisite volume and do not spoil it. The matching set at M. Miq. 7:1-2, things which invalidate and do not raise the level of the pool, again takes for granted that drawn water is excluded. The other items consist of water which has been deprived of its purity, either by mixture with food or by being turned into something which is neither wine nor water. Yohanan b. Nuri knows that liquids other than water are not acceptable for the pool. Accordingly, by later first century times it was clear (1) that only water may be used in an immersion pool; (2) that water in solid form remains suitable; but (3) that water adulterated with wine is unfit, a neat trilogy of mutually complementary rules.

What about invalidating an immersion pool? At M. Miq. 2:4, Eliezer rules that a pool without water is invalidated by a quarter-qab of drawn water; one with water is invalidated by three logs of drawn water. Sages say that invalidation under all circumstances is with three logs of drawn water. The issue before Eliezer and sages is the process of invalidation. Eliezer holds that the three log measure applies only to a pool already containing some, but insufficient water. But if a pool has even a quarter-qab of drawn water before fit water flows in, that suffices to spoil the whole. Eliezer therefore has two invalidating measures in hand, quarter qab and three logs. Sages deny that the quarter-qab measure bears any relevance whatsoever. Under all circumstances, a pool lacking requisite volume is invalidated only with three logs of drawn water. What lies behind the dispute therefore is the three log measure. Eliezer wishes to investigate the application of the inherited measure of three logs. So, too, do other authorities at the end of the first century. But Eliezer's distinction is his own. Does the invalidating measure apply under all circumstances, or do we distinguish an empty pool from one containing some water, but not the requisite volume?

M. Miq. 2:7-9 ask about the effect upon rain water of passage through jars. Does this constitute an act of intervention on the part of man, therefore invalidating the water? Eliezer's position is that if the jars are left on the roof and are filled with rain, it is deemed rain water. Why? Because mere passage through the jars suffices to turn rain water into drawn water. Joshua's position is that since the man did not intend to gather the water in the jars, his purpose having been to dry them, the fact that the rain water collected in the jars does not change matters. The rain water remains rain water. Accordingly, as at Makhshirin, to Joshua the issue of intention is paramount. So long as the man did not intend to collect the water in the jars, what happens in the natural course of events does not change the picture. Self-evidently, the man is not to lift up the jars. Joshua will agree that if he removes the water by lifting the jar of water, pouring it out, emptying it into the cistern, he indeed turns the rain water into drawn water. Accordingly, Joshua will not reject the view that one's deed in connection with the water is paramount. What will he say of Aqiba's view that water does not spoil the pool unless it is actually raised up and poured into the pool out of a single utensil? He need not disagree, since M. Miq. 2:7F-H explicitly rules out emptying the jars into the cistern. One must not pick up the jar and turn it over. Accordingly, to Joshua the water is fit, and the only concern is that by our *action* we not render it drawn water. The upshot is that systemic interests in the power of human intentionality come to expression here as in so many other discrete areas of the law.

This brings us to other liquids that may be used for purification. We know what water is required for the immersion pool. What about other liquids beside water, for example, wine, milk, honey, and the like? M. Miq. 7:5 begins in the assumption that such liquids are not used for immersion, and, if they fall into the pool of water lacking in the requisite volume, they spoil the pool. Only water may be used for the immersion pool. All other liquids are unacceptable. Yohanan b. Nuri attests the secondary and derivative matter of the relationship between water and wine or milk. So far as he is concerned, the primary concern is the matter of color. But that attests the principle that, if wine changes the color of the water, the water is no longer regarded as water at all and no longer functions, to spoil the pool, as does water when it is drawn.

To summarize: all water in its origin is fit for purification in that it derives either from rain water or from springs. But all water may be rendered invalid through human agency, that is, if it is drawn and carried, or may be invalid by reason of insufficient volume. The processes by which water invalid for either reason may be used for immersion are two.

1. We mingle unfit water with a fit pool, through apertures of various sizes and by various means, so that the fit water purifies the unfit;
2. Or we remove the invalid water from a pool or annul its affects upon the pool.

Joshua, M. Miq. 3:1, holds that we restore the usefulness of the pool simply by removing a very small quantity of water, in the assumption that in whatever we remove is a portion of the invalidating water which has fallen in. Accordingly, a pool has been "purified" if we remove ever so little water, as against removing the whole volume and a bit more. Joshua maintains that the mingling of the drawn and fit water is so complete that, if we remove a tiny amount of water, we thereby diminish the drawn water in the pool to less than the disqualifying volume. The diametrically opposite view is that we remove the entire volume of the pool and a bit more.

What about the process of purification itself? In using the pool, one must make certain that the water touches all parts of a person or object which are to be purified. At M. Miq. 9:2-3, Eliezer maintains that whatever one takes note of interposes between the water and the flesh, and whatever ones does not take note of does not interpose. Eliezer proposes the simple criterion, dependent upon the individual's attitude, that if the water reaches all those parts of the body with which one normally is concerned, then there has not been interposition. When we come to utensils, the principal rule, at M. Miq. 10:1, is that if the handle is not integral to the utensil, it interposes, that is, it is not deemed connected. The important consideration is that the water reach all parts of the utensil. If the utensil is immersed upside down, air pressure builds up and prevents the water's reaching all parts of the utensil. If even turning the utensil upside down will not assure the water's touching the inside, then we make a hole in the utensil so that air will escape, and water will flow throughout the utensil.

The late first-century materials thus develop the antecedent conceptions at the following points:

1. Rain water is required for purification, and drawn water spoils the pool; utensils therefore are not to be used in connection with the collection of rain water.
2. Rain water is required for the formation of an immersion pool. This carries in its wake the distinction between rain water and spring water or still water.
3. Drawn water spoils the pool.
4. Water collected in utensils (under certain circumstances) is deemed drawn water.
5. Water is purified in an immersion pool, other liquids are not.
6. A pool is purified by removing the invalid volume of water or part of it.
7. When immersing, one must not permit anything to interpose between the body and the water.

IV. Breaking an Object as a Mode of Purification

The secondary developments of this scriptural conception are predictable. The Houses debate the point at which an object becomes insusceptible. The Shammaites invoke the principle of breakage (M. Kel. 14:2), the Hillelites, the view that what is affixed to the ground or to an insusceptible object is insusceptible. The object under discussion is metal, not clay. The Hillelites' position then would seem to wish to limit the principle of breakage to clay utensils in particular and to find a different basis for insusceptibility or purification for metal objects. M. Kel. 20:6 has the Houses apply the Hillelite view of M. Kel. 14:2. Now the issue is a permanent change in the object's utilization. In this context, the Shammaite position appears to be the more interesting. Scripture specifies breakage as purification solely for clay utensils, for example, the oven. But the Shammaites treat the principle as generic and generative. If breaking purifies a clay object, it is not because the object is clay, but because the process of *breaking* effects purification. The same process therefore applies to objects not made of clay. The mode of thought is similar to that which deems what is important about the tent to be not its formal traits but its functioning, the fact that it *overshadows* something. Therefore anything which overshadows both a corpse and another object brings uncleanness to said object and may or may not serve to interpose between the corpse uncleanness and the object. In both instances we find stress on the action – overshadowing, breaking – and not on the state or characteristic of that which does the action or to which it is done, the tent, the clay utensils in particular. Accordingly, Scripture is read as something other than a series of concrete and limited statements, but rather as a set of principles which yield important generalizations, with stress on the generalization of the process described by Scripture, breaking or overshadowing, respectively.

Second-century opinion builds on first century propositions and refines them. The useless object is clean. The later authorities then add: But if the broken object still works more or less as before, it is not really regarded as useless at all. So the meaning of "breaking" or "damage" is clarified. Not merely a break in the form but a considerable revision in the function is required for insusceptibility. The matter of the secondary purpose of course will be important. Meir's view is that a utensil which can carry out a subsidiary function, even if it cannot perform its original one, is still susceptible. Consideration of the stages by which an object falls into uselessness, or, more pertinently, loses its primary traits and therefore enters a diminished degree of susceptibility or uncleanness, clearly is a secondary development as well. At the same time both new questions and new principles are joined to the old, so that the law is a mixture of the basic principles of the first century intertwined with secondary developments of these same points in the second century. The first matter is the receptacle. How is it to serve for it to be susceptible? Second comes the question of distinctive character. Is that consideration determined solely by form, or do we ask about the way the parts of a utensil as a whole function? Then, third, the issue of normal use is greatly expanded by asking, Is this normal use directed toward meeting the needs of man or of utensils? The later view, that the susceptible utensil normally serves man, or normally serves both man and a utensil at once (as the case may be, depending on the authority), once again revises the given law. The later authorities, fourth, ask of a useful object: How shall we know that it is useful? What are the uses to be taken into consideration, those primary to the object, or secondary and derivative, perceived only when the object is no longer functioning in the normal way? Then, granting that normal use is determinative, they wonder whether use is determined by the traits of the object only, or also by the function to which an otherwise shapeless object is put. Form and function again are intertwined in reference to additions to an object.

One consideration original to the second century authorities is the distinction between the ordinary person and the craftsman. Do we take account of the way in which an adaptation, or the completion of the process of manufacture, is to be carried out? The distinction is attempted between whether anyone can routinely carry out the action, and whether only a skilled person can do it. Along these same lines is the distinction between what is useful to a poor person and what is useful to a rich one. A third complicating consideration is the question of whether one actually must carry out a deed, or merely intend to do so, before an object becomes insusceptible. A fourth innovation is the question of changing something into another object. This is parallel to the matter of connection: form versus function. Now the issue is this: Granted that changing an object alters its status as to susceptibility, what do we say about the nature of that change? If something is changed in function, it is clean in respect to its former status. Later on, therefore, one of three things will happen to principles laid down earlier:

1.   Either the principles will continue without significant alteration or development; or
2.   The development and application of established principles will be greatly expanded; or
3.   Subtleties and refinements will be introduced drastically to revise the original conception.

The course of the development of the law therefore seems clear: Breaking is purifying (Scripture). Breaking is signified by inability to carry out the former function, meaning to hold 1/96th of the former capacity. Breaking is signified by inability to carry out the former function meaning to hold what it formerly held, without regard to a fixed ratio. The sherds thereafter are susceptible when serviceable. The earlier view of the end of a utensil's susceptibility is that if a utensil's function is changed, its susceptibility also will be revised. "Breaking is purifying" therefore is treated with considerable subtlety. When, further, we take into account the changing of a utensil's function, we also ask about the maker's original intent. The second century masters add some fairly obvious corollaries to received principles. If a useless object is clean, a broken utensil which still serves its former purpose is then not useless, but still susceptible. Secondary purpose remains important. Changing the function or use of a utensil may take place by stages. An object which works but not in its normal way is not susceptible. This is further refined. First, the distinction is made between the work of the ordinary person and that of the craftsman. Second, the purpose of intention of the poor man is distinguished from that of the rich. Third, the actual accomplishment of an intention is introduced, distinguishing among the gradations of intention. Fourth, changing the status of a utensil is defined in terms either of form or of function. Finally, sherds and remnants are going to be open to susceptibility. There we ask how continued usefulness is determined.

V. Preparation of Purification Water by Burning a Red Cow

Purification from corpse uncleanness is accomplished in a different way from purification from other kinds of uncleanness, for example, that imparted by dead creeping things. A person who has been made unclean by corpse matter has to be sprinkled on the third and seventh days after contamination with purification water, the preparation of which is described in great detail at Mishnah-tractate Parah. The preparation of the ashes for mixing with running water to make purification water, as required at Numbers Chapter 19, provides some of the generative principles of that tractate, but not all of them. These are the guiding rules:

1. The cow must not be used for common labor.
2. A. The cow is not offered in the Temple, therefore is not subject to the Temple's rules.

   or

   B. The cow is not offered in the Temple, but, since it is called a *hat'at* (purification-offering), it is subject to the Temple's rules.
3. A. The cow must be perfectly red by nature.

   or

   B. The cow may be perfected by human action.
4. Details of the rite worked out: kindling fire, throwing in hyssop, etc., garments of priest, flaying, collecting ashes, collecting blood.
5. The water mixed with the ash must be unadulterated by dirt or other unsuitable materials and liquids.
6. All persons and objects involved in the rite must be free of all uncleanness. The cow is brought to the Mount of Olives in such wise that it never is exposed to uncleanness. A degree of purity even higher than applies to the Temple on the Day of Atonement is required.
7. Purification water which is suitable and sufficient for sprinkling causes uncleanness when moved. Unfit water does not do so to one clean for the rite of burning the cow.

8.   An act of labor not connected with the rite spoils the cow, the
     water, and all other aspects of the conduct of the rite.
9.   All objects used for lying and sitting are unclean for the rite.
10. The jar of water must be kept in a clean place.

Among these data of the earliest strata of the Mishnah's thought on the
subject, let us now eliminate two sorts, first, those which repeat the
obvious sense of Scripture and the Scriptural origin of which may be
taken for granted; and second, those which seem to reflect disputes fresh
at Yavneh, not about the application of principles available to, and
shared by, all parties. In the first category are No. 1; the supposition of
No. 3, that the cow must be red; No. 5, which is commonsense; No. 7,
which is explicitly stated in Scripture; and No. 10, also contained in
Scripture. In the second category are Nos. 2 and 4 (which simply repeats
the primary principle of No. 2), not to mention No. 10. What remains are
the following:

> Nos. 6, 8, and 9: The strict rules of cleanness applied to all
> who participate in the rite and to all objects used in that
> connection.
> No. 8: An act of labor not connected with the rite spoils the
> water, not to mention the cow and other aspects of the conduct of
> the rite.

These two matters, rules of cleanness different from, and higher than,
these applying even to Holy Things, on the one side, and the taboo
against doing labor not connected with the rite of burning the cow, on
the other, form the foundation for the first century stratum.

The priestly code (Num. 19:1-10) stresses that the rite of burning the
cow takes place outside the camp, in an unclean place. Anyone involved
in the rite is made unclean by participation in it. The priestly legislator
takes for granted that the rules of purity which govern rites in the
Temple do not apply to the red cow. Only to the Temple do the
cleanness rules pertain, which is why a rite done outside it is not going to
have to be protected by them. The predominant concern of the earliest
stratum of Parah, by contrast, is that people in the rite must be clean, and
that water used in the rite is to be drawn and protected with great care.
Since the Priestly author assumes that the rite produces uncleanness and
is conducted outside of the realm of cleanness, his version of the rule of
burning the cow does not involve keeping the Levitical rules of
cleanness. Parah is interested in that matter specifically because it takes
for granted cleanness is to be attained outside of the cult and not only in
the Temple. Indeed, as I said, the rule set forth by the Mishnah-tractate
demands a degree of cleanness even higher than that required for the

cult itself. Protecting the water by declaring unfit any water between the drawing and mixing of which there has been an intervening act of extraneous labor likewise is beyond the imagination of the priestly code. Thus the Mishnaic authorities have exactly the opposite conception from that of Numbers. Water used for the mixing must be mixed without intervening acts of labor so that it can be suitably protected from uncleanness. So the fundamental conviction of Parah is that rules of purity can be and are kept outside the Temple.

M. Par. 4:1 asks whether the rite is comparable, because of its rigid requirement of purity, to the Day of Atonement, done by the high priest in golden garments. The net result is that whatever priest – high or ordinary or prefect – does the rite, he is garbed in ordinary garments. In this regard then we exclude the analogy of the burning of the cow to the sacrifice on the Day of Atonement. Ishmael's willingness (expressed at Sifré Num. 124M) to admit a woman's participation in an aspect of the rite – the gathering of the ashes – is possible only within the supposition that the burning of the cow is so utterly divorced from the requirements of the Temple cult that women are admissible as participants. Since women have no role whatever in the Temple cult, it is an important opinion, based upon the fact that the sacrifice of the cow takes place outside of the Temple, to some precincts of which women were not admitted.

It is assumed that an act of labor not connected to the rite of drawing water for mixing, done between drawing a bucket of water and mixing it with the ashes, spoils the water. The same principle, that an extraneous act of labor spoils the procedures, applies to the rite of burning the cow itself. The principle of M. Par. 7:6-7 is clear. If one does an act of labor, such as returning a borrowed rope used for drawing the water to its owner, en route to the mixing of the water and the ash, the water is not spoiled. If he goes out of his way to return the rope, he spoils the water. Accordingly, the innovation is the distinction between labor intrinsic to the rite and that which is not.

At M. Par. 7:11 the rule is given that if a person entrusted the water to an unclean person, the water is made unfit. If he gives it over to a clean person, it is fit. The issue is whether the drawn water leaves the owner's domain. The anonymous rule holds that it does. Therefore the guard must be clean. Eliezer says that it does not. So if the guard is unclean, there is no effect on the water. The force of the gloss of Eliezer's saying is to introduce the issue of work. If the owner worked, the water guarded by the unclean person is spoiled. Rather than reviewing further details in sequence, let us turn to the main issue that is expressed in debates on details. That requires us to identify the myth – or competing myths – that are in play in the consideration of the particular rules.

VI. Addressing a Common Agendum: Ritual without Myth

The laws at hand, like many others considered in earlier chapters on Judaism, constitute ritual entirely lacking in mythic, let along theological, explanation. The processes of making those laws themselves constituted the rabbis' mode of thinking about the same issues investigated, in other circumstances, through rigorous theological thought, on the one side, or profound mythic speculation, on the other. So far as the laws describe a ritual, the ritual itself is myth, in two senses. First, the ritual is myth in the sense that it was not real, was not carried out. Second, while lacking in mythic articulation, the ritual expresses important ideas and points of view on the structure of reality. What people are supposed to do, without a stage of articulation of the meaning of what they do, itself expresses what they think. The explanation of the ritual, the drawing out of that explanation of some sort of major cognitive statement, is skipped. The world is mapped out through gesture, the boundaries of reality are laid forth through norms on how the boundaries of reality are laid forth. Accordingly, we deal with laws made by people who never saw or performed the ritual described by those laws. It is through thinking about the laws that they shape and express their ideas, their judgments upon transcendent issues of sacred and profane, clean and unclean. It follows that thinking about the details of the law turns out to constitute reflection on the nature of being and the meaning of the sacred. The form, the ritual lacking in myth, is wholly integrated to the content, the mythic substructure. The structure of the ritual is its meaning.

We turn now to a particular ritual, the burning of the red cow for the preparation of ashes, to be mixed with water, and sprinkled upon a person who has became unclean through contact with a corpse. The ritual is described in two sources, Numbers 19:1-10, and the tractate of Mishnah called Parah, the cow.

Let us first consider the way the priestly author of Numbers 19:1-10 described the rite, the things he considers important to say about it:

> Tell the people of Israel to bring you a red cow without defect, in which there is no blemish, and upon which a yoke has never come. And you shall give her to Eleazar the priest, and she shall be taken outside the camp and slaughtered before him. And Eleazar the priest shall take some of her blood with his finger and sprinkle some of her blood toward the front of the tent of meeting seven times. And the heifer shall be burned in his sight; her skin, her flesh, and her blood, with her dung, shall be burned; and the priest shall take cedar wood and hyssop and scarlet stuff and cast them into the midst of the burning of the heifer. Then the priest shall wash his clothes and bathe his body in water, and afterwards he shall come into the camp and the priest shall be unclean until evening. He who burns the heifer shall wash his clothes in water and bathe his body

> in water and shall be unclean until evening. And a man who is clean shall gather up the ashes of the heifer and deposit them outside the camp in a clean place; and they shall be kept for the congregation of the people of Israel for the water for impurity, and the removal of sin. And he who gathers the ashes of the heifer shall wash his clothes and be unclean until evening (Num. 19:1-10a).

How is the ash used? Num. 19:17 states:

> For the unclean they shall take some ashes of the burnt sin-offering and running water shall be added in a vessel; then a clean person shall take hyssop and dip it in the water and sprinkle it upon the tent... (in which someone has died, etc.).

Let us now ask, what to the biblical writer are the important traits of the burning of the cow and the mixing of its ashes into water? The priestly author stresses, first of all, that the rite takes place outside of the camp, which is to say, in an unclean place. He repeatedly tells us that anyone involved in the rite is made unclean by his participation in the rite, thus, 19:7, the priest shall wash his clothes; Num. 19:8, "the one who burns the heifer shall wash his clothes"; Num. 19:10, "and he who gathers the ashes of the heifer shall wash his clothes and be unclean until evening." The priestly legislator therefore takes for granted that the rules of purity which govern rites in the Temple simply do not apply to the rite of burning the cow. Not only are the participants not in a state of cleanness, but they are in a state of uncleanness, being required to wash their clothes, remaining unclean until the evening, only then allowed back into the camp which is the Temple. Accordingly, the world outside the Temple cannot be clean; only to the Temple do the cleanness taboos pertain; and it follows that a rite performed outside of the Temple is by definition not subject to the Temple's rules and is not going to be clean.

What is interesting, when we turn to the Mishnah tractate on the burning of the red cow, Parah, is its distinctive agendum of issues and themes. If I may now summarize rapidly the predominant concerns of Mishnah-tractate Parah, which we have already considered in some detail, they are two: first, the degree of cleanness required of those who participate in the rite and how these people become unclean; second, how the water used for the rite is to be drawn and protected, with special attention directed to not working between the drawing the water and the mixing of the ashes referred to in Num. 19:17. The theoretical concerns of Mishnah-tractate Parah thus focus upon two important matters of no interest whatever to the priestly author of Numbers 19:1-10, because the priestly author assumes the rite produced uncleanness, is conducted outside of the realm of cleanness, and therefore does not involve the keeping of the Levitical rules of cleanness required for participation in the Temple cult. By contrast, Mishnah-tractate Parah is chiefly interested in that very matter. An important body of opinion in our tractate, as we have already seen, demands a degree of cleanness higher than that required for the Temple cult itself. Further, the matter of drawing water, protecting it, and mixing it with the ash, is virtually ignored by the priestly author, while it occupies much of our tractate and, even more than in quantity, the quality and theoretical sophistication of the laws on that topic form the apex of our tractate. Accordingly, the biblical writer on the rite of burning the red cow wishes to tell us that the rite takes place outside the camp, understood in Temple times as outside the Temple. The rite is conducted in an unclean place. And it follows that people who are going to participate in the rite, slaughtering the cow, collecting its ashes, and the like, are not clean. The Mishnah authorities stress exactly the opposite conception, that people who will participate in the rite must be clean, not unclean, as if they were in the Temple. And they add a further important point, that the water which is to be used for mixing with the ashes of the cow must be mixed with the ashes without an intervening act of labor, not connected with the rite.

The laws of the ritual themselves contain important expressions about the nature of the sacred and the clean, I shall now attempt to illustrate how the articulation of the laws, through the standard legal disputes of the late first- and second-century authorities, contains within itself statements about the most fundamental issues of reality, statements which, in describing the form of the ritual, also express the content of the ritual, its myth. The first dispute concerns which hand one uses for sprinkling the blood toward the door of the Holy of Holies; the second asks about how we raise the cow up to the top of the pyre of wood on which it is going to be burned; and the third deals with whether intending to do the wrong thing spoils what one actually does. The texts are simple and pose no problems of interpretation. The first is at Mishnah Parah 3:9:

> They bound it with a rope of bast and place it on the pile of wood, with its head southward and its face westward.
> The priest, standing at the east side, with his face turned toward the west, slaughtered it with his right [northern] hand and received the blood with his left [southern] hand.
> R. Judah says, "With his right hand did he receive the blood and he put it into his left hand, and he sprinkled with [the index finger of] his right hand."

Before analyzing the pericope, I should add the corresponding Tosefta supplement (Tosefta Parah 3:9):

> They bound it with a rope of bast and put it onto the wood pile.
> And some say, "It went up with a mechanical contraption."

R. Eliezer b. Jacob says, "They made a causeway on which it ascended. Its head was to the south and its face to the west."

In the present set, therefore, are the first two of the issues mentioned earlier: which hand we use for sprinkling the blood, and how we raise the cow to the top of the pyre of wood.

Let us notice, first of all, the placing of the cow and the priest. The rite takes place on the Mount of Olives, that is, to the east and north of the Temple Mount in Jerusalem. Accordingly, we set up a north-south-east-west grid. The cow is placed with its head to the south, pointing in the direction of the Temple Mount, slightly to the south of the Mount of Olives, and its face is west – that is, toward the Temple. The priest then is set east of the cow, so that he, too, will face the Temple. He faces west – toward the Temple. When he raises his hand to slaughter the cow, he reaches over from north and east to south and west, again, toward the Temple. We have, therefore, a clear effort to relate the location and slaughter of the red cow, which takes place outside the Temple, toward the Temple itself. In fact each gesture is meant to be movement toward the Temple. Just as Scripture links the cow, outside the camp, to the camp, by having the blood sprinkled in the direction of the camp (a detail which Mishnah takes for granted), so that the sprinkling of the blood, which is the crucial and decisive action which effects the purpose of the rite – accomplishes atonement, or *kapparah,* in Mishnah language – so all other details of the rite here are focused upon the Temple.

This brings us to Judah's opinion, which disagrees about slaughter with the left hand. As observed, we have to set up a kind of mirror to the Temple, with the whole setting organized to face and correspond to the Holy Place. The priest in the Temple slaughtered with his right hand, and received the blood in his left. Likewise, the anonymous rule holds, the priest now does the same. In other words, our rite in all respects replicates what is done in the Temple setting: What is done there is done here. Judah, by contrast, wants the blood received with the right hand and slaughtered with the left. Why? Because we are not in the Temple itself. We are facing it. Thus if we want to replicate the cultic gestures, we have to do each thing in exactly the opposite direction. Just as, in a mirror, one's left is at the right, and the right is at the left, so here, we set up a mirror. Accordingly, he says, if in the Temple the priest receives the blood in his left hand, on the Mount of Olives and facing the Temple, he receives the blood in his right hand. All parties to the dispute, therefore, agree on this fundamental proposition, that the effort is to replicate the Temple's cult in every possible regard.

This brings us to the dispute about how we get the beast up to the top of the woodpile. The anonymous rule is that we bind the sacrificial cow and somehow drag it up to the top. But in the Temple the sacrifices were not bound; they would be spoiled if they were bound. Accordingly, Eliezer b. Jacob, a contemporary of Judah, imposes the same rule. He says that there was a causeway constructed from the ground to the top of the woodpile on which the cow will be slaughtered and burned, and the cow walks up on its own. Self-evidently, both parties cannot be right, and the issue is not what really was done in "historical" times – let us say, seventy-five years earlier. As in the dispute between Judah and the anonymous narrator, the issue is precisely how we shall do the rite, on the Mount of Olives, so as to conform to the requirements of the rite on the Temple Mount itself. To state matters in general terms, it is taken for granted by all parties to the present pericope that the rite of the cow is done in the profane world, outside the cult, *as if* it were done in the sacred world constituted by the Temple itself.

How is the contrary viewpoint expressed? The simplest statement is in Mishnah Parah 2:3B-D:

> B.   The harlot's hire and the price of a dog – it is unfit.

That is to say, if the red cow is purchased with funds deriving from money spent to purchase the services of a prostitute or to buy a dog, the cow is unfit for the rite. The pericope continues:

> C.   R. Eliezer declares fit,
> D.   since it is said, "You will not bring the harlot's hire and the price of a dog to the house of the Lord your God (Deut. 23:18)." But this [cow] does not come to the house [of the Lord, namely, the Temple].

The issue could not be drawn more clearly than does the glossator (D). Eliezer holds that since the burning of the cow takes place outside of the Temple, the Temple's rules as to the acquisition of the cow simply do not apply. Let us proceed to the secondary developments of this point. The first item, Mishnah Parah 4:1, is as follows:

> The cow of purification which one slaughtered not for its own name [meaning, not as a cow of purification, but for some other offering], or the blood of which one received and sprinkled not for its own name, etc., is unfit.
> R. Eliezer [Eleazar] declares fit.

What is at issue? In the sanctuary, we have correctly to designate the *purpose* of a sacrifice. Eleazar holds that this is not a rite subject to the rule of the Temple cult. The rule continues,

> And if this was done by a priest whose hands and feet were not washed, it is unfit.

R. Eliezer declared fit.

Priests of the Temple of course had to be properly washed. Since the rite is not in the Temple, Eliezer says that the priest need not even be washed. In this connection, Tosefta supplies:

> If one whose hands and feet were not washed burned it, it is unsuitable.
> And R. Eleazar b. R. Simeon declares fit, as it is said "When they come to the tent of meeting, they will wash in water and not die" (Ex. 30:20) – so the washing of the hands applies only inside [the Temple, and not on the Mount of Olives].

The issue seems to me fully articulated, and the glosses in both the matter of the harlot's hire and the matter of washing spell out the implications. The law which describes the ritual – the *structure* of the ritual itself – also expresses the meaning of the ritual. The form imposed upon the ritual fully and completely states the content of the ritual. If now we ask, What is this content? we may readily answer. The ritual outside of the cult is done in a state of cleanness, as is the ritual done inside the cult. The laws of the cult, furthermore, apply not only to the conduct of the slaughtering of the cow (the cases I have given here), but also to the preservation of purity by those who will participate in the slaughtering (cases not reviewed here).

The Mishnah presupposes what Scripture takes for granted is not possible, namely, that the rules of purity apply outside of the Temple, just as the rules of Temple slaughter apply outside of the Temple. And the reason is, of course, that the Mishnah derives, in part from the Pharisees, whose fundamental conviction is that the cleanness taboos of the Temple and its priesthood apply to the life of all Israel, outside of the Temple and not of priestly caste. When Israelites eat their meals in their homes, they must obey the cleanness taboos as if they were priests at the table of God in the Temple. This larger conception is expressed in the laws before us. Let us now proceed to a matter which is by no means self-evident, and which was not understood in the way in which I shall explain it even by the second-century authorities. It concerns the issue of drawing the water. The rule is that if I draw water for mixing with the ashes of the red cow, and, before actually accomplishing the mixture, I do an act of labor not related to the rite of the mixing of the ashes, I spoil the water. This is stated very succinctly, "An act of extraneous labor spoils the water." This conception is likely to have originated before the destruction of the Second Temple in 70, because a very minor gloss on the basic rule is attributed to the authorities of the period immediately after 70:

> He who brings the borrowed rope in his hand [after drawing the water with bucket suspended on a rope, the man plans to return the rope to the owner] – if [he returns it to the owner] on his way [to the rite of adding ashes to the water], it is suitable [that is, the bucket of water has not been spoiled by the act of extraneous labor], and if it is not on his way, it is unfit.

Appended is the following observation:

> [On this matter] someone went to Yavneh three festival seasons [to ask the law], and at the third festival season, they declared it fit for him, as a special dispensation.

Taken for granted, therefore, is the principle, evidently deriving from Pharisaism before 70, that an act of extraneous labor done between the drawing of the water and the mixing of ashes and water spoils the drawn water.

The rule lies far beyond the imagination of the priestly writer of Numbers, because he tells us virtually nothing about the water into which the ashes are to be mixed. But that is of no consequence. What is interesting, second, is the language which is used, *unfit*, not *unclean*. So the matter of the cleanness of the water – its protection against sources of contamination – is not at issue. Some other consideration has to be involved. Third, the drawing of the water is treated as intrinsic to the rite. That is: I burn the cow. I go after water for mixing with the ashes of the cow. That journey – outside of the place in which the cow is burned – is assumed to be part of the larger rite. Now this matter of extraneous labor is exceedingly puzzling. We have to ask, to begin with, for some sort of relevant analogy. Do we know about other rites in which we distinguish between acts of labor which are intrinsic and those which are not? And on what occasion is such a distinction made? The answer to these questions is obvious. We do distinguish between acts of labor required for the conduct of the sacrificial cult, and those which are not required for the conduct of the sacrificial cult, in particular we make that distinction *on the Sabbath*. On the Sabbath day labor is prohibited. But the cult is continued. How? Labor intrinsic to the sacrifices required on the Sabbath is to be done, and that which is not connected with the sacrifice is not to be done.

When we introduce the issue of extraneous labor (and the issue extends to the burning of the cow itself), what do we say about the character of the sanctity of the rite? Clearly, we take this position: the rite is conducted by analogy to the sacrifices which take place in the Temple, so that the place of the rite and all its participants must be clean, exactly as the place of the Temple and all the participants in the Temple sacrifices must be clean. So, too, with the matter of labor. When we impose the Temple's taboos, we state that the rite is to be conducted in clean space. When we introduce the issue of labor, we forthwith raise the question of holy time, the Sabbath. For it is solely to the Sabbath that the matter of labor or no labor, labor which is intrinsic or labor which is extrinsic, applies. When we impose the taboos applicable to the Temple on the Sabbath, we state that the rite is to be conducted in holy *time.* The cleanness laws in the present instance create in the world outside of the cult a *place of cleanness* analogous to the cult. The Sabbath laws in the present instance create in the world outside of the cult a *time of holiness* analogous to the locus of the cult. The ritual constructs a structure of clean cultic space and holy Sabbath time in the world to which, by the priestly definition, neither cleanness nor holiness (in the limited sense of the present discussion) applies.

The laws, it is clear, do not contain explanations. The issues themselves are trivial, ritualistic, yet even the glossators at the outset introduced into the consideration of legal descriptions of ritual extralegal conceptions of fundamental importance. Accordingly, the processes of thought which produce the rabbis' legal dicta about ritual matters also embody the rabbis' judgments about profound issues. The final stage in my argument is to consider other sorts of sayings, in which the rabbis speak more openly and directly about matters we should regard as theological, not ritual, in character. These sayings are general, not specific, treat questions of salvation, not of the conduct of a ritual, and constitute a quite distinct mode of expression about these same questions. These theological sayings contrast, therefore, to the ones about ritual law, showing a separate way in which the authorities of the same period form and express their ideas. The issue at hand, in particular, is the relationship between cleanness and holiness. We have already considered the matter in our interpretation of the ritual laws, showing that cleanness is distinct from holiness, and the two are related to and expressed by the laws about burning the red cow. Pinhas b. Yair gives us a statement which links the issue of cleanness and holiness to salvation:

> R. Pinhas b. Yair says, "Attentiveness leads to [hygienic] cleanliness, cleanliness to [ritual] cleanness, cleanness to holiness, holiness to humility, humility to fear of sin, fear of sin to piety, and piety to the holy spirit, the holy spirit to the resurrection of the dead, and the resurrection of the dead to Elijah of blessed memory."

Pinhas therefore sees cleanness as a step in the ladder leading to holiness, thence to salvation: the resurrection of the dead and the coming of the Messiah. Maimonides, the great medieval philosopher (1135-1204), much later, introduces into the messianic history the burning of the cow of purification. Referring to the saying that nine cows in all were burned from the time of Moses to the destruction of the Second Temple, he states (*Red Heifer* 3:4):

> Now nine red heifers were prepared from the time this commandment was received until the Temple was destroyed the second time...and a tenth will King Messiah prepare – may he soon be revealed.

Maimonides thus wishes to link the matter of the burning the red cow which produces water for ritual purification to the issue of the coming of the Messiah. Both sayings, those of Pinhas b. Yair and Maimonides, show that it is entirely possible to speak directly and immediately, not through the language of ritual law, about fundamental questions. And when we do find such statements, we no longer are faced with ritual laws at all. Yet it seems to be clear that Pinhas b. Yair and Maimonides saw in the issues of purity, even in the very specific questions addressed by the rabbinic lawyers who provide the ritual law, matters of transcendent, even salvific, weight and meaning.

Let us now return to the issues raised at the outset and summarize the entire argument. It is now clear that the sages at hand express their primary cognitive statements, their judgments upon large matters, through ritual law, not through myth or theology. Indeed, we observe a curious disjuncture between ritual laws and theological sayings concerned with the *heilsgeschichtliche* meanings of the laws. The ritual laws themselves describe a ritual. Since the ritual was not carried out by the authorities of the law, the purpose and meaning of legislation in respect to the ritual of burning the cow are self-evidently not to describe something which has been done, but to create – if only in theory – something which, if done, will establish limits and boundaries to sacred reality. The issue of the ritual is *cleanness* outside of the Temple, and, if I am right about the taboo connected with drawing the water, *holiness* outside of the Temple as well. The lines of structure, converging upon, and emanating from, the Temple, have now to be discerned in the world of the secular, the unclean, and the profane. Where better to discern, to lay out these lines of structure, than in connection with the ritual of sacrifice not done in the Temple but outside of it, in that very world of the secular, unclean, and profane. As I have stressed, the priestly author of Numbers cannot imagine that cleanness is a prerequisite of the ritual. He says the exact opposite. The ritual produces contamination for those who participate. The second-century rabbis who debated the details of the rite held that the rite is performed just as it would have been done in the Temple. Or, in the mind of Eliezer and Eleazar b. R. Simeon, the rite is performed in a way different from the way it would have been done in the Temple. The laws which describe the ritual therefore contain important judgments upon its meaning. With remarkably little exegesis of those laws – virtually none not coming to us from the glossators themselves – we are able to see that their statements about law deal with metaphysical reality, revealing their effort to discern and to define the limits of both space and time.

The structure of the ritual contains its meaning. Form and content are wholly integrated. Indeed, we are unable to dissociate form from content. It follows that what is done in the ritual, the sprinkling with one hand or other, the binding of the cow or the use of a causeway to bring it to the pyre, the purchase of cows with the wrong sort of money, the employment of unwashed priests, the exclusion of the issue of the wrong intention – all of these matters of rite and form *alone* contain whatever the rabbis will tell us about the meaning of the rite and its forms. The reason is that the rabbis think about transcendent issues primarily through rite and form. When they choose another means of discourse and a different mode of thought entirely, matters of rite and form fall away. Theological and mythic considerations to which ritual is irrelevant take their place. Judah, Eliezer, Eleazar b. R. Simeon, Eliezer b. Jacob, and the others cited, however, refer to no myth, make use of neither mythic nor theological language, because they think about reality and speak about it through the norms of the law. Since the law concerns a ritual which these authorities have never seen and certainly would never perform, *the law itself constitutes its own myth,* the fabulous myth of a ritual no one has ever done, and the transcendent myth of the realm of the clean and the sacred constructed through ritual and taboo in the world of the unclean and the secular. That is why I claim that the ritual *is* the myth. What people are told to do is what they are supposed to think, the gestures and taboos of the rite themselves express the meaning of the rite, without the mediation of myth. And what we have said about this particular purification rite applies to the entire Judaic system of uncleanness and cleanness – seen in context and interpreted correctly.

Appendix One

Comparing Judaic and Zoroastrian Law: The Pahlavi Rivayat Accompanying the Dadestan i Denig and the Talmud of Babylonia

To validate the comparison of a given topic, we have to show prima facie evidence that two sets of writings are sufficiently alike to sustain comparison. For that purpose, I present the comparison of Mishnah law with two Zoroastrian law compilations. We find episodic intersections of a striking order, and these justify the hypothesis that comparison is feasible: like to like, to identify the unlike. The Pahlavi Rivayat Accompanying the Dadestan i Denig is found among the manuscripts associated with the Dadestan i Denig of Manushchihr, high priest of Pars and Kirman, and forms part of that writing down of the great tradition that took place in the ninth century under his sponsorship.[1] At that same time, Sherira, a principal authority of Judaism in Babylonia, was explaining that the Talmud of Babylonia was written down to preserve the great, originally oral tradition from disappearance. So both legal documents were assigned the same purpose.

The Bavli's authors will have found much of Pahlavi Rivayat analogous to their own Talmud. That is the part of this rivayat made up of questions and answers, whether of legal or theological character. In

---

[1] All translations are by A.V. Williams, *The Pahlavi Rivayat Accompanying the Dadestan i Denig* (Copenhagen, 1990: The Royal Danish Academy of Sciences and Letters through Munksgaard). Williams, 1:8: "[It] is placed in the manuscripts with works by authors from one well-known family of learned priests and it is likely that a member of the family might have compiled this Rivayat."

general, most of the chapters "are in some ways answers either to a question, explicit or implied, or to a predicament." It is "neither speculative, philosophical, nor in any narrow sense theological; it is pedagogical, for here, above all, the doctrines of purity, righteousness, and just, meritorious action are extolled to the reader by every available means. Clearly, the voice is that of a priest."[2] Then the colloquy between Zoroaster and God is the priest's recording of the received tradition, as much as the Mishnah represents Judah the Patriarch's allegation of having preserved in fixed and readily memorized form – thus published in an odd way – the received tradition.

Closer to the trait of the Bavli still, this rivayat contains numerous citations of prior, authoritative writings. So the work is traditional in another sense parallel to the Bavli: received authoritative writings are the sources for much that is said, so Williams: "Much of the material appears to come directly from a knowledge of the Pahlavi versions of the Avesta with the Zand, either oral or written." Williams comments:

> [The text] was addressed to Zoroastrians living in Muslim Iran, at a time of great insecurity for those who adhered to the older religion. The text was intended not only to impart information, whether practical, ritual, or theological, to the community; rather it intends to preach solidarity and faithfulness in the community.[3]

In this context, Williams cites Jacques de Menasce's comment:

> The documents of this type do not generally insist on what, in a faith, is the most current and the most actual. Interest is turned more on what is in danger of being forgotten and on what is the object of controversy. Thus one will not find a balanced and complete account.

Whether or not the same may be said in specific passages of the Bavli, the highly contentious and argumentative character of the Bavli's unique writing (as distinct from kinds of writing it shares with other documents, for example, the Mishnah, not only cited but imitated in authoritative formulations of law) points to the same intentionality. Let us undertake the comparison of episodic points of law, at which the two codes intersect.

I. The Transmission of Uncleanness

Comparison of episodes at which the two documents – the Rivayat Accompanying Datestan i Denig and the Bavli (inclusive of the Mishnah) – address the same question and even say the same thing. But

---

[2]Williams, 1:9.
[3]Williams, 1:10.

the Rivayat forms only a part of a much larger set of writings, and its rules testify to only one component of a complete legal and theological system. The severely limited range of comparison, to be sure, is not because, even at their most arcane, the two writings do not cover the same ground in the same way. The contrary is the fact. Anyone familiar with the Judaic law of uncleanness will find himself at home in a statement such as the following, concerning the transmission of uncleanness through being affected by the motion of, without direct contact with, the source of uncleanness:

> If they are carrying a dead [body] over a bridge of wood or of stone, if it trembles, if everyone who is standing on the bridge [is standing] still, [they are] not polluted, but if anyone keeps going he will indeed be polluted.

The principle here is that the corpse uncleanness is conveyed through motion, but not at rest; the criterion (who has to be moving) is, the person who is a candidate for contamination.

Let me paraphrase the Iranian rule. If a corpse is carried across the bridge, and if others are moving on it, too, if the bridge trembles under the weight of the corpse, then all other persons on the bridge are made unclean, the movement of the bridge transmitting the corpse uncleanness to third parties if they, too, are moving. But if they are not moving, then the uncleanness is null. It then follows that [1] if the bridge is firm and does not shift, [2] and if occupants of the bridge also do not move, then others standing on the bridge are unaffected. The upshot is simple. Corpse uncleanness is transmitted through the motion of an object that bears its weight.

In the following the same principle of the physics of the transmission of uncleanness pertains, though it works itself out somewhat differently. The datum is the category of uncleanness described at Lev. 15, called in Hebrew the Zab, a person afflicted with flux uncleanness. Such a person transmits uncleanness to objects that bear his weight, even though not touching those objects – just as the corpse does in the Zoroastrian case – if the other party also is in motion by reason of the same cause, the movement of the ship or the raft or the beast.

Mishnah-tractate Zabim 3:1

A. The Zab and the clean person who sat in a ship or on a raft,
B. or who rode [together] on a beast,
C. even though their clothes do not touch –
D. lo, these are unclean with midras uncleanness.
E. [If] they sat on a plank, or on a bench, or on a bed frame, and on the beam,
F. when they are infirm –
G. [if] they climbed up on a tree which was shaky,

H.   on a branch which was shaky on a firm tree –
I.   [if they climbed up] on an Egyptian ladder when it is not fastened with a nail,
J.   on the bridge,
K.   and on the beam,
L.   and on the door,
M.   when they are not fastened with clay –
N.   they are unclean.
O.   R. Judah declares clean.

At Eff. we come to precisely the case before us: the Zab and the clean person are on the same plank, bench, bed frame or beam or tree or ladder or bridge; if these are shaky, then the clean person is made unclean. Why? Because the uncleanness of the Zab is transmitted to the clean person through the motion of the infirm bridge or other object. And that is the exact counterpart to the Zoroastrian detail, if the persons on the bridge are moving, too. The point of difference proves equally obvious: for the Mishnaic law, it is the bridge that is moving, for the Zoroastrian, the afflicted parties. For the one, the uncleanness is transmitted by the movement of the weight bearing component of the tableau, for the other, the movement of the candidate for uncleanness. In the following, we find the same principle:

M. Negaim 13:7

A.   The unclean [person] stands under the tree, and the clean person passes –
B.   he is unclean.
C.   The clean person stands under the tree, and the unclean passes –
D.   he is clean.
E.   If he stood, he is unclean.
F.   And so with the stone which is afflicted with plague – he is clean.
G.   And if he put it down, lo, this one is unclean.

Now if the unclean person is at rest (put the corpse down on the bridge) and the clean person walks by (add: and overshadows it, in line with Num. 19), then the clean person contracts uncleanness. The opposite is also the rule: if the uncleanness is in motion and the clean person or object at rest, then the clean person or object remains clean. So the distinction recurs, and makes the same difference, but, for the Judaic system, in reverse. The point of this arcane exercise should not be missed: we can readily identify, even in the most remote and hermetic chapters of the law of uncleanness of Iran and Israel, more than a few points of intersection, where the same principles and the same cases generate decisions that are either the same or the opposite: a fine problem for comparison and contrast indeed. And, I am sure readers will agree to stipulate, a search through the ninth-century documents (all the more so prior ones) will yield countless points of parallel and even intersection.[4] But until we have formed a theory of the whole, each system compared in its entirety to the other, these details remain inert facts, generating nothing beyond themselves. That is why, for the present purpose, a clear view of what we wish to find out has always to remain in plain sight. It is to compare the two traditions when they go over the same theme and reach comparable conclusions, a comparison that, once more, shows us how the documents differ where they are alike.

II. Master-Disciple Relationships

Certainly the two systems' orbits come close in their address to the relationship prized by each, that is, the one upon which the formulation and transmission of the great tradition ultimately depends: the relationship between master and disciple. That is how God's word has come down in both traditions. The myth of the Oral Torah, beginning with Moses at Sinai, rests upon that relationship; the claim of the ninth-century priests to set down the great tradition depends upon it as well.

In the Judaic case, it is through the chain of master-disciple relationships, extending forward from Sinai, that the tradition is formulated and transmitted. In the Zoroastrian case, in the two rivayat writings before us and also in the Pursishniha, the literary form – question, answer – and much of the contents as well presuppose the relationship of master and disciple, the one answering, the other asking questions. And in both cases, the model derives from the original moment of revelation: God instructing Moses at Sinai, Ohrmazd instructing Zoroaster. The Bavli's presentation – functioning as counterpart to the colloquy language utilized by our rivayat, is as follows:

Bavli Erubin 54B-55A

43.　A.　*Our rabbis have taught on Tannaite authority:*
　　　B.　What is the order of Mishnah teaching? Moses learned it from the mouth of the All-powerful. Aaron came in, and Moses repeated his chapter to him and Aaron went forth and sat at the left hand of

---

[4]A systematic comparison of the two systems' purity rules, encompassing the entirety of their respective canons (on the side of the Mishnah and Talmuds, Leviticus and Numbers and the Tosefta, for instance) would certainly yield a hypothesis on how the entirety of the two systems compare. One can work from details to the whole – and has to. Nonetheless, episodic intersection such as what is before us leaves open too many variables to allow for the forming of hypothesis on the comparison and contrast of the systems at hand. A fine preliminary effort in just the right direction is in A.V. Williams, "Zoroastrian and Jewish Purity Laws. Reflections on the Viability of a Sociological Interpretation," to be published in a future volume of *Irano-Judaica*.

Moses. His sons came in and Moses repeated their chapter to them, and his sons went forth. Eleazar sat at the right of Moses, and Itamar at the left of Aaron.

C.   R. Judah says, "At all times Aaron was at the right hand of Moses."

D.   Then the elders entered, and Moses repeated for them their Mishnah chapter. The elders went out. Then the whole people came in, and Moses repeated for them their Mishnah chapter. So it came about that Aaron repeated the lesson four times, his sons three times, the elders two times, and all the people once.

E.   Then Moses went out, and Aaron repeated his chapter for them. Aaron went out. His sons repeated their chapter. His sons went out. The elders repeated their chapter. So it turned out that everybody repeated the same chapter four times....

What we see here is characteristic of the Bavli: presentation of the fact, then systematic analysis of that fact.

Not only in myth, but also in law, the master-disciple relationship proves of critical interest to both traditions. For instance, the merit of a disciple accrues to the master; not only so, but if the disciple then teaches other disciples, "The merit of teaching the disciple to teach other disciples shall verily be unto the teacher. Unto those who shall so practice it, just as it is." Even those acts which the other teacher performs, it is just as if they perform [i.e., that which the disciple performs goes over to the teacher, and that which goes over to the disciple from other persons does not go over to the teacher]."[5] In the Judaic counterpart, the teacher enters into the status of the father and deserves the respect owing to the disciple's father by the disciple; and takes precedence over the father. The principle is the same, the details, diverse.

In that context, we compare rules of conduct delivered by masters to disciples. The form is essentially the same: an instruction by a named master to a disciple, consisting in both case of a long set of rules of proper attitude and action. I find the "counsels of Adurbad" and those of the Judaic sages in tractate Abot to serve the same purpose and to take the same form. For the sake of brevity, I give only the initial part Adurbad's counsels, also abbreviating the repertoire in tractate Abot:

Chapter Sixty-Two
Counsels of Adurbad, Son of Mansarspand,
from the Sayings of his Teacher Mihr Ohrmazd

There was a disciple of Adurbad of immortal soul, son of Mansarspand; he was with Adurbad for a long time.

---

[5]See Kaikhusroo M. Jamaspa and Helmut Humbach, *Pursishniha. A Zoroastrian Catechism* (Wiesbaden, 1971: Otto Harrassowitz), Part I. *Text, Translation, Notes*, p. 29-31.

And this indeed he said to Adurbad: "Instruct me, so that when I go forth from the presence of the teacher instruction of my soul can then [proceed] better on account of that."

Adurbad said: "Be certain [in faith] in the yazads. Keep your thought, speech and action honest and true. Neither think nor speak nor do any sin whatsoever, and may you be blessed."

And the disciple said: "O teacher, I am not perfect in this, give me special instruction, so that I shall practice it and I shall be blessed."

Adurbad said: "Consider the twenty-two precepts of Mihr Ohrmazd, my teacher; understand all [of them], put them into practice and may you be blessed!"

The disciple said: "If you consider me as worthy, please tell [me the precepts], so that I may understand and practice [accordingly]."

Adurbad said in reply: "The precepts [are] these three kinds of generosity, fourth truthfulness, fifth virtuousness, sixth diligence, seventh intercession, eighth trustworthiness, ninth peace seeking, tenth law-abidingness, eleventh union, twelfth laying down of weapons, thirteenth moderation, fourteenth lowliness, fifteenth humility, sixteenth modesty, seventeenth pleasantness, eighteenth completeness [of mind], nineteenth patience, twentieth love for people, twenty-first contentedness, twenty-second oneness [of mind].

"The best generosity: first, he who is not asked but gives; second, he who is asked [and] gives immediately; third, he who is asked and fixes a time and does [his giving] on time. He [is] best, who, when he gives, entertains no hope as regards that [receiver of his generosity, thinking]: 'He will give (it) back to me'; he does not give for the sake of acquiring trade, nor for the sake of covetousness...."

What we have is a catalogue of virtues, systematically expounded as a handbook for the good life. I fail to see any material differences, in the chosen form of transmitting a tradition on good attitude and action, from the mode of tractate Abot, in the following (also abbreviated) reprise:

Tractate Abot Chapter Three
Chapter Four

4:1 Ben Zoma says, "Who is a sage? He who learns from everybody, as it is said, 'From all my teachers I have gotten understanding' (Ps. 119:99). Who is strong? He who overcomes his desire, as it is said, 'He who is slow to anger is better than the mighty, and he who rules his spirit than he who takes a city' (Prov. 16:32). Who is rich? He who is happy in what he has, as it is said, 'When you eat the labor of your hands, happy will you be, and it will go well with you' (Ps. 128:2). ('Happy will you be – in this world, and it will go well with you – in the world to come.') Who is honored? He who honors everybody, as it is said, 'For those who honor me I shall honor, and they who despise me will be treated as of no account' (1 Sam. 2:30)."

In both cases an important component of the master-disciple relationship is the transmission of wisdom on proper conduct. In both instances, the master is named, and in both cases, a liturgy is tacked on to the end of the catalogue of virtuous attitudes and behavior. To be sure, this kind of writing would have presented no surprise to sages and disciples who flourished from the remotest times of writing onward; Sumerian, Akkadian, Egyptian, not to mention Greek and Roman writers recorded the same kind of advice, and even much the same advice (recommendations of arrogance are vastly outnumbered in the literature by the counsel of humility, but, to be sure, praise of masters' humility is outweighed in volume by complaints about their arrogance). But in the Zoroastrian and Judaic writings, the master-disciple relationship finds definition in not only generalizations but detailed rules, and that is what makes the comparison particular to the two cases and distinctive as well.

III. Father-Son or Master-Disciple Relationships

The comparison of the relationship of father to son and master to disciple comes to expression in this rivayat in the revelation by Ohrmazd to Zoroaster on the rule – parallel in the two relationships – governing law suits between persons of said classifications. The tradition tells the judge how to adjudicate a case in which each party presents evidence of the same weight as that of the other. In that case, the judge is to favor the master or the father, who has nurtured him. Indeed, the father, and, by extension, the master, owns the earnings of the son or disciple and the merit of his good deeds, as though the father of the master had done those deeds himself:

Chapter Twenty-Nine
The Privileges of Seniority

This also [is] revealed, Ohrmazd said to Zoroaster: "If a father is engaged in a lawsuit with his son, or a herbad with his pupil, or a father-in-law with his son-in-law, and if the father [has] one witness on his side, and the son one witness on his, make the decision in favour of the father, and entrust the property [at stake] to the father, for this reason that the good that the father does for his son, the son can never repay that goodness. He has nurtured him from childhood and immaturity until that [time] when he becomes an adult. Indeed according to this saying: 'Until a son is 15 years old his nurture [comes] from his father,' then also so long as he [i.e., the father] [is] alive the [son's] earnings belong to the father, and all the good deeds which the son does will thus belong to the father as if he had done them with his own hands."

What attracts our attention is two facts, first, the reason – the father has nurtured the son, and the master is in the status of the father and so is deemed to have nurtured him, too – and second the consequence, the father or master owns the son's earnings and merits. We find the same issue worked out along intersecting lines in the following:

Mishnah-tractate Baba Mesia 2:11

A. [If one has to choose between seeking] what he has lost and what his father has lost,

B. his own takes precedence.

C. [If he has to choose between seeking] what he has lost and what his master has lost,

D. his own takes precedence.

E. [If he has to choose between seeking] what his father has lost and what his master has lost,

F. that of his master takes precedence.

G. For his father brought him into this world.

H. But his master, who has taught him wisdom, will bring him into the life of the world to come.

I. But if his father is a sage, that of his father takes precedence.

J. [If] his father and his master were carrying heavy burdens, he removes that of his master, and afterward removes that of his father.

K. [If] his father and his master were taken captive,

L. he ransoms his master, and afterward he ransoms his father.

M. But if his father is a sage, he ransoms his father, and afterward he ransoms his master.

The issue is framed in different terms, of course, since it is the son who has the decision to make, not the judge. And the son has to give priority to his own interest, for a reason that the Talmud will immediately want to uncover. At issue is when he (not the judge) has to choose between his father and his master. The answer, however, would have interested the author of our rivayat, since the Mishnah rule carries forward the same principle as the Zoroastrian one: the master enters into the status of the father. The Mishnah cannot imagine that the master or father will take over the property or the merit of good deeds of the son.

But the framer of the Bavli wants to know why the son's interests take priority, and that is, I assume, in light of the commandment to honor father and mother. The answer follows:

I.1 A. What is the scriptural source of this rule ["**his own takes precedence**"]?

B. Said R. Judah said Rab, "Said Scripture, 'Except that there shall be no poor among you' (Deut. 15:4). Your own takes precedence over anybody else's."

C. But said R. Judah said Rab, "Whoever treats himself in such a way will end up in such a condition [of poverty]."

II.1 A. [If] his father and his master were carrying heavy burdens, he removes that of his master, and afterward removes that of his father.

B. Our rabbis have taught on Tannaite authority:

C.   "The master of which they have spoken is the one who taught
      him wisdom, not the master who taught him Scripture or
      Mishnah," the words of R. Meir.

D.   R. Judah says, "It is anyone from whom he has gained the greater
      part of his learning."

E.   R. Yosé says, "Even someone who has enlightened his eyes in his
      repetition of a single Mishnah paragraph – lo, this is his master"
      [T. B.M. 2:30D-F].

F.   Said Raba, "For example, R. Sehorah, who explained to me the
      meaning of the words that stand for a certain utensil [at M. Kel.
      13:2]."

II.2 A.   Samuel tore his garment as a mark of mourning for one of the
            rabbis, who had merely taught him the meaning of the phrase, **one
            of the keys goes into the duct as far as the armpit and the other
            opens the door directly [M. Tam. 3:6E].**

II.3 A.   Said Ulla, "Disciples of sages who are located in Babylonia stand up
            in respect to one another and tear their garments in mourning for
            one another.

      B.   "But as to returning a lost object, in a case in which there is a choice
            between his father [and his master], he goes first of all in search of
            his master only when it is his principal teacher."

The Bavli's initial contribution, as is commonly the case, links the
Mishnah's rule to a source in the Written Torah. The proof is such as to
eliminate possibility that the father or master owns the son's or disciple's
property. The Talmud's next step is to enrich the discussion through the
qualification produced by Tosefta's supplement: defining the master who
counts. Here we recall the rivayat's distinction between a disciple who
does not teach others and the one who does; the master gets credit for the
good deeds of the disciple who teaches others. We find ourselves
moving in the reverse direction: the identification of the master who
enjoys the status that is subject to discussion here. No. 3 pursues the
same matter. The difference in the presentation of the rule becomes
apparent here: the rivayat gives rules, the Bavli undertakes a systematic
analysis of them. Information by itself is insufficient; sustained, applied
reason and practical logic transform information into truth and insight.
The next point of intersection yields the same formal contrast between
the two writings.

IV. Husband-Wife Relationships: The Wife's Perfect Obedience

The Zoroastrian code finds it possible to say in a few words precisely
what the wife owes the husband, which is perfect and unquestioning
obedience to his will in all matters; and anyhow, she shouldn't torment
him. Between the ritual ideal, on the one side, and the concession to the
everyday, on the other, presumably lies what can be expected. On the
Judaic side, the same thing is spelled out in more concrete ways, the

Mishnah being a far more detailed document than the two rivayats before us (or the Pursishniha, for that matter):

Chapter Thirty-Nine
Wife and Husband

This [question]: how should a wife behave towards her husband?

The wife of *padixsay* [status] should consult her husband three times every day saying: "What do you require when I think and speak and act, for I do not know what is required when I think and speak and act, tell [me], so that I will think and speak and act as you require?" Then she must do everything that the righteous husband tells her, and she should refrain from tormenting and afflicting her husband.

The concrete obligations of the woman to the man in Judaism convey the same attitude, but because of their specificity, place some (few) limits on the husband's caprice:

Mishnah-tractate Ketubot 5:5

A. These are the kinds of labor which a woman performs for her husband:

B. she (1) grinds flour, (2) bakes bread, (3) does laundry, (4) prepares meals, (5) gives suck to her child, (6) makes the bed, (7) works in wool.

C. [If] she brought with her a single slave girl, she does not (1) grind, (2) bake bread, or (3) do laundry.

D. [If she brought] two, she does not (4) prepare meals and does not (5) feed her child.

E. [If she brought] three, she does not (6) make the bed for him and does not (7) work in wool.

F. If she brought four, she sits on a throne.

G. R. Eliezer says, "Even if she brought him a hundred slave girls, he forces her to work in wool,

H. "for idleness leads to unchastity."

I. Rabban Simeon b. Gamaliel says, "Also: He who prohibits his wife by a vow from performing any labor puts her away and pays off her marriage contract. For idleness leads to boredom."

The Bavli's reading of the rule follows, in abbreviated form. The traits we have found characteristic recur here.

I.1 A. **Grinds flour:**

B. *Under what circumstances [can we imagine that a woman would grind flour, which involves moving heavy machinery]?*

C. *Read:* taking charge of the grinding.

D. And if you prefer: grinding with a hand mill.

I.2 A. *Our Mishnah paragraph is not in accord with R. Hiyya, for R. Hiyya set forth the following Tannaite rule:*

B. [Marrying] a woman is only for her beauty, only for children.

C. *And R. Hiyya set forth the following Tannaite rule:*

D. A wife is for wearing women's ornaments.

E. *And R. Hiyya set forth the following Tannaite rule:*

F. *He who wants his wife to be attractive should dress her in linen clothes. He who wants his daughter to have a bright skin should feed her young chicken and give her plenty of milk to drink as she comes toward her first period.*

II.1 A. **Gives suck to her child:**

B. *May one say that this does not accord with the position of the House of Shammai? For it has been taught on Tannaite authority:*

C. **If she took a vow not to give suck to her child,**

D. **the House of Shammai say, "She pulls her teats from the child's mouth."**

E. **And the House of Hillel say, "He can force her to give suck to her child."**

F. **If she was divorced, however, they do not force her to give suck to him.**

G. **If her son recognized her as his mother, they give her a wage, and she gives suck to him, because of the danger to the child's life. The husband cannot force his wife to give suck to the child of his fellow, and the wife cannot force her husband to permit her to give suck to the child of her girlfriend [T. Ket. 5:5A-H].**

H. *Well, you may even maintain that the House of Shammai stand behind our Mishnah paragraph. Here with what case do we deal? It is a case in which she took the oath and he confirmed it for her. The House of Shammai take the view that he has put his finger between her teeth [the vow is his fault], and the House of Hillel maintain that she put her finger between his teeth....*

III.1 A. **[If] she brought with her a single slave girl, she does not (1) grind, (2) bake bread, or (3) do laundry:**

B. *But the rest of the duties she has to do.*

C. *But why can't she say to him, "I brought you another woman in my place [for all manner of work, not just for this]"?*

D. *Because he can say to her, "That slave girl works for me and for herself, who's going to work for you?"*

IV.1 A. **[If she brought] two, she does not (4) prepare meals and does not (5) feed her child:**

B. *But the rest of the duties she has to do.*

C. *But why can't she say to him, "I brought you another woman in my place [for all manner of work, not just for this], and she's going to work for me and for her, and the first one will work for you and for herself"?*

D. *Because he can say to her, "So who's going to work for our guests and visitors?"*

V.1 A. **[If she brought] three, she does not (6) make the bed for him and does not (7) work in wool:**

B. *But the rest of the duties she has to do.*

C. *But why can't she say to him, "I brought you a third one still, to work for our guests and visitors"?*

D. *Because he can say to her, "The bigger the household, the more numerous the guests and the visitors."*

E. *If so, then even if she brought in four, you could have the same colloquy!*

F. *If there are four, since they are that many, they help one another.*

This drastically abbreviated presentation of the Bavli's analysis points in an obvious direction, which we may discern by noting that what is of special interest to us in the Bavli is not the rule, but the mode of representing it. Here, clearly, we come to the principal point of difference between this Rivayat and the Bavli, when the two writings intersect.

To state the difference in a simple way: What should we have found in the Rivayat, had the words, "The wife of *padixsay* [status] should consult her husband three times every day saying: 'What do you require when I think and speak and act, for I do not know what is required when I think and speak and act, tell (me), so that I will think and speak and act as you require,'" been followed by:

1. What is the source [in the Avesta or Gathas] of this rule? or
2. Under what circumstances?
3. This rule is not in accord with the following, known in some other compilation?

Then again, if we had the same rule, following by, "may we say this does not accord with the position of...," followed by a contrary view in some other source, what should the rivayat have looked like? Or if we had, "if the husband said...," and then, "but does she have to do no more?" what shape would the writing have taken? The answer is simple: we should have had something very like the Bavli. And we do not have anything like the Bavli.

V. Commercial Relationships: True Value

Our final specific comparison of the two traditions as they intersect on the same matter concerns the conception of true value. That theory maintains that an object possesses an intrinsic and inherent value, which is distinct from the price that the market sets on the same object (that is, what an informed buyer and informed seller are willing to pay and to receive for the object to change hands). The notion of true value logically belongs together with the conception of money as an item of barter or meant merely to facilitate barter, because both notions referred to the single underlying conception of the economy as a steady state entity in which people could not increase wealth but only exchange it. Fraud involves not adulteration of a product or misrepresentation of the character or quality of merchandise, such as we should grasp but simply charging more than something is worth, and that can only mean, than something is worth intrinsically.

The Zoroastrian formulation maintains that if an object has a true value of four, and one sells it elsewhere for ten, he may not retain six; he may keep the four that he paid, plus his expenses and his wages, and the rest of the profit goes to a meritorious purpose. Now the given is that, in that other place, the object has a true value of ten. Then the man is governed by the criterion of the true value set by the place in which he bought the object, not the place in which he sold it.

Trading and Acquisition of Wealth

This [question]: How should trading take place so that there will be no sin in it?

When [a trader] buys for four drachms a single piece of clothing, worth four drachms, and he takes it to another town, and [in] the place where he takes it it is worth ten drachms, he sells it for ten drachms, and takes out of it wages and daily sustenance for himself and his horse, and he gives away what remains [of it] as a righteous gift, it is a [work of] great merit.

"True value" then is negotiated in relationship to market value. That is, the "true value" of four, set at the time of purchase, has to be brought into relationship with the true value of ten, which the market has placed on the object in that other place. We take account of the difference between the true value, which is the purchase price where the trader lives, and the market value, by refunding the difference between the market price and the true value in acts of piety.

The Mishnah expresses the identical notion, that an object possesses a true value. But it sets forth the idea in a different context. It speaks of an "overcharge," meaning, what the market has paid for an item that exceeds true value; true value then is a fixed and known value, and "fraud" or overreaching is whatever the market pays over and above that value, which is anything more than 16.667 percent above true value. The difference has to be refunded:

Mishnah-tractate Baba Mesia 4:3

A.   Fraud [overreaching] is an overcharge of four pieces of silver out of twenty-four pieces of silver to the sela –
B.   one-sixth of the purchase price.
C.   For how long is it permitted to retract [in the case of fraud]?
D.   So long as it takes to show [the article] to a merchant or a relative [who will know the true value of the object that one has bought].

Fraud here is simply a charge higher than the intrinsic worth of the object permits. That definition rejects the conception of "free" and "market," that redundancy that insists upon the market as the instrument of the rationing of scarce resources. If an object has a true value of twenty-four and the seller pays twenty-eight, he has been defrauded and may retract. Tarfon gave and took, E-K. What is expressed here are, first, the notion of a just price, second, the emphasis upon barter. The reason is that the logic of the one demanded the complementary logic of the other. Once we impute a true value to an object or commodity, we shall also dismiss from consideration all matters of worth extrinsic to the object or commodity; hence money is not an abstract symbol of worth but itself a commodity, and, further, objects bear true value.

The Talmud's amplification of the matter addresses ambiguities in the Mishnah's rule – once more the point of departure of the Talmud from the Rivayat:

I.1   A.   It has been stated:

       B.   Rab said, "What we have learned to repeat in the Mishnah is, 'a six of the purchase price [reckoned at true value]' [**one-sixth of the purchase price**]."

       C.   And Samuel said, "A sixth of the money paid also was taught."

       D.   *Obviously if something worth six was sold for five or seven, all parties concur that we follow the purchase price and if there was overreaching by one-sixth, [the law of fraud is invoked]. Then what is at issue? It would be a case in which something worth five or seven was sold for six.*

       E.   *As to Samuel, who has said that we follow the money paid as well, in both instances there is a valid claim of fraud.*

       F.   *But in the view of Rab, who has said that we follow only the purchase price, then if something worth five went for six, the sale is invalid, but if something worth seven is sold for six [so it is only a seventh of the true value of the purchase price], then the seller is deemed to have renounced part of what is really coming to him.*

       G.   *And Samuel said, "When do we maintain that there is renunciation by the seller or invalidation of the sale? Only if there is not a sixth variation from true value on either side [whether we regard the true purchase price or the money paid (Freedman)], but if there is a sixth of variation on one side, then it is a case of fraud."*

Enough of the Talmud is before us to show how a sustained analysis of the secondary issue raised by Rab and Samuel is set forth. So the simple rule at hand requires amplification and clarification. Had this Rivayat's author wished to address the problem, he could well have given us an entirely factual statement along the same lines; he certainly could have told us how to calculate the overcharge, if his formulation (4/10) had left any point of unclarity. So in comparison, the issue is not where the presentations of the rule differ, rather, it is the mode of discourse. When the two great traditions make the same or similar points, they do so in strikingly different ways, and that fact points to the paramount definitive trait of the Judaism put forth by the Talmud of Babylonia. Any account of the history of Judaism must answer the simple question: How shall we account for the remarkable power of that Talmud to define Judaism? In this comparison one answer is adumbrated.[6] One point is clear from the comparison at hand: the Bavli conveys its messages at two levels, one, on the surface, a message of rules, regulations, theological requirements; another, beneath the surface, a measure conveyed through hermeneutics.[7] Now, when we come to hermeneutics, we return to our starting point: the fine scholarly record of Lou H. Silberman, who carried forward the Talmudic tradition of saying one thing, but conveying many, through the depth of thought set forth in clear and lucid ways.

---

[6]In the following monograph in seven parts I have given my answer to this larger question in a systematic comparison of the two Talmuds and an identification of how the second is intellectually unique: *The Bavli's Unique Voice. A Systematic Comparison of the Talmud of Babylonia and the Talmud of the Land of Israel. I. Bavli and Yerushalmi Qiddushin Chapter One Compared and Contrasted; II. Yerushalmi's, Bavli's, and Other Canonical Documents' Treatment of the Program of Mishnah-Tractate Sukkah Chapters One, Two, and Four Compared and Contrasted. A Reprise and Revision of* The Bavli and Its Sources; *III. Bavli and Yerushalmi to Selected Mishnah-Chapters in the Division of Moed. Erubin Chapter One, and Moed Qatan Chapter Three; IV. Bavli and Yerushalmi to Selected Mishnah-Chapters in the Division of Nashim. Gittin Chapter Five and Nedarim Chapter One; V. Bavli and Yerushalmi to Selected Mishnah Chapters in the Division of Neziqin. Baba Mesia Chapter One and Makkot Chapters One and Two; VI. Bavli and Yerushalmi to a Miscellany of Mishnah Chapters. Gittin Chapter One, Qiddushin Chapter Two, and Hagigah Chapter Three; VII. What Is Unique about the Bavli in Context? An Answer Based on Inductive Description, Analysis, and Comparison.*

[7]And this second clearly forms a theological statement of considerable profundity, made through the medium of hermeneutics. This I spell out in my *Judaism States its Theology: The Talmudic Re-Presentation* (in press).

Appendix Two

Comparing Judaic and Zoroastrian Law: The Pahlavi Rivayat of Aturfarnbag and the Mishnah and the Talmud of Babylonia

What we shall see in this second of the two exercises in comparative law confirms what is already clear. Where the two compilations – Judaic and Zoroastrian – deal with the same thing and even make the same general point about public policy – the provision of a share of the father's estate for the daughter, the inviolability of a prenuptial agreement with the wife, the return of stolen goods, the status of a vow concerning something not then in existence – they differ in a predictable way. And where they intersect, asking the same questions about the same legal relationships, they tend to reach the same conclusions as well. What this and the preceding appendix therefore demonstrate therefore is that comparison is entirely justified: we really are comparing like to like, to uncover points of difference.

In the first of the two Pahlavi law books we shall consider, *The Pahlavi Rivayat of Aturfarnbag and Farnbag Srosh,* translated by Behramgore Bahmuras Anklesaria, (Bombay, 1969: Kaikhusroo M. Jamasp Asa), Aturfarnbag answers 147 questions; his questions and answers were collected in book form; but the unit of thought is the question and the answer. Following Anklesaria's summary, we note that Nos. 2-5 deal with the problem of a wife whose husband apostatized, that is, abandoned the religion; what is the status of his wife, who now is without a guardian, her guardianship having been vested in the husband: "As she could not remarry without being given away by her guardian, who could not be an independent wife without being handed over in marriage by her guardian, so she is in the status of one who has married without her guardian's consent." Nos. 6-17, 19-20 deal with guardianship in other aspects. Nos. 18, 21-28 deal with a man who has no son to inherit his wealth and who accepts a person as his adoptive child, male or female. Nos. 29-30 deal with the wickedness of a wife or child. Nos. 31-33, 34-36, 37-50, 54-55, 63-65, deal with purity rules, corpse uncleanness, and the like. Nos. 51, 56-59 deal with personal injuries, 52-53 with those who commit the sin of removing the sacred thread girdle. Nos. 66-69, 72 deal with civil suits, involving lending and borrowing, mortgage of property, and the like; also jailing debtors. Further issues of purity rules follow, to the end.[1] We shall now undertake some episodic comparisons between Aturfarnbag's rivayat and comparable statements of the Talmud of Babylonia. We take up family, then civil law.

I. Exercising the Right of Refusal

A minor girl may be assigned by her father to a man as wife, but, when she comes of age (generally: puberty) both Talmudic and Zoroastrian law accords her the right to confirm or nullify the marriage. The issue is, what is the status of the relationship during the girl's minority? And what is her status should she exercise the right of refusal and decide to leave the relationship altogether? The issue is, does she revert to the father's control, so that he can marry her off again (Bavli) or does she revert to his control so he can assign her guardianship to someone else (Rivayat)? Specifically, once he has given her away, has the father any further rights over the daughter, or is she now an independent woman (both)?

XII

Question

1. When a man gives a three-year-old daughter to a man in wifehood; and that daughter attains to majority, and says: "I do not consent to marry this man," with whom will the guardianship rest? If that man says: "Unless thou wilt be my wife, I will not give thee to anyone under guardianship," can that daughter secure a guardian? If she marries, will her status be of an independent woman or not?

Reply

2. As I understand: the wifehood cannot take place; the guardianship shall have been given; and if her father will not

---

[1]Anklesaria, pp. 36-44.

withdraw the guardianship during the length of his life, the guardianship will rest with him to whom he will give after the father; and if he says, "If thou will not be my wife, I will not give thee to thy husband," he is rightful; if the husband is agreeable to cause the menstruation month to pass in marriage and the spouse be not agreeable, the sin of the menstruation month originates with the spouse.

Aturfarnbag's formulation of the problem rests on the fact that no woman can remain without a guardian; if the woman's guardian died without appointing another in his place, or without appointing her as her own guardian, she becomes the ward of the community, who finds a guardian for her. Now in our case, the father gives the daughter at the age of three years in marriage; she gets the husband as guardian. If she comes of age after the father's death and becomes independent, she would have the right to reject her husband as guardian, but then she has to have some other guardian in his place (Anklesaria, pp. 38-39). So, while the father as guardian may give her in marriage, the girl being forbidden to marry without his consent, the father also may appoint another person as the daughter's guardian during his lifetime and he can also revoke the guardianship if she agrees. Now the husband would take over as guardian.

Here is the Mishnah's and Talmud's treatment of the same matter. The issue is framed differently. But the basic principle is the same, namely, the girl married off prior to puberty has the right, at puberty, to dissolve the relationship. The Mishnah's concern is, what kind of prior relationship may be dissolved, for the Mishnah knows two stages in which a woman is designated for a particular man, betrothal and the fully consummated marriage. Here the dispute is, may a girl upon reaching puberty leave a fully consummated marriage?

Mishnah-tractate Yebamot 13:1

A. The House of Shammai say, "Only girls who are [merely] betrothed exercise the right of refusal."

B. And the House of Hillel say, "Those who are betrothed and those who are married."

C. The House of Shammai say, "[The right of refusal is exercised] against the husband, but not against the levir" [the deceased childless husband's surviving brother, with whom the girl has entered into levirate marriage, as dictated by Deut. 25:5-10].

D. And the House of Hillel say, "Against the husband and against the levir."

E. The House of Shammai say, "[It must be exercised only] in his presence."

F. And the House of Hillel say, "In his presence and not in his presence."

G. The House of Shammai say, "[It must be exercised] in a court."

H. And the House of Hillel say, "In a court and not in a court."

I. Said the House of Hillel to the House of Shammai, "She may exercise the right of refusal while she is a minor, even four or five times."

J. Replied to them the House of Shammai, "Israelite girls are not to be tossed around like so much ownerless property.

K. "But: She exercises the right of refusal and waits until she reaches maturity, or she exercises the right of refusal and remarries [forthwith]."

I.1 A. [The House of Shammai say, "Only girls who are [merely] betrothed exercise the right of refusal":] Said R. Judah said Samuel, *"What is the operative consideration in the mind of the House of Shammai?* It is because a stipulation may not be attached to a marriage, so if a girl who is married should exercise the right of refusal, *people will come to maintain that* a stipulation may be attached to a marriage.

B. "If the girl had entered the marriage canopy but not had sexual relations, *however, what is to be said?*

C. "It is because a stipulation may not be attached to entry into the marriage canopy.

D. "If the father had already handed over the daughter to the agent of the husband, *however, what is to be said?*

E. *"Rabbis made no such distinction [as to the phases of the marriage procedure].*

F. *"What is the operative consideration in the mind of the House of Hillel?*

G. *"People in general are informed that the marriage of a minor is only on the strength of rabbis' authority."*

I.2 A. *Rabbah and R. Joseph both say, "The operative consideration in the mind of the House of Shammai is that* a man does not treat an act of sexual relations on his part as one of mere fornication.

B. "If the girl had entered the marriage canopy but not had sexual relations, *however, what is to be said?*

C. *"It is because the husband doesn't want his marriage canopy to involve a forbidden act.*

D. "If the father had already handed over the daughter to the agent of the husband, *however, what is to be said?*

E. *"Rabbis made no such distinction [as to the phases of the marriage procedure].*

F. *"What is the operative consideration in the mind of the House of Hillel?*

G. *"Since the process involves a betrothal and a marriage contract, people are never going to say that* an act of sexual relations on his part is one of mere fornication."

I.3 A. *R. Pappa said, "The operative consideration in the mind of the House of Shammai is on account of the usufruct [of the plucking property that belongs to the minor].*

B. *"And the operative consideration in the mind of the House of Hillel also is on account of the usufruct [of the plucking property that belongs to the minor].*

C. *"The operative consideration in the mind of the House of Shammai is on account of the usufruct: For if you say that a married girl has the right of refusal, her husband will grab the fruit and eat it up, since she may leave him any time.*

D.   *"The House of Hillel? To the contrary, if you say that she may exercise the right of refusal, he is going to improve the property, thinking that, if not, her relatives will advise her and take her from him."*

I.4   A.   *Raba said, "This is the operative consideration of the House of Shammai:* A man will not go to the trouble of making a banquet and then lose all he has spent.

    B.   *"And the House of Hillel? Both parties are glad to be married to one another, so that they may be known as married."*

The issue is a vital one: What is the status of the marriage of the prepubescent girl? The House of Shammai treat it as an ordinary marriage, once the marriage has been consummated, and they will want a writ of divorce, not merely a public declaration of refusal. The further explanations of what is at stake present no surprises and speak for themselves. The contrast between the Bavli's presentation of the rule of the prepubescent marriage and the Rivayat's hardly requires extensive explanation. Aturfarnbag gives us the rule, the Mishnah provides a dispute and the Bavli, an explanation of the issues that inhere in the dispute (with the proviso that all parties know that the law follows the position of the House of Hillel).

Now if we set the statements side by side, we see reasonable justification for comparing the passages in the shared problem. But dealing with the dissolution of the prepubescent marriage, each party has its distinctive considerations, which render further comparison somewhat puzzling. The issue of guardianship does not intersect with the issue of the status of the marriage that may or may not be dissolved. To be sure, our sages of blessed memory know the issue of the future standing of the girl who has exercised the right of refusal, and this is discussed in later passages of the present chapter of the Mishnah and Talmud But the details of the presentation serve to distinguish the one from the other treatment of the common issue. At the same time, we may legitimately point to an obvious point of difference. In presenting the same subject, the two documents differ in a fundamental way. Aturfarnbag provides information: question and answer. Had he chosen to present his ideas in the form of the Mishnah, he could readily have done so, for example:

> When a man gives a three-year-old daughter to a man in wifehood; and that daughter attains to majority, and says: "I do not consent to marry this man," the guardianship shall have been given; and if her father will not withdraw the guardianship during the length of his life, the guardianship will rest with him to whom he will give after the father; and if he says, "If thou will not be my wife, I will not give thee to thy husband," he is rightful; if the husband is agreeable to cause the menstruation month to pass in marriage and the spouse

be not agreeable, the sin of the menstruation month originates with the spouse.

All I have done is restate the language before us from question and answer to declarative sentence to come up with a statement that, with the required changes, could have taken up a comfortable residence in the Mishnah; or it could have stood in the Talmud as a proposition awaiting analysis, for example:

> Rabbah said, "When a man gives a three year old daughter to a man in wifehood; and that daughter attains to majority, and says: 'I do not consent to marry this man,' she has not got the right [the marriage is valid despite her wishes]. Under what circumstance? If the marriage was consummated. But if she was only betrothed, she has the right."

Someone then has to tell us that Rabbah has taken the position of the House of Shammai, and that problem will have to be resolved in one of the various ways available for that purpose.

So, except for "Rabbah said," and its ubiquitous counterparts throughout the Bavli, I find nothing that distinguishes the question-and-answer form from the propositional statement of the law. Where the Bavli differs is at the point that the Bavli takes over the Mishnah paragraph and conducts its analysis. Here, our interest not in the rule but its theory or premise or underlying principle does carry us far from the stated concerns of Aturfarnbag, who rarely tells us more than the rule. So while, making provision for obvious differences, we can treat Aturfarnbag's work as analogous to that of Judah the Patriarch, to whom authorship of the Mishnah is attributed, it most certainly is not analogous to that of the authors of the Talmud.

II. When Equal Shares in an Inheritance Have Been Guaranteed

At issue for both legal systems is a prenuptial agreement, assuring the wife that her children will take equal shares of his estate. Is the husband bound by that agreement, or may he give more to one and less to another? Further, if a daughter marries during the husband's lifetime, is her status changed in respect to that original agreement? The issue is phrased fairly clearly in our Rivayat, the answer being: the agreement is firm.

LXII

Question

1. There is a man who makes an agreement with his wife and says: "The children who are born of thee are made co-partners and joint owners"; and thereafter, to the children

who are born of that wife; can that man give a greater share
of his property to some one of the children, and less to some
one? The father hands over to the husband the daughter
who is born of that wife; is a share of the property hers after
the father or not?

Reply
2.   An equal share belongs to sons and daughters, and one
cannot do otherwise; if the daughter takes a husband when
her father is alive, even then the share goes to her by way of
justice and lawfulness.

The two important points, which can have been stated as a legal
proposition, contain no ambiguity: the agreement stands firm, even if the
daughter marries while the father is alive. The framing of the issue in the
Mishnah and Talmud focuses upon a different problem, namely, a
conventional stipulation that is left unarticulated. If the husband made
no commitment regarding the wife's offspring in the union, nonetheless,
the stipulation that is routine is held to prevail. The topic is the same,
but the problematic quite different.

Mishnah-tractate Ketubot 4:10

A.   **[If] he did not write for her, "Male children which you will have
with me will inherit the proceeds of your marriage contract, in
addition to their share with their other brothers,"**

B.   **he nonetheless is liable [to pay over the proceeds of the marriage
contract to the woman's sons],**

C.   **for this is [in all events] an unstated condition imposed by the
court.**

It is clear that the rule as stated by the Mishnah expresses the same
fundamental policy as in the Rivayat, namely, the wife's expectations in
regard to the disposition of the husband's estate are to be honored,
whether circumstances change (the Rivayat) or the expectations are not
even articulated.

III. Disposing of an Inheritance of Thievery

How a family disposes of an inheritance that has been amassed
through the father's sinfulness presents a problem to the framers of the
rules for both communities. Aturfarnbag's question is framed in his
circumstance, use of the money for ceremonies for the father's soul or for
the souls of those who inherit the wealth, the Talmud's addresses their
problem: how to right the wrong done by the father.

CXLI

Question

1.   Can the man who obtains from his father wealth which is
     accumulated with unrighteousness, enjoy that wealth, and
     make a provision for duty and good deeds or not? And if he
     performs out of it ceremonies for his own soul and even that
     of his father, will they reach their souls or not ?

Reply

2.   For all the wealth which the father had accumulated before
     the coming forth of the child, I cannot understand his child
     to be a sharer in his sins or good deeds; and then when it
     comes into the possession and authority of the child, he shall
     return, whatever he knows as having been obtained from the
     thief or the robber; a half or one-third, just as the Dasturs
     may direct, and he shall restore the rest, that which is worthy
     of him; and he shall make provision according to religious
     usage, just as may be very helpful, for the expiation of the
     sins of his father; as to that of which he does not know
     anything, as he himself is authorized to keep the wealth in
     his possession, it is good that he shall, in all respects perform
     ceremonies, votive-offerings, and other works of merit for
     the soul of his father, for making the atonement of the sins of
     his father and by way of good deeds even for the sake of the
     soul of his father, so that he may expiate the sins and
     impurities, and the indebtedness of his father; for the
     expiation of sin is the most compulsory work of merit,
     whereby glory and radiance are increased.

The child is in no way responsible for what the father has done, but the
child has nonetheless to seek to restore part of what is known to have
been stolen, as he is instructed to do. But as to what is not known to
have been stolen, he can keep it and do good with it, for both himself and
his father's soul. The key then is knowledge and intentionality. If one
knows something has been stolen, he cannot keep it but must restore it in
the proper manner; if he does not know that an object has been stolen,
then mere suspicion is null; one does good with what he has.

10:1A-C

A.   He who steals [food] and feeds [what he stole] to his children, or
     left it to them –
B.   they are exempt from making restitution.
C.   But if it remained something which could serve as security [e.g.,
     subject to a mortgage, that is, real estate], they are liable to make
     restitution.

The Mishnah's distinction is a different one. If what has been stolen is movable or intangible and has been consumed, the beneficiaries are exempt from all further obligation. The reason has yet to be explained; the operative consideration is whether or not title is retained by the victims of the theft or has passed to the thief. As to the heirs, the rule is unambiguous. If they cannot restore what they have received from the father's wrongful action, they are not responsible. But if it is a matter of real property, that has to be restored. The rule is then simpler and does not invoke the consideration of intentionality; and the disposition of the property also is not subjected to extraneous considerations, for example, doing good with it. What is the heirs' is theirs, and what should not be theirs is restored. But the Talmud immediately adds the issue of intentionality – now with reference to the victim.

I.1   A.   Said R. Hisda, "If one stole something [such as an animal], and, before the owner had despaired of getting it back [at which point the thief acquires title to the object], someone else came along and ate up what he stole, the owner has the choice of collecting the payment from the one or the other." *How come? The reason is that, for so long as the owner did not despair of getting the thing back, the stolen object is still in the title of the original owner.*

Our problem is tangential to the Mishnah's rule and immediately revises the discussion by introducing a distinct problem. That problem then is referred back to our Mishnah rule for solution.

B.   *But have we not learned in the Mishnah:* **He who steals [food] and feeds [what he stole] to his children, or left it to them – they are exempt from making restitution. But if it was something which is subject to a mortgage, [that is, real estate], they are liable to make restitution?** *Does this not contradict the position of R. Hisda?*
C.   *R. Hisda will say to you, "When that is set forth as a Tannaite rule, it pertains to the situation that prevails after the original owner has despaired of getting the thing back [and so title has passed to the thief]."*

Clearly the two codes have introduced the same operative consideration, that of intentionality, but each negotiates matters in its own way. Aturfarnbag concerns himself with the intentionality of the heir to the stolen property; if he knows it is stolen, he has to restore it. But that of course is the very point at which the Mishnah's case commences: we know as fact that the food was stolen. The children have eaten it. Now do they have to return the stolen food or its value? Not at all. Why not? Because the intentionality of the victim of the theft is such that he has relinquished, by his despair of recovering his food, title to the stolen property. So while intentionality comes into play, it is for a different consideration altogether from the one operative in the Zoroastrian law.

And yet, once more, we have to say, had Aturfarnbag had the advantage of a talmud to make his rules dense and suggestive, the first thing that talmud would have said is, well isn't it obvious that if the property is known to have been stolen, it has to be returned? If it is not returned, then the heir becomes a thief; if it is returned, then what's the problem?   And the answer can well have been, what might you otherwise have imagined? That if the heir knew it was stolen, he has under all circumstances to return it? Not at all. If the food is no longer available, no restitution is required – the heirs having no part in the theft and having eaten the food in good faith; if the stolen property of course can be returned, it is to be returned. So, in all, the diverse expressions of somewhat awry cases turn out to conceal a community of viewpoint, despite the rather different consideration – the original owner's despair and the transfer of title on that account – that animates the Bavli's thinking.

IV. Relations to the Outside World

The Rivayat makes a simple, factual statement, which contains its entire message. The substance of the rules varies only slightly; for Israel, the other worships idols, and therefore his food is taboo; for Zoroastrian Iran, the other fails to observe the menstrual taboo, so his food is taboo, too. The one finds theology, the other, sexuality, intrinsically related to food, at which point social differentiation takes place. Not eating what the outsider produces – wine in particular, other edibles in general – is what designates the outsider as other; and eating what "we" produce makes us us. What marks the outsider – wrong faith, yielding sins of commission, idolatry, or omission, failure to observe the menstrual taboo – then accounts for the alterity of the other.

We should not, therefore, find striking the difference between the laconic way in which Aturfarnbag makes his statement; it is all that has to be said, and, when we examine the Talmudic counterpart, with its prolix and elaborate restatement, we shall in the end know more than Aturfarnbag tells us in fifty words or less.

CXXV

Question
  1. Can we purchase wine and other eatables from the Christians or not?

Reply
2. We cannot purchase but during helplessness, for they do not abstain from the menstrual impurity which they hold as lawful.

While I cannot claim to understand quite how Anklesaria has formulated the English counterpart to the Pahlavi, the sense is clear: no, because they do not abstain. Obviously, "our sages of blessed memory" concur that the wine and some other edibles of gentiles will be prohibited; at issue for us is how the Bavli sets forth these prohibitions.

The Mishnah, elucidated by the Bavli, has a great deal to say on the same topic, which occupies a considerably larger place and receives a far more dense discussion, in detail and in generative principle, than the rather routine observation just now cited. The entire issue is clear at the outset: idolatry, pure and simple; anything that has been used or that has been left over from what has been used or dedicated for use for an idol's service is forbidden.

Mishnah-tractate Abodah Zarah 2:3-5

A. [29B] These things belonging to gentiles are prohibited, and the prohibition affecting them extends to deriving any benefit from them at all:

B. (1) Wine, (2) vinegar of gentiles which to begin with was wine, (3) Hadrianic earthenware, and (4) hides pierced at the heart.

C. Rabban Simeon B. Gamaliel says, "When the tear in the hide is round, it is prohibited. [If it is] straight, it is permitted."

D. "Meat which is being brought in to an idol is permitted.

E. "But that which comes out is prohibited,

F. "because it is like *sacrifices of the dead* (Ps. 106:28)," the words of R. Aqiba.

G. With those who are going to an idolatrous pilgrimage it is prohibited to do business.

H. With those that are coming back it is permitted.

Clearly, sages take many more words to say what Aturfarnbag has told his faithful about their gentiles. But they raise a variety of issues that pertain to food, making distinctions of no interest to the Zoroastrian counterpart: not using but at least trading in a product is considered, so there are distinctions that extend beyond eating to other kinds of transactions. But that seems to me to inhere in the matter: if the concern is uncleanness, then, if one can avoid contracting the uncleanness, there can be no objection to trading in what one cannot eat. But if the concern is one of the relationship of the object to idolatry, then the intrinsic character of the object, not only its function (serving as food, serving as an object of trade) is going to form a consideration and yield distinctions.

V. Oaths Imposed on Children in Connection with
the Father's Estate's Debts

We turn from relations between the group and outsiders to those within the group, between generations. Here we revert to a theme already introduced, the situation of the heirs of a wicked father, but the issues are not merely public and civil: correct procedure in the community at large; not merely moral and ethical: a private decision on what is to be done or not done with stolen goods. In the problem at hand, a father takes a loan and dies without repaying it. The wife and children deny the loan. Both traditions solve the problem in the same way, by imposing an oath on the heirs that they know nothing of the matter and deny it. The oath is owing by the heirs to the estate; it then frees them from any further obligation. Here is the Zoroastrian version:

Children Take an Oath That They Did Not Know of
a Loan Claimed Against the Parents' Estate

LXVI

Question
1.   There is a man who gives a loan to a man; that man departs from this world; he has a wife and children in this family; the widow does not return the loan taken from the man; when she departs from this world, and there are sons and daughters in the family, and the man asks the return of the loan from a son; and the son is perverse and says, "I do not know it"; the man who is this creditor says, "Swear that thy father did not take this loan from me, and I and other heirs of my father have neither to return nor give this property to thee; their returning or giving is not lawful"; the man who took the loan says, "Let us you and I so undergo the ordeal"; "I and other heirs of my father have no knowledge of this event" – what is the advice?

Reply
2.   As I understand: then he shall certainly undertake the ordeal, saying, "My father and mother did not take this loan from thee, O Man! And we who are the heirs of our father and mother have not to return this loan to thee."

The Talmud introduces exactly the same issue at M. Ketubot 7:7E, below, but has the oath taken by heirs of an estate with the consequence that they have the power to collect an amount owing. Now they allege that they have proof of the loan but no proof of payment, F. The basic principle – appeal to the oath – is the same; the sole point of difference is, who takes the oath and with what consequence. That the imposition of the oath in this case is anomalous is announced at the outset of the Bavli's exposition of the larger passage of which this item forms a part, which finds scriptural evidence for the principle at hand, the oath itself:

Mishnah-tractate Ketubot 7:7

A. Just as they have said [M. Ket. 9:7], (1) A woman who impairs her marriage settlement collects only by taking an oath,

B. [and] (2) [if] a single witness testifies that it has been collected, she collects it only by taking an oath;

C. [and] (3) she collects from indentured property and from property belonging to the estate only by taking an oath;

D. [and] (4) she who collects her marriage settlement not in her husband's presence collects it only by taking an oath,

E. so (5) heirs of an estate collect [debts owing to the deceased] only through an oath:

F. "(1) We swear that Father gave us no instructions [in this matter], (2) Father said nothing to us about it, and (3) we did not find among his bonds evidence that this bond had been paid off."

G. R. Yohanan b. Beroqah says, "Even if the son was born after the death of the father, lo, this one must take an oath before he collects [what is owing to the estate]."

H. Said Rabban Simeon b. Gamaliel, "If there are witnesses that the father had stated when he was dying, 'This bond has not yet been paid off,' [the son] may collect [the debt] without taking an oath."

I.1 A. All those who are subjected to oaths which are [required] in the Torah take [said] oaths and do not pay [the claim against them]:

B. *How do we know this on the basis of Scripture?*

C. "[The oath of the Lord shall be between them both, to see whether he has not put his hand unto his neighbor's goods.] And the owner thereof shall accept it and he shall not pay" (Ex. 22:10). [The owner accepts the oath, and the bailee does not have to pay (Silverstone).]

D. So the person who would have to pay has to takes the oath [so that he does not have to pay].

XIII.1 A. ...So (5) heirs of an estate collect [debts owing to the deceased] only through an oath: "(1) We swear that Father gave us no instructions [in this matter], (2) Father said nothing to us about it, and (3) we did not find among his bonds evidence that this bond had been paid off." R. Yohanan b. Beroqah says, "Even if the son was born after the death of the father, lo, this one must take an oath before he collects [what is owing to the estate]." Said Rabban Simeon b. Gamaliel, "If there are witnesses that the father had stated when he was dying, 'This bond has not yet been paid off,' [the son] may collect [the debt] without taking an oath":

B. *From whom is the debt collected? Should we say from the borrower? The father could have gotten back his money without an oath, and should they have to take an oath? Rather, it means,* And so also orphans cannot collect payment from orphans without taking an oath.

C. *And both Rab and Samuel say,* "This rule pertains only if the lender died in the lifetime of the borrower. But if the borrower died in the lifetime of the lender, the lender is already obligated to take an oath to the children of the borrower, and someone may not then leave as an inheritance to his children the requirement to take an oath."

XIII.4 A. *R. Nahman came to Sura and went to see R. Hisda and Rabbah b. R. Huna. They said to him, "Will the master come and uproot this rule of Rab and Samuel [that someone may not bequeath the requirement to take an oath to his son]?"*

B. *He said to them, "Have I gone to the trouble of coming this vast distance merely to uproot this rule of Rab and Samuel [that someone may not bequeath the requirement to take an oath to his son]?"*

C. *"So then give us this: Don't add to it [and apply it only to the case of which they spoke]."*

D. *"For instance?"*

E. *"For instance what R. Pappa said, 'He who impairs his bond and died – his oaths may take the oath of heirs and collect on the strength of the bond.'"* [The bondholder admitted having collected part, so has to take an oath to get the rest; if he dies, his oaths can swear the oath of heirs, and here we do not apply the ruling of Rab and Samuel about not bequeathing the right to take an oath and collect (Silverstone).]

XIII.5 A. *A certain man who died left a guarantor [for the loan, who, upon the man's death, became surety for the loan; the borrower died as well, so the creditor has to take an oath to collect; then the creditor died, and his heirs claim the money from the guarantor of the loan]. R. Pappa considered ruling, "In a case of this kind the principle, don't add to it [and apply it only to the case of which they spoke] applies."*

B. *Said R. Huna b. R. Joshua to R. Pappa, "Will the guarantor of the loan not go after the orphans [to collect what is owing]?"* [So the heirs of the creditor, if permitted to taken an oath and claim the loan from the guarantor, will ultimately be depriving the debtor's heirs because of the oath, and to such a case the ruling of Rab and Samuel applies.]

XIII.6 A. *A certain man died and left as his heir only a brother. [The borrower had died, leaving children; the lender's brother claims the debt from the borrower's children.] Rammi bar Hamma considered ruling, "In a case of this kind, too, the principle, don't add to it [and apply it only to the case of which they spoke] applies."*

B. Said to him Raba, "What difference does it make to me whether the claim is, 'My father did not leave me orders,' or, 'My brother did not leave me orders?'" [There is none, and the lender cannot bequeath such an oath to his sons, so also to his brother.]

XIII.7 A. *Said R. Hama, "Now that the decided law has not been stated either in accord with Rab and Samuel or in accord with R. Eleazar, a judge who rules in accord with Rab and Samuel has done a valid deed, and who rules in accord with R. Eleazar has done a valid deed."*

Enough of the Bavli's treatment of this theme has been given for one point to emerge. The very basis of the rule is challenged at XIII.1, with the result that severe limitations are imposed upon the conception that an oath is required, or imposed, at all. How can the requirement to take an oath be bequeathed to one's children? So, once more, a simple principle of law, that debts can be exacted, or avoided, through the intervention of an oath, yields complexities, such that the rule is transformed beyond recognition. That is the point of No. 4. No. 5 shows us how, nonetheless, the revision leaves in place the social benefit intended by the basic rule: to provide for the guarantee of capital that has been put forth as a loan. Here we contrast a simple rule covering a simple case with an interest in formulating principles that extend over many cases, take account of a variety of conflicting interests – the children's, the estate's, the borrower's, the lender's, the stability and security of financial transactions, the whole guaranteed in the end by supernatural intervention to penalize him who takes a false oath.

VI. Can One Transfer Ownership of What Has Not Yet Come into Existence?

Now we come to an exceptionally striking confluence: not only is the detail, but the principle that generates the problem, the same on both sides. At issue in religious systems that assign to the faithful the power of effective speech is the relationship between words and things, between what one says and the status, as to permissibility of otherwise, of objects out there. Since both Zoroastrian and Judaic traditions recognize the validity of vows and accord to believers the power through vows to transform the status of things, both the priests and the sages had to speculate on theoretical questions concerning vows with intensely concrete consequences for those who took them. And here, as a matter of fact, the intersection is nearly verbatim.

In the present instance, we deal with two distinct questions that meet in a problem of high abstraction: Can one take a vow (Zoroastrianism) or by a statement transfer title of ownership (Judaism) to something not now in existence? The first question concerns the effect of a vow upon what is intangible at this time but will become tangible, for example, an object one will make, a meal one will cook. The second, a deeper, perennial philosophical issue, concerns the reality of the potential. Framed in neutral terms, can I dispose of an oak, when only the acorn is in hand? Is what is potential classified, because of what will come about inevitably and inexorably, as what is actual? Or do we distinguish the here and the now from what might come about? Left as an abstract question, the issue of the potential and the actual could not have come up in either the Talmud or the Rivayat, neither of which knows how to frame philosophical questions in a philosophical way. But stated in concrete terms, both writings prove highly qualified to analyze philosophical problems.

The Rivayat states matters in language that with only slight revision can have appeared in the Mishnah. If one takes a vow to dedicate for someone else whatever actions of merit that he may carry out in the future, is this a valid act of dedication? Aturfarnbag's answer is virtually identical to language that we can find in the Talmud, if we translated the question into the status of "property that has not come to his possession," which is difficult to distinguish from "something that has not yet come into the world." Not only so, but the Talmud knows the problem of whether one can transfer title to something that has not yet come into the world (an unborn baby) or of something that has not yet come into one's possession (a crop in the sowing stage).

LXXIV

Question

1.   Whoever makes a solemn vow with this sort of colloquy: "I have dedicated to such and such person all acts and good deeds which I may perform from this day onward," what is your opinion of this case: this as to whether they will have been dedicated by him or not?

Reply

2.   If he declares as "dedicated" that property which has not come to his possession, it will not have been dedicated; and if he speaks of that good deed which has not become his, he shall not have dedicated in the same manner; if he speaks of that property which has not come to his possession, or of that good deed and property which have not together come to his possession, if a fear, or a difficulty, or a trouble, or depressing thought, or a defect has not come, such as that which is said in detail in the ordeal section of the Husparam, if he speaks of one who is worthy; then when that property came to his possession, or that good deed came to achievement, then he shall have been dedicated, in the same manner, to him to whom they are dedicated, if even now that worthiness has not elapsed; it can be dedicated for that one fear of fears, when one dedicates anything to worthy persons for fear of the wicked existence; if he says, "I will dedicate a good deed, not for any earthly gain, but for the friendship of the soul of a person who is worthy," it will be his to whom he said, "I will dedicate," when he has performed it; and it will not be the less, of him who performed it; it will come to him in the same manner as if he had performed it for the sake of his own soul; since he declared that colloquy, "I will dedicate," for the love of

righteousness, he advances this in the path of a soul, even this munificence which he advances with a good deed will be such as his who performs a worship, without earthly reward and gain, for the souls of persons; then, the recitation by him of what is in the oath ordeal has gone by, which brings out the least preparation of this kind, then he shall recite the words of Rasnu, those which the Avesta has demonstrated, those which he can verily consider, such as one says: (Av.) "Here is such utility," so is this regulation for defense, (Av.) or, "Here is its information unto me," so I have information of it by proof, (Av.) or, "I do not know of it," or "I have not that by knowledge," if by non-recitation of it, I am a sinner who misuses a trust; then, I do not know of any formula to explain that he has to take effectively in reckoning those words which it is not according to the law for him to speak, and to decide the matter.

3. It is instituted that if there has been such a man, a man who, on account of fear, speaks in the presence of judges: "This man had smitten me," the judge understands that he spoke on account of fear, he shall release him on the highway.

4. They shall leave the decision of this, as to for what reason that man spoke in dedicating that good deed, to the Yazats who ordain; they can decide; otherwise, since the judges of this world cannot effectively return to the real holder the property which is invisible, which is known to have been in the keeping of one who carried it away with force, therefore, as an invisible good deed becomes requisite by declaration, he has to atone for the false oath; the punishment of the atonement is evident as determined; they shall not mitigate the penalty of that which is indubitable and that which is doubtful, and they shall adjudicate the material person and property; they shall leave the judgment of the soul and the good deed to Him who knows; it is even due to His power that the righteous is inculpated by that over which he has no power.

Aturfarnbag's answer leaves nothing in ambiguity: one has not got control of what is not now in the world or subject to one's possession. When he rapidly qualifies matters, it is to make an obvious point, one that is irrelevant to the question. Once the deed has been done, it does indeed go to the credit of the person for whom he has dedicated it. What makes the difference is the motive. If one does the act for the sake of his own soul, it serves for the other. The exposition leads on at Nos. 3, 4 to related matters; the main point throughout is that we take account not only of the dedication of what does not exist but also the intentionality of the person who makes that statement. Then, if the intentionality is valid, the statement before the fact takes effect; if the intentionality is invalid – coercion having led to the pledge, for instance – then the act later on is not classified by the initial language.

To state matters simply, the Zoroastrian priest's statement takes account of three considerations, not two: [1] the power of a person to make such an affective statement; [2] the distinction between what is potential and what is actual; [3] the character of the intentionality that has brought about making the statement. The person with the right attitude and intention indeed can make such a statement stick.

Now to the Talmud's discussion of the same matter. It is stated in the very same context as the Zoroastrian, namely, vow taking. The issue is not spelled out in the Mishnah but is invoked as soon as we propose to interpret the Mishnah, at I.1.B: May a person sanctify something that is not yet in existence? The act of sanctification is a statement that a person makes concerning an object that he owns that it is donated to the Temple, for example, for sale with the proceeds to go to the upkeep of the altar and the building. Can he make such a statement concerning what is not now in existence? That is an exact parallel, controlling for the differences in systemic detail, to the problem that interests Aturfarnbag.

M. Nedarim 11:4

A.   [If she said,] "Qonam if I work for Father," or "For your father," or, "...For your brother," he cannot annul that vow.

B.   [If she said, "Qonam if I work for you," he need not annul [that vow, which is null to begin with].

C.   R. Aqiba says, "Let him annul it,

D.   "lest she place a burden upon him more than is appropriate for him."

E.   R. Yohanan b. Nuri says, "Let him annul it, lest he divorce her, and she be prohibited from returning to him."

I.1   A.   Said Samuel, "The decided law is in accord with the position of R. Yohanan b. Nuri."

B.   *Is that to imply that Samuel takes the view: A person may sanctify something that is not yet in existence? And by way of objection:* **He who sanctifies to the Temple the fruits of his wife's labor [her wages], [85B] lo, this woman [continues to] work and eat [maintain herself]. And as to the excess – R. Meir says, "It is consecrated." R. Yohanan Hassandlar says, "It is unconsecrated"** [M. Ket. 5:4]. And said Samuel, "The decided law accords with the position of R. Yohanan Hassandlar," *which proves that [in his view here,] a person may not sanctify something that is not yet in existence. And, moreover, should you say that, when he said, "The decided law accords with the position of R. Yohanan Hassandlar,"*

> *it was only with reference to the excess [but not other wages that she would receive in the future], then he should have said,* "The decided law in respect to the excess accords with the position of R. Yohanan Hassandlar," *or, otherwise,* "The decided law accords with the position of the initial, anonymous authority," *or, otherwise,* "The decided law accords with R. Aqiba."

The issue that interests us enters through a side door, the implication of Samuel's statement being that he takes the position that is specified, even though, in another setting, it is clear that he takes the opposite view. So we harmonize the two positions assigned to Samuel, rather than analyze the issue before us. What this tells us about how the Judaic sages thought it important to set forth the great tradition is clear: part of the power of the tradition lies in its formal perfection; not only does the Mishnah not repeat itself or tell us obvious things, but the authorities of the Mishnah and those in charge of its exegesis are perfectly consistent in all their positions.

Index

South Florida Studies in the History of Judaism

DATE DUE